REVELATION, THE RELIGIONS,
AND VIOLENCE

REVELATION, THE RELIGIONS, AND VIOLENCE

Leo D. Lefebure

ORBIS BOOKS

Maryknoll, New York 10545

The Catholic Foreign Mission Society of America (Maryknoll) recruits and trains people for overseas missionary service. Through Orbis Books, Maryknoll aims to foster the international dialogue that is essential to mission. The books published, however, reflect the opinions of their authors and are not meant to represent the official position of the Society. To obtain more information about Maryknoll and Orbis Books, please visit our website at www.maryknoll.org.

Published by Orbis Books, Maryknoll, New York, U.S.A.

Excerpts from *The New Jerusalem Bible*, copyright © 1985 by Darton, Longman & Todd, Ltd. and Doubleday, a division of Random House, Inc., and les Editions du Cerf, are reprinted by permission.

Manufactured in the United States of America

Library of Congress Cataloging-in-Publication Data

Lefebure, Leo D., 1952–
    Revelation, the religions, and violence / Leo D. Lefebure.
        p.   cm.
    Includes bibliographical references and index.
    ISBN 1-57075-300-8 (pbk.)
      1. Christianity and other religions.   2. Catholic Church—Relations.
   3. Revelation—Comparative studies.   4. Violence—Religious aspects—
Comparative studies.   5. Revelation—History of doctrines.   6. Violence—
Religious aspects—Catholic Church—History of doctrines.   I. Title.

BR127.L39   2000
241'.697—dc21

                                  00-028564

In Memory of Jon Hextell (1952–1976)
Cousin and Friend of My Youth

Contents

Foreword

This is an important book, which fortunately appears at a crucial time in the meeting of world religions. The religions of Asia are now becoming a major concern of Christian theologians and of Christians at large. No longer are these religions merely an object of study by historians of distant and exotic realms of the past. Increasingly mosques and ashrams are becoming a part of the landscape of our neighborhoods. Hindus and Buddhists have entered into the fabric of our lives as medical doctors, scientists, and computer experts. What does this new religious pluralism mean for our lives? For our understanding of ourselves and our religious identity? Do these religions threaten our identity or can they enrich our spiritual journeys?

Writing as a theologian, with the support of the history of religions, Leo Lefebure takes the issues surrounding world religions to a new depth and clarity. He has already published a number of articles and two significant books in this area: *The Buddha and the Christ: Explorations in Buddhist-Christian Dialogue* and *Life Transformed: Meditations on the Christian Scriptures in the Light of Buddhist Perspectives*. In the present book he takes issues further still, breaking new ground in three areas: (1) deepening and broadening understanding of wisdom, which can serve as a foundation of interreligious dialogue; (2) extensively presenting the link between religions and violence; and (3) offering a creative perception of scientific chaos theory, which can throw light on the complex interrelatedness of the world's religions. Lefebure examines these areas with an impressive balance of erudition and precision, presenting the most complex issues with a conceptual and verbal clarity that makes them at once accessible.

Although the wisdom traditions of the Old Testament have been studied by Jewish and Christian scholars, they have not been tapped for the deeper and broader layer of wisdom that forms a link with the wisdom traditions of the world's religions. These teachings have an affinity with the wisdom traditions of Hinduism, Buddhism, and Chinese religion. As this book demonstrates, wisdom literature itself acknowledges that its teachings have a broader context in the traditions outside the geographic limits of Israel. This is especially significant if one takes the point of view of Karl Jaspers, whom Lefebure cites, that there was an Axial Age from

800 to 400 B.C.E., when a new form of consciousness emerged in three disparate regions, through which similar teachings of the major religions of the world took shape. Although we do not have abundant evidence that far Eastern wisdom flowed into Israel, nevertheless there is a foundation in the wisdom traditions for the kind of dialogue that has emerged globally during the last century. Lefebure has opened a major avenue of research that points to the fact that in various ways for over two millennia the East and West have had a basis for the dialogic consciousness that has emerged in our time.

Granted this positive foundation, the religions of the world have a dark side. Tragically and embarrassingly, religions have fostered, incited, condoned, and initiated violence. In our era, this has been increasingly acknowledged by religious leaders. For example, on Sunday, March 12, 2000, at St. Peter's Basilica, Pope John Paul II issued a dramatic statement: "We can ask forgiveness for the divisions of Christians, for the use of violence that some Christians have committed in the service of the truth, and for the attitudes of mistrust and hostility sometimes assumed toward followers of other religions."

The violence that has been interwoven with religion throughout history has rarely been taken into account by theologians. In contrast, Lefebure brings the issue of violence to center stage and provides a treatment of the history of violence in each of the major religions. He draws significantly from the thought of René Girard, although he does not follow Girard's approach in all respects. The issues are still open, but Lefebure has led the way to a comprehensive treatment of violence in the world's religions from a theological and spiritual standpoint.

A third major contribution is toward understanding the interrelation of the teachings of the world's religions. Lefebure surveys various approaches—exclusive, inclusive, and pluralistic—but makes his own contribution through the scientific paradigm of chaos theory. Experienced as he is in one of the most difficult dialogues—the Buddhist/Christian—he is careful to retain the integrity of each tradition, while making creative contacts.

He closes with what may be his most profound contribution to the dynamics of interreligious dialogue—exploring the thought of Karl Rahner and the Buddhist scholar Masao Abe. This dialogue is the culmination of the book. It is the result of his many years of Buddhist meditation and his teaching of Christian systematic theology. The eloquent epilogue, which expresses the richness of the Christian experience of divine love, is also the fruit of the dynamic of the entire book, as it unfolds in the wisdom traditions, the transformation of violence, and the intensity of Zen practice.

EWERT COUSINS

Preface

In July 1996, Buddhist and Christian monastics from the United States, Asia, and Europe gathered at Our Lady of Gethsemani Abbey near Louisville, Kentucky, for a week of meditation and dialogue. The Gethsemani Encounter began with His Holiness Tenzin Gyatso, the Fourteenth Dalai Lama, and Abbot Timothy Kelly, O.C.S.O., planting a young tree in front of the monastery entrance as a reminder of both the Buddha's awakening under a tree and Christ's self-emptying on the cross. The program included discussions of monastic life and practice, the role of a spiritual guide and community, and stages of prayer or meditation.

What none of the planners had foreseen was how strongly the violence of the world would be felt in the monastery at Gethsemani. The outer setting was peaceful and serene, framed by the rhythms of Catholic monastic life, but questions of violence appeared repeatedly in the discussions.[1] One Buddhist participant commented on seeing the body of Jesus on the crosses in the monastery and asked Christians if they felt sad at seeing the suffering figure. One Christian after another came forward to express his or her understanding of Jesus Christ on the cross. Later in the discussions, the same Buddhist stated that he greatly enjoyed chanting the psalms with the monastic choir at the vesper service; but he asked the Christian participants about the bloody, vengeful psalms that call upon God to crush one's enemies in graphic fashion. "What does it mean for Christians to pray such psalms?" he asked. Another Buddhist pressed the question of how the death of Jesus could in any way be salvific: "I just don't get it." As we struggled to explain this central aspect of our faith, Christians went through an internal process of reflection on how to present the mystery of God's presence at the heart of suffering to Buddhists whose religious sensibilities are so different.

Each tradition was challenged to face the violence within its own heritage. One Korean Zen leader recalled the tragic history of Buddhist and Christian collaboration in violence and aggression in Asia; and he lamented the silence of Chinese, Korean, Burmese, Thai, and Japanese Buddhist leaders about injustice and aggression during the twentieth century. He also issued the challenge to Christians: "I think there is something in the Christian teachings that allows its followers to become intolerant to us non-Christians."

The question of how to respond to violence took a poignant turn when Armand Veilleux, O.C.S.O., a French Trappist monk, recounted the background of the recent kidnapping and martyrdom of the French Trappist monks in Algeria by the Armed Islamic Group. After the military takeover of power and the beginning of Muslim fundamentalist violence against foreigners, the monks knew that their lives were in danger, but they decided to stay. While Christians saw this as an act of witness and courage, a Buddhist participant stated that from a Buddhist perspective it might be more compassionate to leave such a situation to prevent one's potential killers from the bad karma (or effects) of murder, which will last for lifetimes. In reply, Dom Bernardo Olivera, O.C.S.O., the abbot general of the Trappist community worldwide, affirmed that the God of Jesus Christ is a God of mercy and compassion and stated that he expected to see the face of the killer with him in paradise: "Forgiveness, there is no other answer."

Interreligious dialogue and violence challenge Christian theology to develop and change in different ways. On the one hand, through contacts with members of other traditions, Christians are increasingly open to recognizing grace and truth in other religious traditions; many sense that divine revelation is not limited to Jews and Christians. On the other hand, Christians are challenged to acknowledge and mourn the violence fostered by many religious traditions, especially our own tradition, from biblical holy wars to virulent anti-Jewish attitudes to countless later expressions of animosity. Christians are moving both to greater openness to other traditions and also to a critical scrutiny of our own tradition's sources and history.

Two different but related themes will shape this discussion. The first is the variety of biblical and Christian perspectives on revelation and other religious traditions, with particular attention to the wisdom tradition. The wisdom tradition of Israel, which strongly influenced the early Christians' interpretation of Jesus Christ, offers a biblical precedent for acknowledging the wisdom of God within other religious traditions. The sages of Israel, as well as their later Christian heirs, assumed that the wise of other nations were illumined by the Wisdom of God. The second major focus is the relation between revelation and violence in the Bible and the Christian tradition. The Bible itself and the later Christian tradition present a variety of conflicting perspectives on violence. In discussing this topic, I will critically and selectively draw upon the work of René Girard. The theory of religion, culture, and violence of Girard explicitly rejects the ancient Israelite sages' assumption of a universal offer of wisdom, restricting revelation to the biblical tradition. While I believe Girard's exclusivist view of revelation is not justified, his naming of the dynamics of revelation as the unveiling of violence is an insightful and provocative contribution. Girard sees the dynamics of human culture as rooted in exclusion and violence. For Girard, religions originally arose from the sacralization of violence in order to channel and contain surging violent energies. Throughout later history, human societies repeatedly established social bonds by targeting certain individuals and groups as scapegoats. Divine revelation unmasks this phenomenon and presents God on the side of the victims. I believe we can learn from Girard even if the totalizing claims of his system must be rejected.

This work will begin by exploring the ways in which the biblical witness and the classical Catholic Christian tradition have understood revelation in relation to other religious traditions and to violence. The opening chapter will discuss the recent shifts in Catholic attitudes toward other religions and the issues arising from interreligious dialogue and from violence. The second chapter will explore the attitudes of biblical authors toward other religions. The Bible offers a sharp critique of the idols of other religious traditions, but it also borrows heavily from other religious traditions in its own naming of God. The third chapter will examine the various stances within the Bible toward violence, ranging from the sacralization of war to the nonviolent teaching of Jesus. The fourth chapter will discuss the attitudes of patristic and medieval Christians toward revelation and the other religions in their context, including Judaism, Hellenistic religions, and Islam. The fifth chapter will explore patristic and medieval perspectives on violence, from the pacifism of many early Christians to papal preaching of the Crusades. The sixth chapter will turn to the major religious traditions of China and India—Confucianism, Taoism, Hinduism, and Buddhism—of which biblical writers and early and medieval European Christians were largely unaware. While some of these religions had no conception of a transcendent God or a divine revelation, each proclaims the manifestation of an insight that transforms human life. The seventh chapter will examine some aspects of the contemporary encounter with other religions, drawing upon the resources of contemporary chaos theory as a metaphor for naming the dynamics of interrelationships among religions. The final chapter offers a conversation between the perspectives of the Japanese Zen Buddhist philosopher Masao Abe on awakening and of the German Catholic theologian Karl Rahner on revelation. There is a glossary of special terms. Terms included in the glossary are marked with a dagger (†) at their first occurrence.

To understand revelation demands both honesty in acknowledging the tragic history of the Christian tradition and a spirit of friendship and concern in relation to other religious traditions. Even though the history of encounters among the world's religions is filled with conflict, the values that we share challenge us to think and work together for the sake of the entire community of life on this planet.

Acknowledgments

This work has been shaped by the contributions of many persons and many encounters, and I owe a special debt to the many persons who have taught me through their participation in dialogue. I would like to express my gratitude to the members of the Colloquium on Religion and Violence, the Research Committee of the Council for a Parliament of the World's Religions, the Board of Monastic Interreligious Dialogue, the Faiths in the World Committee of the National Association of Diocesan Ecumenical Officers, the Jewish–Catholic Scholars Group of Chicago, the participants in the Gethsemani Encounter, and the participants in the various Jewish–Christian, Hindu–Christian, and Buddhist–Christian dialogues and retreats in which I have shared.

I would also like to thank the various audiences who heard and responded to sections of this work in lectures, especially members of the Catholic Theological Society of America, Vanderbilt University Divinity School, the Colloquium on Violence and Religion, and the Society for Buddhist-Christian Studies. Some material in this work has previously appeared in different form in articles in *The Christian Century, Contagion,* and *Chicago Studies.* Chapter 8 appeared in an earlier form as "Awakening and Grace: Religious Identity in the Thought of Masao Abe and Karl Rahner" (*Cross Currents* 47, no. 4 [1998]: 451–72).

I am grateful to Donald Ottenhoff, Lawrence Hennessey, Ewert Cousins, Robert Schreiter, and William Burrows for reading and responding to earlier drafts of this work. I am especially grateful to Ewert Cousins for contributing the Foreword. While this work owes much to so many people, its weaknesses and limitations are truly my own.

1

Revelation, the Religions, and Violence

WISDOM AND EXPERIENCE

Christian faith proceeds from the conviction that God has revealed Godself and God's will for humanity and all creation in the history of Israel and in Jesus Christ. A wide array of narratives, laws, symbols, and concrete images, including the call of God to Abram to leave his homeland, the voice of God from the burning bush calling Moses to go to Pharaoh, the encounter with God and the giving of the covenant at Mt. Sinai, the experience of Isaiah in the temple, the summons of Lady Wisdom at the city gates in the Book of Proverbs, the voice from the whirlwind speaking to Job, the visions of Daniel, the song of the angels to the shepherds proclaiming the birth of a Savior, the voice of God at the Baptism and the Transfiguration of Jesus, the teachings, actions and miracles of Jesus, the suffering and death of Jesus, and the appearances of the Risen Lord, all bear witness to the surprising power of God breaking into this world, challenging people's assumptions and calling them to conversion of mind and behavior and to new and deeper life. For Christians, revelation is the dynamic process through which the unseen and unknowable God addresses humans in historical events, in prophetic calls and apocalyptic visions, in the experiences and reflections of individuals and communities, and above all in the person and event of Jesus Christ. Narratives, symbols, images, counsels, and commands convey this revelation and disclose what is of ultimate value and concern, what is worth living and dying for.

The reception of revelation is life-transforming, healing, and reconciling, clarifying the significance of the past, focusing the present, and summoning new energies for the future. As an authoritative call from God, revelation provides the central point of orientation for human life, the norm for assessing knowledge and action, unifying both personal lives and cultures and calling forth creative energies for witness and action. To acknowledge and accept divine revelation is to experience the ultimate claim on our loyalty, the measure for all other measures.

Revelation comes to humans in the form of symbols that make present the transcendent and immanent reality of God. Symbols point beyond themselves and evoke awareness of a dimension of human existence that cannot be captured in nonsymbolic expressions. Christian symbols proclaim the revelation of God, who is infinite love. Yet in practice, both the biblical commands and later Christian understandings of revelation have been ambiguous, commanding both love of neighbor and also extermination of one's foes. They have supported and enriched countless lives; but they have also repeatedly led to systematic discrimination, persecutions, inquisitions, and wars. The symbols that communicate revelation have supported both holy wars and also traditions of peacemaking. Jesus Christ has been proclaimed the commander of Christian armies, the King of kings who will reward his soldiers' valor, and also the nonviolent Suffering Servant who endures injury and refuses to retaliate with force. The history of later Christian interpretations of revelation is itself a heritage of appropriation and betrayal, of inspiring witness and horrendous atrocities. The intertwining of understandings of revelation and violence is one of the most troubling aspects of the biblical tradition and later Christian history.

In recent years two factors have begun to challenge and reshape Christian understandings of revelation: (1) a new awareness of and openness to the vitality and authentic power of other religious traditions and a corresponding interest in interreligious dialogue, and (2) the tragic experience of massive violence and systemic oppression, and the recognition of the historical role of religions in fostering violence and oppression. Through dialogue Christians have become aware of both profound similarities in values and also radical differences of beliefs and worldviews among religious traditions. Even when religious traditions have sharply divergent views of human existence and the universe, their central values often resonate with those of other traditions. The experience of truth and grace in other religious traditions prods Christians to acknowledge that the range of revelation includes the entire human race. Yet the history of religions is filled with hatred and violence. The very forces that promise to draw humans into union with each other and with ultimate reality time and time again have become forces of division and conflict. The manifold ways that interpretations of revelation have supported violence demand a critical appropriation of the scriptures and the Christian tradition itself.

In recent exhortations Pope John Paul II has challenged Christians to celebrate the third millennium of Christian faith by reviewing their history with attention to the ways in which Christians historically have betrayed the Gospel through violence and intolerance and also by entering into dialogue with members of other religious traditions.[1] This challenge calls for Christian theology to pay attention both to the voices of those who follow other religious paths and also to the violence done by Christians in the name of God through the centuries.

THE TRANSFORMATION OF CATHOLIC ATTITUDES

In the development of the awareness of the Catholic Church, the new openness to other religious traditions was closely related to the experience of massive violence and the willingness to question certain aspects of earlier Christian tradition. Indeed, it is doubtful that Vatican II would have addressed the relation of the church to other religions at all if it were not for the pressing memory of the Shoah, the Nazi attempt to destroy all Jews. For centuries, Catholic thought and practice, shaped by traditional understandings of revelation and teachings of doctors of the church, had fostered hostility toward the Jews, though it had never called for the mass murder of Jews. For hundreds of years, anti-Jewish attitudes seemed to flow from the Christian scriptures and the tradition of the early church. The first and often most difficult step in the process of repentance is to acknowledge that something is wrong and face it in full seriousness. Anti-Jewish attitudes and behaviors were so deeply ingrained in Christian life and practice that they appeared to be natural and justified. Christian consciences were lulled. It took a particularly dramatic event to wake up the Christian community to what should have been obvious all along.

For the Christian community, the Shoah unleashed a massive suspicion not only upon the action and inaction of individual Christians during the horrendous years of Nazi rule, but also upon many elements of traditional Christian thought, life, and practice, including traditional interpretations of revelation which had nurtured anti-Jewish attitudes and actions. For centuries, many Christians believed that the revelation of God in Jesus Christ was so clearly evident that all Jews were personally responsible for rejecting him. Peter the Venerable, bishop of the Benedictine Abbey of Cluny in the twelfth century, even posed the question of whether Jews were human because they did not yield to Catholic arguments about the revelation of God in Jesus: "Really I doubt whether a Jew can be human for he will neither yield to human reasoning, nor find satisfaction in authoritative utterances, alike divine and Jewish."[2] The rhetorical question about the humanity of the Jews helped to foster attitudes of suspicion and disdain that lasted into the twentieth century. A book published in London in 1939 by an author who claimed not to be anti-Semitic bore the title, *The Jews: Are They Human?*[3]

If the revelation of God was perfectly manifest in Jesus Christ, then the Jews had no excuse for not recognizing their Messiah. In light of this judgment, many Christians followed early church fathers in accusing all Jews in every generation of deicide because they refused to believe in Jesus. Many Christians also accepted patristic arguments, rooted in interpretations of New Testament texts, that the Diaspora was God's punishment for Jewish infidelity, and that Jews were deserving of mistreatment age after age. It was widely thought that Jewish misery would testify to God's continuing just judgment upon them. Augustine set the basic framework for papal policy for centuries by maintaining that the Jews were to be preserved, but in misery. The authors of a draft of a projected encyclical condemning anti-Semitism during the pontificate of Pope Pius XI rejected the Nazi form of pseudo-scientific racism, but they repeated the age-old Catholic prejudices against the Jews:

> [B]linded by a vision of material domination and gain, the Israelites lost what they themselves had sought. . . . Moreover, by a mysterious Providence of God, this unhappy people, destroyers of their own nation, whose misguided leaders had called down upon their own heads a Divine malediction, doomed, as it were, to perpetually wander over the face of the earth, were nonetheless never allowed to perish, but have been preserved through the ages into our own time.[4]

These words are all the more striking coming from Catholic authors who were deliberately opposing Nazi anti-Semitism. Similarly, even so courageous an opponent of the Nazis as Karl Barth continued the age-old tradition of seeing Jewish sufferings as witnessing to God's judgment upon them.[5] After the Shoah, many Christians, both Catholic and Protestant, were painfully aware of the Christian tradition's own responsibility for poisoning the atmosphere regarding Jews in Europe for centuries before the rise of modern, pseudo-scientific racism.

One dramatic meeting helped to place this question on the agenda of the Second Vatican Council. On June 13, 1960, Jules Isaac, a French Jewish historian who had studied the history of Catholic teaching on the Jews,[6] obtained an audience with Pope John XXIII. Isaac presented Pope John with a dossier containing a request that the upcoming council of the Catholic Church correct the false and unjust statements about Israel in traditional Catholic teaching. Isaac referred in particular to the claim that the scattering of Israel was a punishment inflicted by God on the people of Israel for the crucifixion of Jesus. He also quoted the catechism of the Catholic Church issued after the Council of Trent, which taught that the guilt of all sinners was the fundamental cause of Christ's death on the cross. Isaac argued that this teaching contradicted the false accusation that Jews in particular were guilty of deicide. After a brief audience of about thirty minutes, Pope John assured Isaac that he had reason for hope.

A few months later, in September 1960, Pope John commissioned Augustin Cardinal Bea, president of the Secretariat for Christian Unity, to prepare a draft of a declaration on the inner relations between the Catholic Church and the people of Israel. During the often heated debates over the declaration at Vatican II, some bishops argued that to change the teaching of the church regarding Judaism would be to reject both scripture and tradition, reversing what the church had always taught in light of revelation. Many passages in the New Testament speak of Jews in very harsh language. For centuries, the common Catholic understanding of revelation was that Jews had completely broken off the covenant with God by rejecting Jesus and that their only hope for salvation lay in conversion to Catholic Christianity. The Council of Florence had solemnly declared that "all those who are outside the catholic church, not only pagans but also Jews or heretics and schismatics, cannot share in eternal life and will go into the everlasting fire which was prepared for the devil and his angels, unless they are joined to the catholic church before the end of their lives."[7] The Council assumed that the gospel had been clearly preached to all nations, and that all who rejected it were guilty before God.

Despite the weight of traditional teachings, after the horrors of the Shoah, the large majority of bishops at Vatican II believed that it was imperative that the Catholic Church express a new attitude toward the Jewish community. It was the painful awareness of massive, unjust suffering in the Shoah and the painful knowledge that centuries of Christian anti-Jewish teaching and practice had fostered animosity and hatred toward the Jews that drove the search for new theological perspectives. Many bishops, especially those from Germany and the United States, insisted on the need for a new statement of the relation of the church to Jews and a clear condemnation of anti-Semitism and religious discrimination, from whatever source. This implied a profound shift in the church's understanding of the reception of revelation and tradition. As Raymond Brown commented: "a very traditional Church was authoritatively and publicly contradicting attitudes toward the Jews uttered by some of its most venerated Fathers and Doctors."[8]

As discussions of the church's relationship with the Jewish people progressed, some council fathers proposed a broadening of the scope of the document to include Hindus, Buddhists, and Muslims as well. The new attitude toward the Jewish community had profound implications for the church's stance toward every other religious tradition. The declaration on the church's relation to the Jewish community was eventually extended to embrace the entire range of humanity's thirst for the Absolute, making specific reference to Hindus, Buddhists, and Muslims.

Without the recognition of how earlier understandings of revelation had fostered a climate of violence against the Jewish community, it is unlikely that the Second Vatican Council would have reflected upon the church's relation to other religious traditions as well.

The final text of Vatican II's Declaration on the Church's Relation to Non-Christian Religions (*Nostra Aetate*; hereafter NA) acknowledges that in the present age the human community's ever closer contacts among nations call for new attention to other religions, especially "to what human beings have in common and what things tend to bring them together" (NA 1; p. 968). The opening words, "*Nostra Aetate*" ("In our age"), proclaim an awareness that the present age is distinctive in its awareness and responsibilities. The council notes that there is a nearly universal religious sense of an unseen power at work in the universe and human life. Since all creation comes from God, is guided by God's providence, and returns to God, the council looks in hope for a fundamental unity among the peoples of the world and calls for dialogue and collaboration to "recognise, preserve and promote those spiritual and moral good things as well as the socio-cultural values which are to be found among them" (NA 2; p. 969).

On the question of whether divine revelation is found in other religious traditions such as Hinduism and Buddhism, the council is cautious, not taking an explicit stand one way or the other.[9] The council sets forth the fundamental principle: "the church rejects nothing of those things which are true and holy in these religions" (NA 2; p. 969). The Catholic Church had long acknowledged that a certain truth about God can be known by natural reason from creation.[10] The term "holy," however, is a category of religious experience, implying a positive reception of God's revealing and saving power. To acknowledge the presence of things that are holy in other religions such as Buddhism and Hinduism suggests that God's revelation and salvation come to people in and through their own religious traditions, however different these may be.

While the Second Vatican Council was cautious in its phrasing, it clearly taught that the Holy Spirit is active throughout all human life, offering grace and salvation to all humans, whether they have known Jesus Christ explicitly or not. If salvation is offered, then so also must the gift of faith be offered. Faith is the acceptance of revelation. Thus, if faith is offered to all humans, then God must be revealed to all humans. It would be strange to imagine this revelation coming to religious persons who are not Christians in some way that bypassed their own explicit religious self-understanding. Thus Vatican II clearly implies that revelation is found in other religious traditions even though the council did not explicitly teach this.[11] Thus the council opened the door to viewing other religious traditions as recipients of divine manifestations and grace.

In July 1998, the Buddhist-Christian Colloquium organized by the Pontifical Council for Interreligious Dialogue in Bangalore, India, issued a statement expressing mutual respect for the scriptures of all religious traditions:

> Buddhists are respectful of the sacred texts of all religions. While they recognize that there are differences between the teachings of different scriptural traditions, they do not criticize views that are different from their own. They encourage their monastics and scholars to study other scriptures in order to understand their proper meaning. The Church respects the sacred texts of other religions and believes that they contain an impressive heritage of religious teachings that have guided the lives of millions of people for centuries. These sacred texts of other religions are seen to contain elements of truth in which Christians are invited to discover seeds of the Word which the bountiful God has given to all people.

These principles open the path for exploring the similarities and differences in the testimonies to revelation from different traditions.

FORMS OF DIALOGUE

More recently, the Catholic Church has declared that "Christians must remember that God has also manifested himself in some way to the followers of other religious traditions. Consequently, it is with receptive minds that they approach the convictions and values of others."[12] The Vatican has distinguished four forms of dialogue.[13] The dialogue of life occurs where members of various traditions encounter each other as neighbors, share their joys, sorrows, and concerns, and seek constructive paths of understanding, cooperation, and exchange. The dialogue of life is increasingly an everyday experience in the United States. Many American Christians encounter Muslims and Jews, Hindus, Buddhists, and members of other traditions as residents in their communities, as fellow workers, as citizens concerned with common issues. Christians, called to love their neighbor, have a responsibility to learn and understand the religious customs and perspectives of their neighbors and to share their own Christian faith and practice with others in appropriate ways. In many religions, such as Judaism, Islam, and Hinduism, revelation plays a major role in shaping people's everyday lives. To the degree that the lives of believers in other religions are shaped by their own experiences and understandings of revelation, Christians face the challenge of relating these perspectives to their own reception of revelation.

A second form of dialogue focuses on action in society for the sake of social justice, development, and liberation. Christians encounter members of other religious traditions in a world of widespread poverty, collective violence, and environmental devastation. Many of the violent conflicts in the world today involve religious animosities. Indeed, the history of the encounters among the world's religions is filled with distrust and hatred, violence and vengeance. The deepest tragedy of the history of religions is that the very movements that should bring human beings closer to each other and to their ultimate source and goal have time and time again become forces of division. In one conflict after another around the world, religious convictions and interpretations of revelation have been used and abused as justifications for violence.

Of the many dimensions of interreligious dialogue, perhaps the most urgent is the need for the religions of the world to cooperate and learn from each other in responding to the worldwide crisis of violence, poverty, economic development, population growth, and ecology. These concerns have been prominent in recent official Catholic overtures to other religious traditions. For example, in his message to Muslims for the end of Ramadan in 1998, Francis Cardinal Arinze, president of the Pontifical Council for Interreligious Dialogue, invited Muslims "to make an 'alliance for peace' in which we renounce violence as a method of solving matters of contention."[14] In a similar vein, Cardinal Arinze's 1998 message to the Buddhist community for the feast of the Buddha, *Vesakh,* "Christians and Buddhists: Together in Hope," juxtaposed the sayings of Jesus on nonviolence from the Sermon on the Mount with Cambodian Buddhist Patriarch Maha Ghosananda's interpretation of the teaching of the Buddha on setting aside all resentment when we are wronged. Cardinal Arinze invited Christians and Buddhists alike to accept each other's differences and work together for the elimination of suffering. In his 1998 message to Hindus for the feast of *Diwali,* Cardinal Arinze noted the multiple crises of violence, poverty, and "globalization without solidarity" in the world today and urged: "We Christians and Hindus, each on our respective spiritual paths, can work together to give increased hope to humanity. Yet first we must accept our differences and show each other mutual respect and true love."

A third form of dialogue involves theological exchange, focusing on the intellectual dimensions of religious traditions, comparing beliefs and visions, often in academic settings. Revelation involves a form of knowing that changes our perspectives on God, on human life, and on all of creation; and many religions have developed sophisticated traditions of reflection on revelation. Yet the knowledge of God given in revelation cannot be equated with knowledge of finite objects in the world because God is never one more finite object among others. For Christians, and in differing ways for Jews, Muslims, and Hindus, the God who is revealed always remains in some way hidden and incomprehensible, transcending human understanding and control. Images, symbols, and concepts orient us to the experience and knowledge of God, but they never fully capture the reality of God. Thus the dialogue of theological exchange faces special challenges of interpretation.

The fourth form of dialogue focuses on religious experience, where practitioners of various traditions discuss the experience of the spiritual life, including prayer and meditation. Some of the most intimate inter-religious dialogues have taken place in an atmosphere of silence, meditation, and prayer.[15] Such conversations include followers of both theistic and nontheistic traditions. For theists, if divine revelation is to be effective, it must become a living experience in each generation. The acceptance of revelation transforms people's lives and calls forth a response in prayer. Buddhists do not believe in or pray to a creating and redeeming God, but some Buddhist traditions have symbols of a divine realm. Moreover, many Buddhists have deeply explored the resources of meditation practice, and there are multiple points of contact among meditation practices in various traditions.

Pope John Paul II invited religious leaders from a wide range of traditions to come to Assisi, Italy, in October 1986, to pray for world peace. Jews and Muslims, Buddhists, Sikhs and Hindus, representatives of traditional African and Native American religions, Shintoists and Jains all participated. The pope noted that such diverse traditions could not make a common prayer together and added "but we can be present while others pray." In his remarks to the assembled leaders, Pope John Paul stressed both respect for the differences among religious traditions and also the importance of affirming a common ground: "If there are many and important differences among us, there is also a common ground whence to operate together in the solution of this dramatic challenge of our age: true peace or catastrophic war."[16] The pope also acknowledged the painful past history of religious conflicts: "But, at the same time and in the same breath, I am ready to acknowledge that Catholics have not always been faithful to this affirmation of faith. We have not always been 'peacemakers.' For ourselves, therefore, but also perhaps, in a sense, for all, this encounter at Assisi is an act of penance."[17] Interreligious dialogue goes hand in hand with repentance for the past violence of our tradition.

In explaining the Catholic Church's position on prayer in interreligious settings, Bishop Jorge Mejía stressed the importance of respecting the differences and the integrity of prayer and meditation in different traditions. To identify the various traditions with each other would be a lack of understanding and respect. But he also stressed that being present while others pray "cannot but enrich our own proper experience of prayer. . . . Indeed, is not our being together to pray, and for no other reason however praiseworthy than to pray, already in itself reality and the proclamation of the harmony of spirits in the pluriformity of choices?"[18] There emerges from the experience of being present while others pray a sense of a deeper harmony and union that respects differences.

Each of the forms of dialogue is closely related to the others. While a theology of revelation involves primarily the dialogue of theological exchange, it is important to keep all the dimensions of dialogue in mind. Reflection on revelation finds its roots not only in the study of texts from scripture and tradition but also in the activities of everyday life, in the quest for justice, and in spiritual experience; and it must be aware of the need for action in a world of suffering.

THE ENCOUNTER OF THE WORLD'S RELIGIONS

The first Parliament of the World's Religions, held in Chicago in 1893 as part of the Columbian Exposition, was symbolic of the growing awareness of other religions. During the opening session, a charismatic young Hindu strode to the podium, opened his arms, and proclaimed: "Sisters and Brothers of America!" The crowd went wild, applauding and cheering. Swami Vivekananda, a disciple of Ramakrishna from Bombay, went on to explain that all the religions of the world arise from revelation coming from God. As a Hindu, he could gladly accept all other religions as true, but he was convinced that his own Hindu tradition expressed the divine revelation most fully and clearly. He hailed the assembly in Chicago as a vindication of the teaching of Krishna, the avatar[†] of Vishnu, in the *Bhagavad Gita:* "Whosoever comes to Me, through whatsoever form, I reach him; all men are struggling through paths which in the end lead to Me." In a later speech, Vivekananda explained his perspective on the plurality of religions: the contradictions among the religions "are only apparent, says the Hindu. The contradictions come from the same truth adapting itself to the different circumstances of different natures. It is the same light coming through different colors."[19] Many Americans who had never heard a Hindu speak before were favorably impressed, and some began to think of Asian religions in a new light.

After the cheers had subsided and the crowds had departed, the challenge posed by Vivekananda remained. While the 1893 Parliament did not immediately usher in the new era of religious peace and understanding for which its organizers had hoped, it did mark a shift in the awareness of many religious leaders. Increasingly, religious thinkers began to interpret their traditions not only for their own followers but also with an awareness of other religions as well.[20] As religious traditions came into closer engagement with one another during the twentieth century, their understandings of the plurality of religions frequently changed. As Christians came to know members of other traditions, they often sensed the wisdom and depth of spiritual insight of these religions. Many Christian missionaries who went to Asia to proclaim the gospel encountered other forms of religious practice which enriched their own lives. The growing numbers of Muslims, Buddhists, and Hindus living in North America and Europe broadens the awareness of many Christians.

The growing openness to the goodness and truth found in other religious traditions promises to shape a new era in the history of religious thought. Even though the conflicts among religions continue to mar communal life, increasing numbers of persons are discovering the vitality and insights of other religious traditions and are incorporating these into their own religious life. Many Christians look to images and stories from other traditions to complement their own tradition. Stories of rabbis and Zen masters, poems from Hassidic and Sufi mystics, and sayings from yogis appear in Christian homilies and writings, shaping the context in which Christians understand the meaning of revelation. The boundaries of religious traditions are increasingly porous, allowing for a variety of exchanges. As we will see in the final chapter, the Zen practice of Masao Abe and the Christian practice of Karl Rahner bear important similarities despite the serious differences in their views of human existence.

Today Christians are more acutely aware than ever before that we are not alone in turning to divine revelation for the source of our religious identity. As Mircea Eliade demonstrated, across the world, a wide variety of traditions has looked to hierophanies to give meaning and orientation to human life.[21] Myths and rituals from around the world recount revelatory events that set the pattern for human existence. For believers in many religious traditions, including Judaism, Islam, and Hinduism, the guidance of divine revelation is one of the most important factors shaping their lives. Jews look to the Exodus and the revelation of the covenant with Yahweh at Mt. Sinai as central to Jewish identity. Muslims find in the revelation of the *Qur'an* to Muhammad the authoritative call from God that shapes their religious identity. Hindus turn to the revelation of the Vedas,[†] the Upanishads,[†] and personal manifestations of gods and goddesses such as Vishnu and Shiva as the sources for their religious self-understanding.

An important exception to this pattern is found in Buddhism, which does not rely on any divine revelation coming from a transcendent God. Early Buddhism remembered Shakyamuni Buddha[†] not as a prophet from God but rather as a pathfinder who said: "I myself found the way. Whom shall I call Teacher? Whom shall I teach?" (Dhammapada 353).[22] Even though later Mahayana Buddhists often saw Shakyamuni Buddha as the manifestation of *dharmakaya*,[†] ultimate reality, this cannot be equated with a theistic notion of revelation from a God who transcends the world. Pure Land Buddhists look to the manifestation of the grace of Amida Buddha to orient their practice, but this cannot be identified with the incarnation of a transcendent God. Nonetheless, despite the profound differences in doctrinal expressions, there is often a convergence in the ways Buddhist and Christian symbols transform human life.[23]

Each religious tradition has developed strategies for interpreting the others within its own framework. Jews traditionally turned to the covenant with Noah as establishing God's relationship with all human-kind; and the contemporary Jewish thinker Abraham Joshua Heschel, sees the God of Israel active in other religious traditions.[24] The early Christian writers Justin Martyr, Clement of Alexandria, and Origen saw the Logos, the Word of God, as present to all human beings but as incarnate only in Jesus Christ. Muslims believe that God has sent messengers to every people and that their central message has always been the same, even though it has often been misunderstood and distorted by those who received it. In the Hindu tradition, Vivekananda acknowledged all religions as proclaiming the truth; and some Hindus have interpreted Jesus himself as an avatar of Vishnu. Many Buddhists see reality as manifesting itself in different ways to different peoples. Tenzin Gyatso, the fourteenth Dalai Lama, welcomes the plurality of religions as necessary and beneficial for the diversity of human beings; just as there are different medicines for the body, so there are different spiritual paths that bring healing to different people.[25] The Japanese Buddhist D. T. Suzuki saw *dharmakaya* (ultimate reality) as responding in different ways to the needs of human beings through all spiritual leaders, including one manifestation in Jesus.[26]

Traditional religious interpretations of other religions have used the central symbols of one tradition to name and judge the role and value of other religions. More recently, John Hick has sought to overcome the limitations of all traditional religious interpretations of other religions by reframing them in his own philosophy of religion as manifestations of one ultimate reality.[27] This strategy shifts the center of interpretation from traditional images and symbols to Hick's own modern Western terminology, which discovers essentially the same reality in all the different manifestations. Even in the quest for openness, there is implicit in Hick's own interpretation a set of value judgments regarding which forms of religion are genuine manifestations of the ultimate. A modern Western framework judges the history of religions, accepting what fits its values and rejecting what does not. Thus Hick's approach does not avoid the problem of criteria in assessing religious claims; it only shifts from traditional religious symbols to a modern Western academic perspective.

Other religions have been present in the awareness of Israel and the Christian church from the very beginning. The strategies of encountering other religions of earlier generations are an important part of the Christian heritage and deserve attention both for the wisdom they teach and for the tragic mistakes they embody.

In this work I am accepting the Christian assumption that God's central revelation is the person and event of Jesus Christ, but I am assuming also that God's revelation is not limited to the history of Israel and the birth of Christianity. The wisdom tradition of Israel and later interpretations of Jesus Christ as the Wisdom of God offer a biblical precedent and foundation for dialogue. The differences among the world's religious traditions are profound and must be respected in dialogue. It is impossible to reduce the wide variety of accounts of hierophanies and revelations to a single common core. Nonetheless, despite radically different perspectives and assumptions, the deepest values of the world's religions resonate deeply with those of other traditions. To build up the community of the world's religions and to develop a global awareness of religious and spiritual values require both respect for the distinctive identities of religious traditions and also a search for the values that unite us.

RELIGIONS IN A WORLD OF VIOLENCE

Religious traditions promise to heal the wounds of human existence by uniting humans to ultimate reality; yet the history of religions is steeped in blood, war, sacrifice, and scapegoating. While many interpreters of religion have focused on the constructive role of religion in human life, the brutal facts of the history of religions impose the stark realization of the intertwining of religion and violence: violence, clothed in religious garb, has repeatedly cast a spell over religion and culture, luring countless "decent" people—from unlettered peasants to learned priests, preachers, and professors—into its destructive dance. Walter Burkert has noted how the bloody sacrifice of a victim was an early experience of the holy, which involved

> terror, bliss, and recognition of an absolute authority, mysterium tremendum, fascinans, and augustum. The most thrilling and impressive combination of these elements occurs in sacrificial ritual: the shock of the deadly blow and flowing blood, the bodily and spiritual rapture of festive eating, the strict order surrounding the whole process—these are the *sacra* par excellence, *ta hiera* [the holy things].[28]

Moreover, texts that have been accepted as revelatory in different traditions, from the Jewish and Christian Bibles to the *Qur'an* to the *Bhagavad Gita*, directly enjoin violent struggle as the will of God.[29]

Violence may be defined as "the attempt of an individual or group to impose its will on others through any nonverbal, verbal, or physical means that inflict psychological or physical injury."[30] While human violence is rooted in the patterns of aggression among primates, humans transform aggression through reflective self-consciousness which uses symbols to justify violence. Human violence is not an instinct but an intentional act. From the dawn of history, religious symbols have played a potent role in supporting violent behavior in holy wars and bloody sacrifices. Religious symbols are not only finite expressions of the infinite reality of God; they have also repeatedly served as concrete incitements to violence.

Violent actions can be understood as symbolic language. James Gilligan, a psychiatrist who has done extensive work with violent criminals, argues that behind seemingly irrational violent acts of mutilation there is a logic of shame and a drive to eliminate the sources of shame. The perpetrator feels ashamed before others and wishes to put an end to the experience, even if it requires the brutal mutilation and murder of the victim. Gilligan notes that eyes, tongues, and lips are frequently the vehicles for shame when people are seen or talked about in ways they do not feel able to endure. The murderer frequently imagines: "If I kill this person in this way, I will kill shame."[31] The result may be seemingly senseless acts of mutilation. Gilligan finds the attempt to escape from shame behind the biblical murder of Abel by Cain (Gen 4:1-6), the blinding of Samson (Judg 16:10-15), the blinding of the men of Sodom (Gen 19:11), and the sometimes violent language of Proverbs (the eye that mocks a father or despises a mother will be plucked out and eaten by birds, 30:17), and various Psalms (12, 52, 55).

Violence involves not only the actions of individuals; it can also be embedded in social, political, and economic structures that systematically subordinate some persons to others. Slavery and poverty are forms of systemic violence; indeed Mohandas Gandhi commented that poverty is the deadliest form of violence.[32] Poverty has been endemic to most traditional societies for centuries. The social structure of Western culture from the ancient Near Eastern societies through the Hellenistic, Roman, and medieval worlds until the rise of the industrial age was dominated by a landed aristocracy that controlled most wealth and dominated religious, intellectual, and political life.[33] The dominant political and socioeconomic structures were generally accepted because they were believed to be the will of God or the gods. Thus religion was implicated in maintaining social structures of violence from the earliest historical records. There does, however, emerge an alternative vision, in early Egyptian literature, in the Hebrew prophets and sages, and in the example of Jesus, which protests against such inequities and demands justice. Religion again and again has been ambiguous, at times supporting established structures of inequality and yet at other times calling for change.

For many in the late twentieth century, the greatest challenge to belief in divine revelation is the sheer enormity of evil done by humans to each other and the traditional role of religion in supporting or justifying violence. The massive deaths in World War I, the Shoah, the urban bombings and mass killings of World War II, the purges of Stalin, the mass murders under Mao Tse-Tung and the Khmer Rouge, the more recent slaughters in Rwanda and the Balkans raise questions about the very meaning of human existence and challenge the notion of God's presence in history. Bernard Kouchner, a French doctor and leader in the humanitarian group Doctors without Borders, sees evil in the deaths of children around the world and believes that evil is both more powerful than good and also more widespread. Looking at Christians, Kouchner wonders why more Christians in France did not resist the Nazis and the Vichy regime from 1940 to 1945.[34] Despite his efforts, he finds himself unable to believe in God. To speak of a divine revelation in a world of massive unjust suffering seems to many a cruel deception, a forlorn hope, or a futile evasion of reality.

In his early work, the Jewish thinker Richard L. Rubenstein charged that all the traditional schemas of revelation and salvation history, both Jewish and Christian, are meaningless after the horror of the Shoah: "If there is a God of history, He is the ultimate author of Auschwitz. . . . Few ideas in Jewish religious thought have been more decisively mistaken, in spite of their deep psychological roots, than the terrible belief that God acts meaningfully in history."[35] For Rubenstein, the biblical God of covenant and election is an illusion that must die; instead, God can be named "Holy Nothingness," an image informed by the Jewish mystical tradition that is close to some Buddhist understandings of ultimate reality as *shunyata*, emptying or absolute nothingness.[36]

The problems raised by violence press ever more inexorably upon critical reflection in many disciplines, interrupting thought and raising the challenge of exploring nonviolent options for reshaping the world. While some blame religion for increasing humanity's woes and turn to secular forms of thought and action, other thinkers confront the problem of massive suffering while remaining within their religious traditions and looking to revelation as grounds for hope in a world of violence. The world's major religions have given birth to traditions of both peace and violence, and it would be one-sided to dismiss religions because of their historic complicity in violence. In the late twentieth century, religions have indeed been sources of animosity, but they have also been among the most creative forces working for nonviolent resolutions of conflicts. Secular movements, often inspired by Marxist ideals, have sought to right the ancient injustices and inequities of society, but have themselves repeatedly turned to massive levels of violence to enforce conformity with the vision of a new, egalitarian society.

Confronted with the massive evil of the twentieth century, many religious thinkers have admitted that there is no theoretical, conceptual resolution of the problem violence presents. Massive evil is a surd that resists explanation. There are only practical responses of resistance. For Catholic theologian Edward Schillebeeckx, Christianity does not offer us a clear, conceptual explanation of evil. Instead of trying to explain massive evil, Schillebeeckx sees suffering as calling forth a new awareness of our solidarity with all humans and demanding action against injustice.[37] Similarly, Jewish philosopher Emil Fackenheim warns that there is no overcoming of the Shoah in thought. There can be *teshuvah*, repentance, and mending; there can be resistance to massive evil, but no overcoming.[38] For both Schillebeeckx and Fackenheim, revelation offers a way forward in the face of violence but not a comprehension of it.

RENÉ GIRARD:
REVELATION AS THE UNMASKING OF VIOLENCE

Despite the prominence of violence in the Bible, most theologians have devoted little attention to the relation between revelation and violence.[39] René Girard, a French historian, literary critic, and anthropologist, has launched a major effort to find a single explanation for the interpenetration of religion and violence, tracing the roots of all religions *except* Judaism and Christianity to the directing of violence into manageable pathways. Girard proposes an original theology of revelation that finds its focal point in mimesis† and violence. All other religions, according to Girard, establish social order by channeling violence onto surrogate victims or scapegoats, and they justify and sacralize violence in the name of God or the gods. Only biblical revelation takes the side of the victim and exposes the mechanisms of violence so that they may be overcome.[40]

Girard has developed a three-point mimetic theory† that claims to explain the central dynamics of human desire, behavior, patterns of violence, and the meaning of biblical revelation. The first part of Girard's theory involves the construction of desire and is based on the great novelists from Cervantes to Dostoevski, Stendahl, and Proust.[41] Girard claims that from the time we are very young we learn what is desirable from other persons whom we take as models: we imitate the desire of our model. Our most basic needs are shaped by biology, but the way we fulfill these needs depends on models. Girard calls this process "mimesis." He uses the Greek word for imitation to stress that this process can take place without our being aware of it. Often we think our desires are spontaneous, but in fact we have learned them from others. Desire arises from our awareness of a lack within us, a lack not only of possessions but of being. We desire to be by imitating someone else.

Because desire is mimetic, it is triangular. Mimetic desire does not desire the object directly, but only through the mediation of a model. A mysterious ray descends from the mediator or model which makes the object shine with a false brilliance. We see that someone else desires something, and we follow, even though we may not be aware of the dynamics of this process. Though it may be difficult and even humiliating to admit to ourselves, what we really desire is to become ourselves by appropriating the being of the model we imitate. The object receives its luster from the model's desire, but it fails to satisfy. As Hermia says in Shakespeare's *A Midsummer Night's Dream*: "Oh Hell! To choose love by another's eyes" (I, 1, 140).[42]

Girard distinguishes two forms of mediation. In external mediation†, the mediator or model is so exalted that there is no realistic prospect of displacing him or her. In internal mediation†, the subject becomes increasingly a threat to the mediator or model. A kindergarten student desires to be like the teacher but does not threaten the being of the teacher, and so this situation offers an example of external mediation. A sharp Ph.D. student, however, may well challenge the professor, and this rivalry threatens to become internal mediation. Girard notes the cases, especially in mathematics or physics, where students in their twenties occasionally make more brilliant discoveries than their teachers have ever made in their careers. Earlier, their professors had praised their good work, but after a certain point the mentors become threatened and begin to react defensively. Now the model seems to block the way of the disciple.

Models place us in a double bind: They tell us to imitate them; but if, in imitating them, we threaten their own position, they quickly become rivals who tell us not to imitate them. When we imitate the model's thoughts, there is harmony. When we imitate the model's desires and have the power to challenge the model, the model inevitably becomes our obstacle and rival. This double bind is one of the most endemic and enduring of all human relationships, according to Girard.[43]

The second part of Girard's theory focuses on patterns of violence and scapegoating. Mimesis inevitably leads to rivalry, and rivalry leads to violence, whether physical or not. Violence is itself mimetic, rendering humans more and more like each other and calling forth more violence. Thus violence repeatedly threatens to escalate out of control. Girard believes that since the dawn of human history, the dynamic of mimetic rivalry† has led to conflicts that end in violence. Because of mimesis, tensions in any group will increase over time. At the very beginning of human awareness, Girard believes that proto-humans, caught in the grip of mimetic rivalry, discovered that violence could threaten to overwhelm a group, making common life impossible. Just as the group was about to destroy itself in mutual violence, the death or expulsion of a particular individual or group of individuals had a mysterious, calming effect. Once the body of the victim was stretched out on the earth dead, a wonderful peace came over the group. This spontaneous process, repeated incessantly over centuries, taught early humans that the most effective way to prevent uncontrolled violence was to discharge the tensions of the group onto particular individuals.

In time, the spontaneous primal murders were ritualized and sacralized. Thus since prehistory, primal religions have demanded bloody sacrifices, whether human or animal. Girard argues that the primal experience of the sacred is violence directed at a surrogate victim or scapegoat. Because of the mysterious calm that the process brings, the victim is often hailed as the bearer of peace and may even be seen as a divine victim. Girard calls this process the "surrogate victim mechanism,"† popularly known as scapegoating, and he claims that this dynamic lies behind the sacrifices and the mythologies of the world's religions.

Girard discerns a pattern in mythology and primal religions that is repeated over and over again in various ways in later historical cultures. There is first a crisis of distinctions: something is wrong—differences are erased—the usual patterns of order break down. The crisis of distinctions is a social and cultural crisis that threatens community life. The crisis can be caused by illness. For example, a plague is threatening a city, eliminating the distinction between the living and the dead. People seek a moral cause: Who is responsible for the plague? The story of *Oedipus Rex* begins with the question: Who is the culprit who is causing the gods to send the plague? Girard claims that the real referent of the lack of differentiation is the scene of mimetic rivalry rendering the members of a group more and more angry, more and more violent, and more and more like each other.

The second stage is to identify the crimes that have caused the crisis. These are often crimes that themselves eliminate proper distinctions, such as the charges that Oedipus has slept with his mother and killed his father. The group projects its animosities and jealousies and hatreds onto the victim. When successful, the process focuses all the wrath of the community on the scapegoat. His expulsion or execution brings the mimetic rivalry to an end and thus brings peace.

In identifying the scapegoat, there are stereotypical signs of a victim. These are marks that set people apart, rendering them different from most others and thus suspicious. The mark can be a disability: Oedipus limps. It is often a position of marginality: Oedipus is a stranger who rose very quickly to a high position of power. He has a double marginality, first as a foreigner, an outsider, and second as a king, a powerful figure who is above the usual run of society. The victim may be guilty or may be innocent, but the objective guilt or innocence is not as important as the social dynamic of blaming someone. The victim is viewed as powerful, whether this is objectively true or not.

The third stage is the violence itself, either killing or expelling the victim from the group. This is often done in a way that leaves no individual responsible for the death, for example, by stoning, or by a crowd forcing a person to walk ever closer to a cliff until he or she falls off. The lynch mobs in the South of the United States and the anti-Jewish pogroms in Europe played this role of discharging violence onto victims. The anonymous crowd performed the deed. No one could be identified, and no one would be punished.

In the final stage at the end of the pattern, peace returns, and the victim in mythology often becomes transfigured and revered. In the play *Oedipus at Colonnus*, the different Greek cities revere Oedipus at the end of his life and want him to come to their city to die so that his grave will be a healing shrine in their locality. Girard clams that human society begins in the lynch mob, but myths cover up this origin. Exclusion and violence are the most lasting bonds of social cohesion. Traditional social order is purchased at the price of the suffering of surrogate victims.

One example of this pattern lay at the very center of ancient Rome's self-understanding. In Roman mythology, Romulus and Remus were the founders of the city of Rome. Romulus traced the boundaries of the city of Rome, but Remus did not respect them. Thus Romulus killed Remus. In Roman culture Romulus was thought to be perfectly justified in killing Remus. For the city to exist, boundaries had to be respected. Thus Romulus's primordial murder of his brother set the stage for Roman power, which demanded that order and boundaries be respected unconditionally.

According to Girard, every culture without exception arises from the incessantly repeated patterns of mimetic rivalry and scapegoating. Some authors, like the Greek tragedians, caught a glimpse of the underlying dynamics of the cycle and the arbitrariness of the choice of victim; but outside of the Bible there is never a full unveiling of the pattern of violence and a rejection of it.

The third part of Girard's theory focuses on divine revelation in the biblical tradition as God's nonviolent response to mimetic rivalry and the surrogate victim mechanism. The God of Israel and of Jesus Christ is not a mimetic rival of humans and does not demand sacrificial victims. Instead, God rather expresses solidarity with victims even to the point of dying on the cross. According to Girard's interpretation of the Bible, the people of ancient Israel were, like all others, originally steeped in the surrogate victim mechanism. As we will see in a later chapter, some aspects of the holy war ideology in Israel do conform to Girard's model of sacred violence: the will of God demands the destruction of one's enemy.[44]

What is distinctive about Israel, however, is that many biblical authors, especially the psalmists, the prophets, and the sages of Israel, recognized the primordial pattern of scapegoating, exposed it, and denounced it. Many psalms express the perspective of the victim surrounded by the hostile crowd, and the author of the Book of Job sides with the maligned Job rather than his friends. Girard finds in Job an example of a victim of mimetic envy who becomes the scapegoat of his people but is vindicated by God.[45] At the beginning of the story, Job is a prominent, powerful man, at the height of influence in his society and thus the object of jealousy. When struck with misfortune, he becomes a prime candidate for the scapegoat mechanism,[†] and his so-called friends demand that he admit he deserves his sufferings. When he refuses to play along with their script, his so-called friends and others turn on him with fury, heaping up more and more insults. The usual pattern of mythological scapegoating would assume that Job is guilty and deserves to be punished; but at the end of the book, God tells the friends that they have not spoken rightly of God as has his servant Job (42:7).

Similarly, the Suffering Servant poems in Second Isaiah present the age-old mythological drama: a crowd surrounds an innocent victim and heaps abuse upon him (Isa 52:13-53:12). The point of view, however, has changed. The biblical author does not accept the charges; the victim is innocent and is vindicated by God. This sets the pattern for Girard's reading of the New Testament. God appears in history as the innocent victim who goes to his death as the scapegoat. Far from demanding victims, God identifies with the victims and thus exposes the surrogate victim mechanism as a fraud and a deception. God responds to our violence with nonviolent love. Paul's conversion turns on the realization that he is persecuting God. The realization that God is on the side of the victims is, for Girard, the center of biblical revelation.

Girard's theory shapes his interpretation of current events, including the mass deaths of the twentieth century. Prior to biblical revelation, Girard claims, cultures achieved relative levels of social stability through scapegoating certain individuals and groups. After centuries of work, the gospel has largely destroyed the power of the surrogate victim mechanism, and conventional culture is now in a painful process of disintegration. As the age-old patterns of scapegoating are progressively exposed, they begin to lose their power, and thus they can no longer offer the stability and order found in earlier centuries. Paradoxically, however, some humans continue to use the patterns of scapegoating ever more frantically, leading to the massive killings of the twentieth century. History as we have known it for millennia is coming to an end, and we face a dramatic, even apocalyptic, choice: total destruction or total renunciation of violence. While noting that Christianity has historically often failed to understand the implications of its own revelation, Girard gives credit to biblical perspectives for the widespread contemporary concern for the oppressed and the victims of history.

EVALUATION OF MIMETIC THEORY

Girard's proposal does illumine a wide range of aspects of religion and culture. It is sobering to note how frequently societies have turned to exclusion and violence, expulsions, lynchings, and pogroms, often justified by religious imagery, to cement the social order. By focusing attention on mimetic rivalry and the surrogate victim mechanism, Girard has made a major contribution to social theory and to Christian theology.

When mimetic theory is extrapolated into *the* explanation of all institutions of all human cultures, however, doubts arise about the status of the evidence and the assumptions of the argument. Too often discussions of Girard tend toward an all-or-nothing choice: either uncritical enthusiasm or skeptical dismissal. It is helpful to distinguish between the intuitive power of Girard's proposal, which can be quite compelling for many situations, as numerous applications have shown, and the formal logical status of many of the claims advanced, which remain problematic and unproven. Girard has proposed a hypothesis that is most intriguing, but it has by no means reached the stage of empirical verification; and in many cases it is difficult to see how an affirmative judgment could be made.

The theory of the primal murders and the primordial origin of religion and all human culture in the surrogate victim mechanism is highly speculative because we lack adequate data from the period that Girard takes as foundational for all human culture. Girard seeks to reconstruct a form of mimesis prior to symbols, a mimesis that would be the first origin of human consciousness and culture and religious symbolism. There remains a gap, however, between what we can reconstruct of the primitive drives of hominids and the emergence of higher cognitive and symbolic capacities. Girard claims to have found the missing link in the surrogate victim mechanism, but one can question whether the power of mimesis and the effect of the primal murders can really account for the entire range of development of early humans. Was the surrogate victim mechanism really the motor driving the development of the human brain in interaction with cultural factors, as Girard claims? How can we possibly know?

Moreover, the link between the putative crisis of distinctions and the first manifestation of the sacred remains tenuous. According to Girard, "the sole purpose of religion is to prevent the recurrence of reciprocal violence." Girard also claims that "humanity's very existence is due primarily to the operation of the surrogate victim." Furthermore, he argues that "[t]he origin of symbolic thought lies in the mechanism of the surrogate victim," and that this mechanism also "gives birth to language and imposes itself as the first object of language. . . . It is the surrogate victim who provides men with the will to conquer reality and the weapons for victorious intellectual campaigns."[46] All this seems overstated, and it is hard to see what would count as verification for the earliest periods of human existence.

Moreover, the evidence of later ages is itself ambiguous. There are many texts and practices that fit Girard's theory rather well, but others are less clear. Joseph Henninger has pointed out that many cultures have offered bloodless sacrifices, such as fruits, grains, foods from plants, milk and milk products, and alcoholic libations.[47] These are presented to supernatural beings who often do not need them, and the primary motives are thanksgiving and homage. Henninger argues that the offering of firstfruits in many cultures involves intellectual assumptions and emotions that are far removed from the scapegoating patterns that Girard identifies. Moreover, there is no evidence that the sacrifice of humans and animals is older than the offering of firstfruits.

Anthropologist Valerio Valeri argues against Girard that "it is impossible to postulate a 'pure' psychic dynamics that would be considered the 'cause' of culture. Psychic processes take place in culture and presuppose it."[48] Valeri also notes that the sacrifice of vegetable offerings, which are not killed but are simply allowed to decompose, is not accounted for by Girard.[49]

The theory of Girard risks becoming a tour de force that extrapolates far beyond all available evidence. Girard claims that most of historical culture is involved in a conspiracy to cover over its origins, and this sets up a logical difficulty in assessing the evidence. If the surrogate victim mechanism appears only in fragmented form, supporters of the theory can claim that this reflects the attempt to cover over the guilty, violent origins of culture. The problem with a hidden mechanism is that one can find it everywhere and not be refuted. Girard himself admits that his theory is not falsifiable in the sense that philosopher of science Karl Popper required of a scientific theory. It is not clear what evidence could serve to disconfirm the theory as Girard proposes it. The overarching problem of the proposal comes from the strain of an effort to force all human culture into a single pattern, which is itself often disguised.

It is doubtful that scapegoating is as universal and all-encompassing a phenomenon as Girard makes it out to be. Girard is also vulnerable to the charge of continuing the tradition of Christian triumphalism. He typically finds true religion only in Jewish and Christian texts and neglects the resources of other traditions, such as Jainism, Hinduism, and Buddhism, for renouncing violence and fostering forms of life free from mimetic rivalry and violence. Girard's analyses of recent history tend to be one-sided, explaining complex phenomena by a single cause and neglecting other possible factors. Can we really understand the mass murders of the twentieth century as due to the breakdown of the surrogate victim mechanism?

Even though the full-blown claims of Girard's system are dubious, nonetheless his analyses are provocative and significant contributions. While his overarching project does not succeed in its totalizing ambitions, Girard offers many insightful analyses and a helpful vocabulary for naming the dynamics of desire and violence in religion and society. One of his most important contributions is to challenge Christian theologians to attend to data that have been frequently neglected in discussions of biblical revelation. In this discussion I propose a critical appropriation of some of Girard's insights without endorsing his overall theory. Just as many people who are not strict Freudians use terms such as repression, sublimation, superego, and transference while not accepting the full Freudian theory, so Girard's analyses of mimetic rivalry and of the surrogate victim mechanism or scapegoating can be used without acceptance of his entire theory. In this work I will borrow aspects of Girard's theory where it is helpful in illumining the dynamics of revelation, but I will also note some cases where the data of other religions do not support his exclusivist claims or his harsh judgments of other religions.

DIALOGUE AND NONVIOLENCE

The struggle to overcome violence and form a healthy global community is one of the strongest reasons for interreligious dialogue. Indeed, the series of international movements of nonviolent resistance are among the most important fruits of interreligious exchange. The tragic history of religious violence, including that done by Christians in the name of God, is a scandal to the world. One of the central paradoxes of Christianity is that the teaching of Jesus as remembered by the New Testament stresses nonviolence so strongly, and yet the history of Christianity is so filled with violence. One of the greatest surprises of the twentieth century is that it was a Hindu, Mohandas Gandhi, who taught the world how effective and practical the nonviolent teachings of Jesus could be in concrete social and political conflicts. His example inspired Martin Luther King Jr. and countless others around the world in a series of movements of nonviolent protest.

Catholic theologians have long looked to both scripture and tradition to understand the meaning of revelation, and magisterial teachings sometimes presuppose that scripture and tradition are simply positive witnesses to divine revelation. Exploring the relation of revelation, interreligious dialogue, and violence, however, forces Christians to confront the ambiguity of both the scriptures and the later Christian tradition and also to explore the significance of God's entry into a world of violence in Jesus Christ. The most effective response is to acknowledge and learn from the past so that we may shape a more peaceful world and a healthy community of the world's religions.

From the beginning of the history of Israel, understandings of revelation have involved defining the community's identity in relation to other religious traditions; this process has often been conflictual, repeatedly involving violence. The Bible participates in the life of the religious traditions of the ancient world and emerges from it, so that there is both similarity in images and themes and also a distinctive identity of the religion of Israel and, later, of Christianity. Amid the variety of voices in the Bible, the wisdom tradition offers a precedent for acknowledging the presence of God in other religious traditions and for participating in dialogue. Because the wisdom of God is always present in the world, Israel's sages acknowledged that they could learn from others. However, there is another side to the biblical trajectory. In the repeated conflicts of Israel with its neighbors, violence was frequently believed to be the sacred will of God. Later, Christianity defined its own identity in relation to the Jewish tradition from which it emerged and in relation to the religions in its early environment. This process of identity formation involved both a critical appropriation of elements of other traditions and also a vehement rhetoric of abuse, which would prepare the way for later physical violence.

To proclaim the revelation of God in Jesus Christ today calls for Christians critically to appropriate our own tradition in dialogue with other religious voices. This work will explore the various ways in which biblical and classical Christian authors understood other religions and violence, and it will survey selected voices from major religious traditions of South and East Asia. The biblical wisdom trajectory, as well as its influence on early and medieval Christian thought, will provide one leitmotif, offering a positive basis for dialogue. The theory of religion and violence of Girard will provide a secondary leitmotif, offering one way to name the ways in which religions have sacralized violence in the name of God.

I make no pretension of completeness either in the selection of other religious traditions or in the discussion of history. For reasons of space, I will not discuss the primal religions or other traditions such as Jainism and Sikhism. My historical surveys from the Bible and Christian tradition are also necessarily selective. I will discuss classical Jewish and Muslim perspectives during the historical periods in which Christians first defined their relations with these traditions.

At the center of Christian revelation are the life, death, and resurrection of Jesus Christ; God enters into the situation of human suffering and violence, suffers and accepts our violence without retaliation, and overcomes it. To a world with a multitude of religions and incessant violence, Christians proclaim that God has revealed Godself and God's will for humankind in the life of Israel and in Jesus Christ. The Christian tradition has long proclaimed that God is incomprehensible and hidden even in revelation, but the terrors of the twentieth century have given a new and frightening meaning to incomprehensibility and hiddenness. In a world of violence, the grace-filled encounters with other religious traditions are themselves signs of hope.

2

Biblical Revelation and Other Religions

The revelation of God to the people of Israel and the early Christian community is unique in being rooted in the particular history, narratives, events, and traditions of one nation and in being centered on the person of Jesus Christ. It also participates in the broader history of the world's religions. The images and narratives of divine revelation in the Hebrew Bible emerge from the religious world of the ancient Near East and share many of the assumptions of Israel's neighbors. The boundary between the religion of Israel and the religions of other ancient Near Eastern peoples was not an impermeable, fixed barrier, but rather a constantly changing, complex process of appropriation and resistance. While biblical authors sharply rejected the gods and many of the religious practices of other nations, they also drew heavily upon the imagery and language of other traditions to describe Yahweh. In Israel's relation to other religions, the polemic against idols is intertwined with the repeated appropriation of themes and perspectives from other traditions. Israel's experience of God's revelation was both distinctively its own and also part of the broader horizon of contemporary religious experience. Similarly, the New Testament's witness to Jesus Christ participates in the broader horizon of Hellenistic religions. Both the Bible's resistance to idolatry and its openness to drawing upon other religions' images and values provide important precedents for Christianity's contemporary encounter with other religions. One of the greatest challenges in interreligious dialogue is to respect both the uniqueness and the distinctive identity of each tradition and also to acknowledge the ways in which different traditions share important values and perspectives. To assert either similarity or difference alone would distort the relations among religions.

Gabriel Moran has helpfully distinguished two senses of uniqueness.[1] The uniqueness of a thing in a universe of independently existing substances consists in its exclusivity and unrelatedness. To be unique in this sense is to be different from others and set apart from them. There is, however, another way of viewing uniqueness. To be a unique reality in a universe of interpenetrating relationships is to be inclusive and related to others. Uniqueness in the second sense comes not from standing apart or being wholly different but rather from the modes of participation in relationships with others. In contemporary cosmology the world of independent things has given way to a universe of mutual relationships. As we will see in chapter 7, the recent discoveries of chaos theory[†] shape a vision of the interconnectedness of the entire universe in which each part can be understood only in dynamic interrelationship with the whole. In light of both historical scholarship on the ancient world and also the insights of recent cosmology, we can see that religious traditions are not self-contained units unto themselves but rather ongoing, self-organizing systems that live through processes of feedback and exchange with their environment.

Revelation can be viewed as unique in Moran's first sense only by being an exclusive possession of something not available elsewhere. Moran proposes that revelation can be better understood in the second sense as a participation in an ongoing process: "Revelation would not be a thing to apply to people; it would not be a thing at all, but a complex relation."[2] The presentation of revelation in the biblical witness is unique not by being completely different from other traditions but rather in the distinctive way in which it participates in the broader religious life of the human community.

METHOD OF CONTRAST

Many earlier biblical scholars sought to identify revelation in the Hebrew Bible by a method of sharp contrast in relation to other ancient religions. Revelation was understood to come in sharp contradiction to the expressions of other religions. In the middle of the twentieth century, many discussions of revelation in the Hebrew Bible stressed the distinctiveness of Israel's confessions of God acting in historical events.[3] This sense of a sharp antithesis between Israel and its neighbors suited the neo-orthodox climate of the time. Karl Barth proclaimed that the revelation of God to ancient Israel and in Jesus Christ had nothing in common with any other revelation in a different religious tradition.[4]

Biblical scholars frequently portrayed other nations as having mythological, nature religions that celebrated the cycles of nature's fertility year after year; and they drew a dramatic contrast to biblical revelation, which rejected these cults as idolatrous and proclaimed the God of Israel who acted in specific, nonrepeatable historical events such as the Exodus or the return from exile in Babylon. The biblical God was revealed not in the cycles of nature but in "mighty deeds." Where other religions were based on myths, the religion of Israel was thought to be solidly rooted in history. G. Ernest Wright, the leader of the Biblical Theology Movement in the United States in the 1950s and 1960s, held that the Old Testament served the Christian church as "a bulwark against paganism," reassuring Christians that other religions could not prepare for the Messiah. According to Wright, it was crucial for Christians that the faith of ancient Israel from its earliest days be "an utterly unique and radical departure from all contemporary pagan religions."[5] The titles of Wright's books were programmatic for his theology: *The God Who Acts: Biblical Theology as Recital* and *The Old Testament against Its Environment*.[6] Wright meant the term "against" in a strongly adversarial sense.

The Biblical Theology Movement insisted that God was not an immanent power in nature discernible through human reflection. The transcendent God had acted in a unique way in the history of Israel, and these unparalleled actions were the heart of divine revelation. Thus biblical theology consisted in a recital of the acts of God, and Christian theologians and preachers often focused on themes of salvation history in the Old Testament. The Biblical Theology Movement also stressed the difference between Israel's experience of God in history and Greece's philosophical quest for understanding. Hebrew thought was praised for being concrete, dynamic, and historical, in sharp contrast to the allegedly abstract, static, atemporal categories of the Greeks. Biblical revelation was thought to come not in natural cycles or in abstract propositions but in historical events.

In such a climate, the biblical wisdom tradition, with its affinities to early Egyptian and Mesopotamian sources and its later openness to Hellenistic Greek thought, appeared to have little to offer a contemporary Christian theology of revelation. The wisdom books of the Hebrew Bible, Proverbs, Job, and Qoheleth, never mention Abraham or the Exodus or any other event in the history of Israel. These books did not fit the model of historical revelation that was enshrined as distinctively Israelite. Indeed, the wisdom books were sometimes judged not to be authentically Israelite precisely because they borrowed so heavily from other nations. The German Old Testament scholar H. D. Preuss went so far as to deny that there is any significant difference between the wisdom traditions of Israel and other ancient Near Eastern cultures. Preuss, after persuasively demonstrating the common heritage of Israelite and foreign wisdom, proceeded to deny the value of wisdom for Christian worship and theology.[7]

A number of difficulties brought about the demise of the Biblical Theology Movement. Its reconstruction of the history of Israel came into question, and the exclusion of the wisdom tradition from theological relevance became increasingly doubtful. Walter Brueggemann stressed both the importance of wisdom for biblical theology and also its difference from the perspectives of the Biblical Theology Movement.[8] Scholars also discovered more and more links between the wisdom books and other portions of the Bible.[9] Though defining "wisdom influence" remains problematic, it became increasingly difficult for scholars to isolate the wisdom trajectory as an anomaly or to reject it as inauthentic. The wisdom tradition belongs with the historical and prophetic works as a witness to Israel's faith and a source for understanding revelation.

A further difficulty was that the sharp contrast that the Biblical Theology Movement had drawn between Israel and its neighbors did not hold up to close scrutiny. In 1952 Morton Smith identified elements of the common theology of the ancient Near East that Israel shared with the other religious traditions of that environment.[10] The underlying structure of belief was common, with different forms of expression. According to Smith, Israel accepted the common ancient Near Eastern belief in one god who is accorded the highest worship; Israel, like other nations, thought that its god was an effective agent both in nature and in historical events; Israel represented its god with symbols of power; and the god combined the attributes of justice, mercy, and power. The relationship of the Hebrew people to the god is contractual, and there are prophets who interpret the relationship between the god and the people.[11] Smith argued that points of similarity between Israel and its neighbors need not all have been due to direct borrowing; similar situations and assumptions pervaded the Near East.[12]

The Biblical Theology Movement had claimed that Yahweh was unique in acting in historical events. However, Bertil Albrektson demonstrated that the gods of other ancient peoples were also seen as acting in history, especially in political and military actions.[13] Scholars have found points of similarity for virtually every aspect of Israelite religion.[14] More recently, Mark S. Smith has argued that early Israelite and Canaanite cultures were fundamentally similar and that early biblical descriptions of Yahweh incorporated many traits of Canaanite deities.[15] Smith proposes a model of convergence and differentiation, with many characteristics of various gods converging in Yahweh. The main difference was that Yahweh never engaged in sexual activity or went through a process of dying, as Canaanite deities did.[16] Smith notes that even polemics against other gods often include a positive element of incorporation of the characteristics of other deities.[17]

Similarly, Robert Karl Gnuse has argued that the emergence of monotheism in Israel was not as early, sharp, and revolutionary as previous scholars had assumed, but rather took place through a gradual process of evolution which included dialogue with other cultures and moments of dramatic transformation. Often, when biblical prophets and the Deuteronomic historians were attacking polytheism, idolatry, child sacrifice, and the use of images, they were rejecting earlier accepted practices in Israel itself.[18]

RENÉ GIRARD

The method of contrast appears in a new framework in the work of René Girard, who insists on the difference between other religions and biblical revelation. According to Girard, from the dawn of history religions have channeled sacred violence into particular patterns focused on surrogate victims or scapegoats so that unrestrained violence would not destroy the entire community. The patterns of primeval violence shaped the ancient Near Eastern world, and thus it is not surprising that the Hebrew Bible shows signs of divine justification of violence, as in the holy war narratives of the conquest of Palestine. What is remarkable about the Bible, for Girard, is that it repeatedly reverses the otherwise universal pattern of scapegoating, taking the side of the victim. Whereas pagan gods demand victims and promise peace only at the price of blood, the God of Israel and of Jesus vindicates the victim, exposes the surrogate victim mechanism as a fraud, and offers a genuine peace.

Girard draws a sharp contrast between the points of view of mythology and biblical revelation; even when the themes are the same, the vantage point of the author is different. Roman religion justified the murder of Remus by Romulus and incorporated it into the founding myth of the city of Rome. By contrast, when in the Bible, God asks Cain, "Where is Abel, your brother?" there is no justification for the murder. Abel is a victim of his brother's jealousy, but he is innocent. Where myths justify murder and then try to cover up the traces, the Bible condemns the murder and draws it out into the open. The blood of Abel cries out from the earth to God (Gen 4:3-16).

Girard contrasts the story of Joseph in Genesis with the story of Oedipus.[19] The story of Joseph and his brothers begins in rivalry among siblings (Gen 37:2-36). The brothers are jealous because of their father's preference for Joseph and because of Joseph's dreams that he will lord it over them. They are about to kill him, but they decide to expel him instead. This is a classic scenario of mimetic rivalry leading to violence or expulsion. Rivalry leads to tension, and Joseph is threatened with death and finally driven out to keep the peace.

Joseph goes to Egypt, is taken into the house of Potiphar, where he begins to rise to power, becoming like a son to Potiphar. Thus the sexual advances of Potiphar's wife are almost incestuous. When Oedipus, another powerful foreigner, was accused of incest, the charge was accepted. Instead of blaming Joseph, however, the author of Genesis clearly presents him as innocent; and in the end he is vindicated. When famine hits Palestine and the brothers have to come to beg for food from their unrecognized brother, Joseph has the power to continue the scapegoating pattern. The usual patterns of mimetic violence would dictate that he treat the brothers as they had treated them. Joseph refuses to do this, however, and instead decides to scrutinize his brothers. On the brothers' second visit to Egypt, he proposes a test to see if the brothers have learned anything. By falsely accusing Benjamin of theft, Joseph sets up a situation where the brothers are invited to scapegoat another younger brother who is dear to their father. They can abandon Benjamin and return home free of another younger brother. When Judah refuses to sacrifice Benjamin and offers his own life instead, the scapegoat mechanism is exposed and overturned (Gen 44). Then Joseph can reveal himself as their brother, and reconciliation takes place. The scapegoating patterns of the myth of Oedipus are reversed point by point in the narrative of Joseph.

In a similar vein, Girard interprets the Exodus as a reversal of the age-old mythological pattern of scapegoating. According to the usual mythic pattern, the Egyptians would tell the story of the foreign people who entered the land, became very powerful, and brought plagues and misfortune. After the foreigners were driven out, peace returned and life could continue. The mythic pattern justifies the primordial murder or expulsion that lies at the foundation of social order. The Bible tells the same story, but from the point of view of the victims. In the Book of Exodus, the Israelites are not the scapegoats but the object of God's affection. The Egyptians are not the guarantors of order but the opponents of God. The mythological pattern of blaming the surrogate victim is reversed, and a new possibility for human existence is opened up. This, according to Girard, is "absolutely unique in the foundation of Judaism."[20] For Girard, what is distinctive in the biblical witness is the unmasking of the patterns of scapegoating and violence by God's entering history on the side of the victim.

Girard's insights into the patterns of violence and scapegoating are important and at times profound; however, he greatly simplifies the relation between Israel and its neighbors and neglects the similarities of values shared by Israel and its neighbors. Egypt and Mesopotamia had developed their own sense of social justice and concern for victims centuries before Israel. The Egyptian *Tale of Two Brothers* told of the trials and eventual vindication of a virtuous youth who was falsely accused in a manner very similar to Joseph. Indeed, it was probably one source that was later incorporated into the biblical story of Joseph. In the Egyptian tale, Bata, the unmarried younger brother, is living with his older brother Anubis and his wife.[21] Bata is industrious and virtuous. The wife, attracted to the physical strength of Bata, invites him to share her bed for an hour during the day. Bata rejects her vehemently and returns to the fields. The wife, frightened of what has happened, falsely accuses

Bata of trying to seduce her and of beating her. Anubis plans to kill his younger brother, but the brother escapes—thanks to the warning of his cows. Bata prays to Re-Harakhti, castrates himself, and flees. After many adventures, he becomes the Pharaoh of all Egypt and has the opportunity to judge his brother. He could practice mimetic violence by taking revenge on his brother, but instead he forgives him and installs him as crown prince. The Egyptian tale anticipates point by point Girard's analysis of rivalry, incest, and violence; but it directly contradicts Girard's claim that only biblical revelation takes the side of the victim. The Egyptian tale had vindicated the scapegoat long before the birth of Israel.

Egyptian culture expressed a widespread concern for impartial social justice in the late third millennium.[22] The Egyptian *Wisdom of Ptahhotep,* the address for the *Installation of the Vizier,* and the *Tale of the Eloquent Peasant* are powerful expressions of the claims of justice for all persons, especially those in the underclass. While rulers were to be impartial, they were to show a special concern for the widow and the orphan, the poor, the timid, and the defenseless.[23] Egyptian writers insisted that every person had rights and even rulers had a duty to respect and defend these rights. Mesopotamian kings and temple priests were also to have special concern for the widow and the orphan, the poor and the marginalized.[24]

The method of drawing a sharp contrast between biblical revelation and other religions gives a clear sense of identity and superiority for Christian theology, but it does not do justice to the complexity of the relationship between Israelite religion and other ancient traditions. The method often conceals a theological assumption that if something was revealed by God, then it must have been unique to Israel; if something was known to other nations as well, it could not have been revealed. There is no logical necessity for this assumption; indeed, the similarities between Israel and its neighbors and the biblical practice of appropriating elements from other traditions argue against it. Israel did not simply reject the religions of its neighbors; it frequently drew elements of other religious traditions into a new synthesis of its own. The originality of Israel's religion often lay not in formulating absolutely new ideas, but in reconfiguring ideas and practices of other traditions into a new whole.

REVELATION IN THE EXODUS

The most common and familiar presentation of revelation in the Hebrew Bible is that of God acting in history and calling particular individuals to speak on behalf of God. Above all, the narrative of the events of the Exodus, including the call of Moses at the burning bush, the struggle with the Pharaoh, the deliverance at the Sea of Reeds, the giving of the covenant at Mt. Sinai, and God's dealings with Moses on the mountain, constitutes the central account of revelation in the Hebrew Bible. The narrative of these events discloses to Israel the power and faithfulness of God, what God demands of Israel and who Israel is called to be; it establishes images, patterns, and norms for understanding later revelatory experiences.

The Biblical Theology Movement hoped to reconstruct the historical events behind the biblical narratives, confident that biblical archeology would confirm Christian faith by providing plausible historical settings for the biblical revelation. Highlighting the Exodus as the center of the mighty deeds of Yahweh, scholars reconstructed the events at the Sea of Reeds in Exodus 14-15 in what was thought to be a plausible, realistic historical scenario that did not require supernatural divine intervention in violation of the laws of nature. According to this reconstruction, the fleeing Israelites were trapped between the Egyptian army and the sea during their attempt to escape. When all seemed lost, a storm at sea blew up and a strong wind drove back the waters so the Israelites could pass. When the Egyptians tried to follow, however, the wind died down, and they were drowned. To a neutral observer, the wind was an act of nature; to "the eyes of faith," it was the action of God in history. As John Bright commented: "If Israel saw in this the hand of God, the historian certainly has no evidence to contradict it!"[25] Faith could see the power of God in revelatory events that did not break the laws of nature. The action of God revealed God's power and fidelity and set the pattern for Israel's faith for all generations to come. It was often thought that only Israel's God acted in such historical events. This allowed scholars to posit a sharp contrast between biblical historical revelation and ancient Near Eastern myths.

In time, however, many scholars became more skeptical of our ability to reconstruct the early history of Israel, and some spoke even of "the collapse of history."[26] While for Wright it was very important that historical events conformed to the biblical accounts, other scholars concluded that the archeological and extrabiblical textual evidence did not support the biblical descriptions of the Exodus and the conquest of Canaan.[27] Some argued that the sources are considerably later and reflect the concerns and perspectives of later centuries.[28] It became increasingly difficult to determine what the historical events behind the revelatory narrative were. In recent years, many historians have concluded that Israel did not come into being through a large, single movement from Egypt, but rather emerged through a slow, gradual process involving a wide variety of peoples in Canaan.[29]

The revelation of God to early Israel turned out not to be found in a literal historical event that could be reconstructed with confidence but rather in the vision of possibilities that the early narratives opened up for the future. The memory of the Exodus, whatever the original experience may have been, was preserved in the structure of the narrative in the Book of Exodus, in other biblical recollections, and in the ritual of the Seder service. Each celebration of the Seder meal re-presents the Exodus from Egypt. By being remembered and proclaimed again, the Exodus became contemporaneous with each generation of Jews. This process of reactualization is already recognized in the Book of Joshua, when God tells the generation born in the wilderness after the flight from Egypt: "Your own eyes have seen what I did to the Egyptians" (Josh 24:7). The Exodus would remain available to the prophets of Israel and the wisdom teachers of the Hellenistic period and to Jews and Christians of later centuries as an event with ever new possibilities of meaning. There is no one way of retelling or recapturing the meaning of the story of the Exodus. The revelation occurs in the ongoing tradition, in the dialogue between the narrative and its later readers and hearers.

Jewish scholar Jon D. Levenson has commented that we can know almost nothing about "what really happened" on Mt. Sinai, but "the historical question about Sinai, important as it is in some contexts, misses the point about the significance of this material in the religion of Israel."[30] Whatever the historical events may have been, the Exodus and the conquest became the formative archetype for Israelite and Jewish identity, available to be experienced afresh in every generation.

The description of the deliverance at the Sea of Reeds in Exodus 14-15 draws upon images familiar from other religions, interpreting the rescue in mythic terms that make the event available to later generations in vivid imagery. One central role of mythic language is to furnish a model or paradigm for a people's self-understanding and activities. The Rumanian historian of religions Mircea Eliade argued that myth explains the world by telling a story that reveals how the world works. He quotes G. Van der Leeuw: "The original time is the model for all times. What took place once upon a day is forever repeated. One need only know the myth to understand what life is about."[31] By setting forth the archetypes for understanding the world, myth plays a major role in the shaping of a people's self-consciousness. Eliade asserts that for primal peoples, "true history . . . is myth."[32]

Frank Moore Cross demonstrated that the presentation of the most distinctive moment of Israel's identity, the deliverance of the people at the Sea of Reeds, used the mythic language of a god slaying a sea monster, which was the common mythical language of creation in the ancient Middle East, to describe the significance of the account.[33] More recently Bernard F. Batto has argued that the use of myth to interpret history was very similar in Israel and Mesopotamia: "Myth is paradigmatic for the society in which that myth is operative."[34]

The Babylonian epic the *Enuma Elish* had described the creation of the world as the outcome of a great battle between Marduk and Tiamat. At the climax of the battle, Marduk drove a wind into the mouth of

Tiamat and then split the watery Tiamat in two and from her body fashioned the world.[35] Humans were created after the end of the battle from
the blood of Tiamat so that they could serve the gods. Each year the
Babylonians reenacted the drama of Marduk's victory over Tiamat. The
victory of Marduk kept the forces of chaos at bay; it also legitimated the
reign of the Babylonian king and the control of the aristocracy over the
power and wealth of the empire. One implication of the story was to justify social inequities: slavery is the will of the gods. Walter Wink, following Paul Ricoeur, points out that in the Babylonian myth violence is
responsible for creation: "Creation is a violent victory over an enemy
older than creation. . . . Evil is an ineradicable constituent of ultimate
reality, and possesses ontological priority over good."[36] The implication
for human existence follows: "Our very origin is violence. Killing is in
our blood."[37]

While Ricoeur and Wink rightly stress that Genesis 1 proposes a nonviolent story of creation in sharp contrast to the Babylonian battle, the
use of the imagery in Exodus brings Israel's own foundational narrative
into the realm of mythological violence as well. In Exodus 15, the
imagery of Marduk is applied to the Sea of Reeds: Yahweh splits the sea
in two to allow the Israelites to pass over. After defeating the enemy,
Yahweh terrifies the other nations and goes in a triumphal march up to
his abode on his holy mountain (Exod 15:14-18). The problems posed
by the sacralization of violence flowing from this image will be discussed
in the next chapter.

The use of myth to interpret history was common to Israel and its
neighbors. Batto comments:

> Like his ancient Near Eastern contemporaries, the Priestly Writer
> was enculturated into a mythological worldview that assumed the
> cosmos is maintained in existence by the vigilant rule of the divine
> sovereign who keeps at bay the nihilistic forces of chaos, whether
> these be the chaos monster itself, or one of the many historical
> incarnations of evil.[38]

Later biblical authors would return to the mythical language of slaying the sea monster again and again. Second Isaiah drew upon this image
in a rhetorical question to Yahweh: "Is it not you who cleaves Rahab in
pieces, who pierces the Sea-dragon?" (Isa 51:9; translation by Batto).
Batto suggests that the verbs in this sentence, participial constructions
which are usually translated in the past tense, should be translated in the
present tense and interpreted as a mythic present. The constant mythic
struggle between God and the sea dragon rages in the present.[39]

The Psalmist proclaims: "You split Rahab in two like a corpse, scat-
tered your enemies with your mighty arm" (Ps 89:10).[40] Isaiah looks forward in hope to the slaying of the dragon: "That day Yahweh will

punish with his unyielding sword, massive and strong, Leviathan the fleeing serpent, Leviathan the coiling serpent; he will kill the dragon that lives in the sea" (Isa 27:1). Apocalyptic writers from Daniel to the Book of Revelation turned to the ancient myth of monsters rising out of the sea to symbolize the continuing struggle of evil against order. The use of myth provided Israel with the language to express its self-understanding. The narrative of what happened in the Exodus revealed the structure of Israel's universe and served as a mythic paradigm for later historical events. Like the mythic narratives of the ancient Near East, the Torah furnishes an account of the time of origins of the people of Israel. The creation of the world in Genesis set the stage for the creation of the people of Israel in Exodus.

The ancient Near East understood chaos as a perennial threat to be conquered and subdued through symbolic reenactment of the mythical combat. But chaos also holds possibilities of new configurations. In a very different context, contemporary cosmologists have taken up the ancient Babylonian image of chaos and the figure of a watery dragon emerging from chaos as symbols of the more positive evaluation of chaos in contemporary chaos theory, which we will examine in a later chapter.[41]

MOUNT SINAI

The central scene of revelation in the Hebrew Bible takes place at Mt. Sinai, where a theophany occurs. Amid peals of thunder and flashes of lightning, a dense cloud and a loud trumpet blast, Moses speaks to God, and God answers in thunder (Exod 19:9-25). The people are warned not to break through the barrier that separates them from the mountain, lest Yahweh break out against them and destroy them. The dynamics of the scene are not without parallels in other traditions. Rudolf Otto's famous description of the experience of the holy as *fascinans et tremendum* applies: The divine presence is experienced as an attractive and terrifying power, nonrational and paradoxical.[42] The presence of the Holy lures the people forward but also frightens them. It seems that the people would rush up onto the mountain, but they cannot bear the presence of God and so they must be restrained (Exod 19:21-25).

This strangely ambiguous moment is an important scene for the later consciousness of Israel. People are scared to see God lest they die, for no one can see the face of God and live. Anyone who would touch the mountain will be put to death. According to the description in Exodus, it was an altogether terrifying experience, very different from the domesticated expectations of many contemporary seekers of religious experience. God is really other and radically frightening—one whom we cannot control or manipulate. People tell Moses to go up and talk to

Yahweh. They will remain below and will listen to Moses. What is at stake in the experience of God at Mt. Sinai, prior to any talk of morality and obligation, is sheer human contingency before the incomprehensible power of God. This overwhelming, terrifying power reveals itself as loving, as inviting to a relationship, as offering an invitation to live in covenant. The revelation of God oscillates back and forth between the two poles: the terror of sheer power with the warning to keep one's distance and the alluring offer of intimacy. The people's response itself is ambivalent in the narrative. When Moses asks them if they want to be God's people, they say yes; but when he is gone for too long, they build a golden calf (Exod 32). Almost as soon as the covenant is made, it is broken.

Moses' own encounter with God is described in various ways. Moses goes up the mountain into a cloud of smoke, and God speaks to him with the sound of thunder (Exod 19:18-19). In some passages Moses speaks to God directly, "mouth to mouth" (Num 12:8) or "face to face" (Deut 34:10). But the most famous scene presents Moses as unable to see the face of God; instead he sees only God's "back parts" (Exod 33:21-23). The image preserves a sense of the transcendence of God and suggests the depth to the divine mystery that remains incomprehensible even in the moment of revelation itself.

The conversation is not one-sided: Moses responds to God quite vigorously as an active partner in the dialogue, pleading for the people and dissuading God from destroying the Israelites after their infidelity in the wilderness (Exod 32:11-14). According to the narrative, God listens to Moses and acts differently because of what he has said. Moses has a unique role as recipient and mediator of revelation in the Hebrew Bible and the later Jewish tradition. Four times God speaks with Moses alone about the divine name or pronounces the divine name (Exod 3:13-22; 33:19; 34:5-7; 34:14). When Moses descends Mt. Sinai, his face is radiant with the afterglow of the divine presence, and the people are again afraid.

The giving of the covenant seals the relation between Yahweh and the people of Israel and becomes the foundation of the social ethics of Israel. Laws in Israel were understood to be revealed directly by God on Mt. Sinai. Nonetheless, the form of covenant law, both conditional, casuistic law and unconditional, apodictic law, is similar to that of laws throughout the ancient Near East.[43] The unique relation of God to Israel emerged from the common patterns of law-giving in the ancient world.

Batto argues that the entire narrative has a mythic character similar to other ancient Near Eastern foundational myths. When Moses makes his second ascent of Mt. Sinai, the glory of God rests on the mountain for six days, reminiscent of the six days of creation in Genesis (Exod 24:15-31:18). On the seventh day, Moses enters the cloud at God's command and there receives the heavenly model for the tabernacle. Moses then constructs the tabernacle as an image of the divine model (Exod 35-40); Israel's worship replicates the divine model. Batto comments: "The divine archetypes revealed 'in that time' formed the basis by which the historical Israel lived and worshipped in the 'here and now.'"[44] The mythic patterns common to the ancient Near Eastern world provided the framework for the most important revelatory narrative in the history of Israel.

REVELATION AND THE RELIGIONS IN THE PROPHETS

Like the mythological accounts of gods acting in history, prophecy was a widespread phenomenon in the ancient world, and also in later societies.[45] Many societies had intermediary figures who carried messages back and forth between gods and humans. Jeremiah was aware of prophets, diviners, dreamers, magicians, and sorcerers in Edom, Moab, Ammon, Tyre, and Sidon (Jer 27:1-11); and Elijah struggled against the prophets of Baal (1 Kgs 18:17-40). In the Book of Numbers, Balaam appears as a seer (Num 22-24). Moses as a prophet has been compared to Arabic seers, as have Deborah and Miriam; Samuel has been thought to be similar to later Sufi sheiks presiding over dervishes.[46]

Despite important differences in the content of the messages, the threefold relationship between the intermediary, the divine or spirit-world, and the audience is remarkably similar across different cultures.[47] The perception that the prophet has received a communication from God constitutes the underlying assumption of the prophetic process. But this special revelation to the individual is also a social event, with implications for the audience; and thus the response of the hearers is an integral part of the communication process. The audience interacts with the prophet; and the prophet, in turn, often deals with God on the basis of the people's acceptance or rejection of the message. After bringing the audience's reaction to God, the prophet often receives a further revelation and makes further pronouncements. There is frequently supernatural confirmation of the message. Often the prophet makes disciples, who may themselves act as intermediaries between the prophet and the audience.[48]

The authority of the prophet comes in principle from the experience of divine communication; but in practice this communication must be recognized by at least some of the audience for the prophet to function as a prophet. Whatever novelty the prophetic revelation contains must engage the expectations of the audience enough to confirm the expectations of at least some listeners. Even biblical prophets who encounter widespread rejection, like Isaiah of Jerusalem and Jeremiah, find at least some disciples (Isa 8:16; Jer 26:24; 36), and their words are preserved for future generations.

The biblical prophets repeatedly attack the gods of other nations as idols; nonetheless, there also emerges from the prophetic witness in Israel a clear affirmation of God's presence to and concern for other nations. Prophets even acknowledged the pure prayers of other nations to God. Amos taunts the people of Israel with the claim of their chosenness. "Are not you and the Cushites all the same to me, children of Israel?—declares Yahweh. Did I not bring Israel up from Egypt and the Philistines from Caphtor, and the Aramaeans from Kir?" (Amos 9:7). While Amos's emphasis in this passage is on the infidelity of Israel and the coming judgment of Yahweh, the affirmation of Yahweh's presence to other nations is clear. Isaiah prophesies not only the destruction of Egypt but also the conversion and healing of Egypt: "Yahweh will reveal himself to Egypt, and the Egyptians will acknowledge Yahweh that day and will offer sacrifices and cereal offerings, and will make vows to Yahweh and perform them. And if Yahweh strikes Egypt, having struck he will heal, and they will turn to Yahweh who will hear their prayers and heal them" (Isa 19:21-22).

As Abraham Joshua Heschel noted, Micah implies that even now people throughout the world worship God; and the prophet sharply contrasts this devotion with the failings of Israel: "I am not pleased with you, says Yahweh Sabaoth; from your hands I find no offerings acceptable. But from farthest east to farthest west my name is great among the nations, and everywhere incense and a pure gift are offered to my name, since my name is great among the nations, says Yahweh Sabaoth" (Mal 1:11). Heschel understood the statement to affirm: "All those who worship their gods do not know it, but they are really worshipping Me."[49]

THE EMERGENCE OF MONOTHEISM

The second part of the Book of Isaiah (chapters 40-55, known as Second Isaiah) was written by an unnamed prophet in the exile in Babylon, who is usually seen as the first to proclaim a true monotheism in sharp contrast to the religions of other nations. This is the revolutionary moment within the ongoing evolution of Israel's religious sensibility. The most serious threat to the Jewish community's survival in Babylon was not so much physical oppression as the religious challenge of interpreting their own defeat and the relation of Yahweh to the Babylonian gods. The obvious and tempting conclusion to draw from the disaster was that Babylon's gods were mightier than Yahweh. Jeremiah and Ezekiel had provided an alternative perspective by interpreting the destruction of Jerusalem not as the defeat of Yahweh by foreign gods but as Yahweh's righteous judgment upon the sins of the nation.

Second Isaiah turns to creation itself to affirm the power of Yahweh (Isa 40:12-26). Yahweh has no rivals. The gods of other nations are challenged to a contest with Yahweh in predicting future events, but not one of the gods can answer (Isa 41:21-26). The conclusion is that the gods are nothing (Isa 41:29). Later, representatives of the nations are called to an assembly and invited to consider the evidence: only Yahweh has announced the present from of old; only Yahweh can save (Isa 45:20-22). The polemic against the gods of the nations looks forward to a universal confession of Yahweh by all the earth. Second Isaiah also offers a biting satire on Babylonians who fashion a divine image from one part of a piece of wood and then use the other half to make a fire to warm themselves and bake bread. One half they burn, the other half they ask for salvation (Isa 44:15-17).

The emergence of monotheism in Israel was an important and distinctive transformation of the ancient Near Eastern religious world. It was not, however, unrelated to developments in other religious traditions. In acknowledging Second Isaiah as the first true monotheist in the Bible, scholars also see relations to other religions. It has been argued that the exclusive devotion of many Babylonians to Nabu, the proclamation of Marduk as universal lord, and the monotheism of Zoroaster were significant factors in the birth of Israelite monotheism.[50] Some scholars have seen monotheism as emerging simultaneously in different areas at the same time, with Xenophanes in Greece, Second Isaiah in the Babylonian exile, and Zoroaster in Persia.[51] There are, however, different forms of monotheism. Gerd Theissen distinguishes a monotheism "from above," such as that of the Egyptian Pharaoh Akhenaton, from a monotheism "from below," which emerges from common people. The latter, according to Theissen, inclines toward an egalitarian critique of social structures, while the former legitimates the imperial status quo. Biblical monotheism, while a major transformation of earlier worship of Yahweh, did not appear in a vacuum.

The appearance of ethical monotheism in the prophets of Israel may be viewed as a revolutionary moment within a broader evolutionary development. A long period of gradual change led to a time of rapid transformation in the belief in one creating God with an ethical vision for the entire human race. Robert Gnuse has used the analogy of contemporary evolutionary theory, in which gradual developments prepare the way for radical changes, such as the emergence of a new species, only to be followed by periods of consolidation.[52]

The emergence of monotheism in Israel coincides with what German philosopher Karl Jaspers called the Axial Age,[†] a time when various nations around the world were going through periods of transformation that set the context for all later religious history in those nations.[53] During the same centuries (roughly 800-400 B.C.E.), Greek philosophy and drama were critiquing and transforming traditional Greek religion; the Upanishads, the Buddha, the *Ramayana* and the *Mahabharata* were transforming religion in India; and Confucius and Lao-Tzu were laying the foundations for later Chinese culture. In all these areas the earlier primal, tribal religions were being radically reshaped. In Greece and Persia there were movements toward monotheism; in India, toward a sense of the unity of all reality. The exile of Israel in Babylon would have exposed Jews to many intellectual and religious currents from other cultures along the trade routes, and these contacts may have helped to stimulate the breakthrough to monotheism: "Had the Jews remained in Palestine, they probably never would have attained pure monotheism, for they never would have experienced a crisis sufficiently great to generate such an intellectual leap."[54]

The prophetic heritage of Israel provides the foundation for the monotheism of later Judaism and Christianity and is the strongest link to the Islamic tradition. Muhammad understood himself as a prophet on the model of the Israelite prophets. When he first began to receive the message of the *Qurʾan,* he feared that he might be being deceived by an evil spirit, but a relative who was a Christian assured him that the prophets of Israel had received similar communications from God.

WISDOM IN ISRAEL

Alongside these dramatic moments of revelation to Moses and the other prophets, there was also Israel's wisdom tradition, which presents a more general, universal revelation of God in the experience of ordinary life, apart from dramatic calls from God or special visions. The biblical wisdom literature was quite open to drawing upon the wisdom books of other religious traditions and provides an opening to dialogue with the religions of South and East Asia, which will be examined in chapter 6.

The search for wisdom is among the most ancient and widespread of all human pursuits. Virtually every culture since those of ancient Egypt and Mesopotamia has passed on proverbs and wise sayings that express the wisdom of previous generations. The pursuit of wisdom (*chokmah* in Hebrew, *sophia* in Greek) in ancient Israel was part of the broader Near Eastern search for wisdom.[55] The sages of Israel assumed that the wisdom they had found was also available to the wise of other cultures, since the universal order of the cosmos was open to human discovery.

The early wisdom tradition in Israel arose from reflection on the patterns of everyday human experience and from trust that the ways of God are revealed therein.[56] Unlike Moses and later prophets who based their message on a special call from God, the wisdom teachers made no claim to extraordinary revelations. In the Book of Proverbs the wisdom teacher calls students to obedience, but obedience meant an attentive listening to the values and observations that earlier generations had found true in their experience. The wisdom teachers promised that wise conduct would bring happiness and success in life, and they warned that disobedience would lead to disaster. Every act has consequences, and it is folly to think that we can ignore wisdom and flourish. The source of authority in the wisdom tradition is found in the experience of life itself.

The teachers of proverbs challenged their students to listen to the authority of the elders, but they also invited students to observe carefully and seek out wisdom for themselves. They occasionally juxtaposed directly contradictory sayings, leaving it to the student to know when to apply each: "Do not answer fools in the terms of their folly or you will be a fool yourself. Answer fools according to their folly, or they will be wise in their own eyes" (Prov 26:4-5). The sages trusted that the order implanted by God in creation could be discerned by careful reflection, but they also acknowledged the limits of all human wisdom and the inscrutability of the ways of Yahweh, who transcends any mechanical notion of order and against whom no human wisdom can stand.

The sages knew that different times call for different decisions. One of the most famous of all wisdom sayings tells us: "For everything there is a season, and a time for every matter under heaven" (Eccl 3:1). There is a time for speech and a time for silence, a time for action and a time for waiting. No one else can tell a person when to apply a particular proverb. The perspective of one proverb may be more fruitful at one time; that of another more fruitful at another time. No one else can discern the proper time for us. Thus the wisdom tradition does not offer definite answers to all questions, but presents a set of values and perspectives to guide our decisions. It shapes character and teaches us to learn how to learn.[57]

There is often a sense of playfulness in the expressions of wisdom, and thus sapiential revelation appears in the form of play. Alongside the commonsense proverbs whose meaning is clear, there are riddles and obscure sayings that challenge our wits to seek out a suitable meaning. Some sayings juxtapose a series of different realities and challenge the reader to find the point of comparison (Prov 30:15-31). Riddles and lists of things are a form of play, a manner of playing at hide-and-seek. One person hides the truth in the riddle; another must search for its meaning.[58] Ultimately this game has its roots in the divine playfulness of hiding wisdom in creation. "It is the glory of God to conceal things, but the glory of kings is to search things out" (Prov 25:2). The playfulness of wisdom hidden in riddles and the juxtaposing of clashing perspectives evokes a sense of seeking out hidden wisdom.

The playful, teasing search for wisdom found expression in poems that personified wisdom as a woman. The Hebrew word *chokmah* originally meant the skill of learning to do something, especially how to navigate through the challenges of life. Wisdom was the practical sense of how to get along and get ahead, how to be virtuous and successful at the same time. At some point in the history of Israel, the word *chokmah* began to be used as a poetic image, a symbolic personification. We do not know when or how or why this poetic, symbolic usage first emerged. It definitely appears in texts after the exile, but it may have already been present as early as the time of King Solomon. Several of the wisdom books personify Wisdom as a woman. In the Book of Proverbs, Wisdom appears in symbolic form as a woman who is an active, assertive force in human affairs. Contemporary scholars variously refer to this figure as Woman Wisdom or Lady Wisdom or Dame Wisdom or, using her Greek name, Sophia.

Personified Wisdom is a many-sided symbol. Many scholars have conjectured that a foreign goddess lurks in the background of the image. Wisdom has been variously seen as the primordial world order and the self-revelation of creation;[59] the personification of the scribal wisdom tradition itself, especially the Book of Proverbs;[60] a replacement for and protection against the foreign love goddess, Astarte or Ishtar; an Israelite analogue to the Egyptian Maat, the goddess of justice, social and cosmic order;[61] and a hypostasis or "quasi-personification" of the divine attribute of wisdom with an independent existence.[62] Because of the uncertainty of dating the poems in which Lady Wisdom appears, her antecedents remain unclear. It is quite possible that personified Wisdom is an Israelite appropriation of a symbol from another religious tradition.

The wisdom tradition began in early family and clan instruction in Israel, became institutionalized in the training of the monarchy, and found its final written expression during the postexilic period. After the destruction of the first temple, the disappearance of the monarchy, and the dispersion of many Jews to other lands, wisdom took on added importance as a way of understanding God and the world without the mediation of the king or temple rituals. In a time in which the particular forms of the earlier faith had vanished and Jews often lived in close contact with other peoples, the wisdom tradition offered a foundation for faith, ethics, and action.

The sapiential appeal to experience open to all persons means that more than any other tradition in the Bible, the wisdom books offer an opening to dialogue with the other religions of the world. The sages of Israel were aware of the wisdom teachings of Egypt and Mesopotamia, and they assumed that the wisdom they discovered was also available to the wise of other cultures. The story of the Queen of Sheba coming to visit King Solomon bears witness to the possibility of a common horizon for conversation (1 Kgs 10:1-13). It is noteworthy that in the story it appears that the Queen is the one who does the testing. She measures Solomon's wisdom and decides that he lives up to his reputation. The biblical authors were not only in contact with the wisdom teachers of other cultures; they borrowed freely from the wisdom traditions of other nations. One portion of the Book of Proverbs (22:17-24:22) is an adaptation of an Egyptian wisdom text, *The Instruction of Amenemope*. Job himself was not an Israelite, and the Book of Proverbs includes sayings from Lemuel, the king of Massa (31:1-9), and Agur ben Jakeh, who appears to be a non-Israelite. Since the sages of Israel based their claims on experience that is open to all humans, it is possible for representatives of different sapiential traditions to find a common ground for discussion. Wisdom is found everywhere, and yet wisdom is also elusive.

The wisdom tradition incorporates perspectives from outside of Israel, and it could also include painful questions about its own fundamental assumptions. The Book of Proverbs promises wisdom to those who seek it and assures students that wisdom is worth more than gold or jewels. Job's reflection on his own experience, by contrast, is an eloquent poem of lament that challenges the confidence of much of the earlier tradition. Job 28 insists that wisdom is hidden from humans and known only to God. Wisdom is the key to the meaning and order of creation, valuable beyond sapphires and pearls, but humans cannot find her dwelling place. The proper wisdom for humans is to acknowledge the limitations of human endeavor and insight.

The revelation of God to Job from the whirlwind at the end of the book (Job 38-41) presents a paradoxical message. Even though God accuses Job of obscuring the divine designs, God does not repeat the accusations of the friends, but rather points to the vast and incomprehensible order of creation itself, suggesting that the suffering of one life cannot be the measure of the universe. But then when Job repents in dust and ashes, God accuses the friends of not speaking truthfully of God as Job has (42:7). Nonetheless, God proceeds to act in accord with the friends' theology of reward and punishment! The instability of the conclusion leaves the reader with a strong sense of the limits of human understanding but with no clear definition or pattern for future experience.

The sage in Ecclesiastes claims to have found more wisdom than anyone else before him in Jerusalem, but frankly questions whether wisdom really confers any advantage at all: even the wise cannot understand the purposes of God, and all must die in the end. The acceptance of Job and Ecclesiastes into the wisdom tradition and the biblical canon indicates that the sages were able to live with conflicting views of God and human life. This holding together of diverse, even contradictory perspectives offers an important principle for interreligious dialogue.

Both Job and Qoheleth demonstrate that figures in the wisdom tradition could appeal to their own experience against the statements of the elders. Job tells his friends: "But I have understanding as well as you; I am not inferior to you. Who does not know such things as these?" (Job 12:3). Later he tells them again: "Look, my eye has seen all this, my ear has heard and understood it. What you know, I also know" (13:1-2). In the Book of Ecclesiastes, Qoheleth repeatedly tells us that he has examined the wisdom of the earlier generations in light of his own experience and finds it wanting. Both Qoheleth and Job insist on their own experience of injustice in the world and reject any attempt to deny this experience.

WISDOM AS UNIVERSAL REVELATION

Some scholars have argued that the experiential approach of wisdom reflection constitutes a form of natural theology. They point out that the books of Proverbs, Job, and Ecclesiastes nowhere mention any of the specific events of Israel's history but rather appeal to experiences open to everyone. John J. Collins used the categories of David Tracy's *Blessed Rage for Order* to interpret the wisdom trajectory as first articulating the religious dimension of common human experience and then later, in Ben Sira and the Wisdom of Solomon, correlating this universal dimension with the historical traditions of Israel.[63] More recently, James Barr, in his 1991 Gifford Lectures, *Biblical Faith and Natural Theology*, has accepted Collins's argument and developed its implications for a critique of Karl Barth's theology.[64] In his famous debate with Emil Brunner in the 1930s, Barth had argued strenuously against any form of natural theology and had insisted that all Christian theology be based on the biblical witness to revelation. In a prolonged and vigorous polemic, Barr stresses that on Barth's own terms the presence of natural theology in the wisdom tradition and elsewhere in the Bible undermines Barth's argument. According to Barr, even though natural theology in the wisdom tradition runs contrary to the major trends in biblical theology in the twentieth century, it constitutes an important and integral part of the biblical heritage.

The use of the term "natural theology" may be somewhat misleading in this context. Collins and Barr both use the term differently from the earlier scholastic usage, which distinguished between "natural" and "supernatural" knowledge of God. According to the medieval scholastics, natural knowledge of God is only the preamble of faith and is not salvific. This usage shaped the Dogmatic Constitution on the Catholic Faith of Vatican I, and Barth accepted the usage of Vatican I as the basis for his own polemic against natural theology.[65]

Collins himself acknowledges that biblical wisdom comes as a gift from God beyond human control and thus it is a type of revelation, even though it does not come through specific supernatural historical events. What is at stake is the universal offer of revelation in and through all experience. Roland F. Murphy proposed another model for interpreting the wisdom literature. He argued persuasively that the sages of Israel saw the revelation and grace of God as pervading the entire world of human experience, including the experience of other religions.[66] Grace and nature, salvation history and profane history, revelation and experience are coextensive. Murphy compared the wisdom tradition's perspective to the anthropology of Karl Rahner, who understood all of experience as shaped by the universal offer of God's revelation and grace. The image of Lady Wisdom symbolizes the presence of God implicit in every moment of experience. We will examine Rahner's view of the experience of God in the final chapter.

Viewed as a form of universal revelation, wisdom offers a cosmic context for understanding the specific historical revelation to Israel. The early wisdom books never mention the specific events of the history of Israel. The relation of the particular experiences of revelation by Israel to the universal presence of wisdom became an explicit concern for the later wisdom writings, the Wisdom of Ben Sira and the Wisdom of Solomon. Written while the Hellenistic influences on Jewish life were presenting new dangers and new opportunities, both works turned to personified Wisdom to mediate between the universal order of the cosmos and the historical experiences of Israel. Ben Sira, worried about the threats of Hellenization, warned against delving into matters too difficult to understand and stressed the availability of primordial wisdom in the Mosaic Law. Undertaking, in James Crenshaw's phrase, "a quest for survival," Ben Sira identified wisdom with fear of the Lord and following the Torah (Sir 19:20).[67] The revelation of the Torah is the dwelling of primordial Wisdom in Israel (Sir 24), and devout Jews will seek her there.

The Wisdom of Solomon adopted a more open and confident stance, making bold use of Hellenistic concepts to describe wisdom. For the Wisdom of Solomon, the natural order itself reveals God, and the historical events recounted in Genesis and Exodus are retold with all proper names omitted as the work of personified Wisdom herself (Wis 10:1-11:1). The particular persons and events of the history of Israel have become paradigms revealing the universal activity of Wisdom. Sophia, the personification of Wisdom, is the form in which God is revealed in the world: "For she is a reflection of eternal light, is present throughout the entire universe, influencing all human life and offering a spotless mirror of the working of God, and an image of his goodness" (7:26). Thus, in coming to know Wisdom, humans can know something of God, seeing as in a spotless mirror.

REVELATION IN THE NEW TESTAMENT

The first language that Christians used to talk about the revelation of God in their lives was the language of concrete testimony, narratives, and poetic images. Christian faith arose not from reasoned arguments about the universe but as a response to experiences of revelation, shared

in the concrete narratives of people whose lives had been transformed by
an encounter with Jesus. The First Letter of John expresses the vividness
of this experience of revelation:

> Something which has existed since the beginning,
> which we have heard,
> which we have seen with our own eyes,
> which we have watched
> and touched with our own hands,
> the Word of life—
> this is our theme. . . .
> That life was made visible;
> we saw it and are giving our testimony. . .
> We are declaring to you
> what we have seen and heard,
> so that you too may share our life. (1 John 1:1, 3)

At the center of Christian revelation is the person of Jesus himself,
always summoning us, always elusive, both comforting and challenging.
Christian language about revelation has a dramatic character—something happens that changes the situation, often something surprising and
unexpected. The stories of Jesus often begin with realistic scenes from
the life of his time and culture, but then the strangest things happen in
them. *Metanoia,* the Greek word in the New Testament that we often
translate as "repentance," literally means a change of mind, a change of
attitudes, a new way of seeing the world. The usual way that we have
been thinking and valuing is deeply flawed, and the revelation of God in
Jesus offers us a new vision.

The New Testament offers a wide range of concrete images of God
entering human lives. In the deliberate clash of these images we find a
glimpse of a God who does not fit human calculations. God is both an
extravagantly generous master and also a thief in the night (Luke 12:35-
40). The Gospels continually add on one image after another. God is a
shepherd who looks for a lost sheep; God is a housewife who searches
for a lost coin; God is a father who waits and watches for his wayward
son to return home; God is nondiscriminating love, sending the sun and
rain upon the just and the unjust in equal measure. Jesus himself told
one story after another to express the experience of the reign of God.
Again and again in the parables of Jesus, God does not appear at
humans' command, does not fit usual expectations, does not act the way
humans expect God to act. Indeed, this is one of the most consistent
themes throughout the Bible: God does not fit people's preconceptions.
Experiencing God in revelation changes people in ways they had never
dreamed of. The biblical tradition of overturning expectations can open
Christians to the unexpected ways in which God is at work in other reli-

gious traditions as well. The dynamic of biblical revelation itself cautions us that we never finally comprehend or control God's movement.

The revelation of God in the person and event of Jesus Christ is unique; it is also deeply rooted in the traditions of Israel, and through them, in the broader religious world of the ancient Near East. The New Testament presents Jesus Christ as a prophet and sage, as the new Moses and Elijah, and as an apocalyptic seer; but it also surpasses all the archetypes by presenting him as the incarnation of Wisdom herself, the one through whom all things were created, the Logos which is God. As the incarnation of Sophia, the revelation of God in Jesus Christ is integrated into the entire process of creation from the beginning. Moreover, because the Christian scriptures were written in Greek for Hellenistic audiences, the first written expressions and interpretations of Jesus Christ directly participate in the religious heritage of the Hellenistic world.[68] Jesus Christ shares in the broader religious history of the human race. In relation to earlier religious imagery, there is both continuity and also revolutionary breakthrough in the descriptions of the Christian revelation.

At the beginning was a change in people's awareness. Ordinary people in Palestine in the first century met a wandering prophet, teacher, exorcist, and miracle worker from Nazareth and experienced the power of God in this encounter. Beginning during Jesus' public ministry, and even more after his death and resurrection, people realized that their lives had been forever changed by meeting Jesus. They were not the same persons that they were before. They experienced the revelation of God's power in the forgiveness of sins, healing, a new sense of their own worth as persons. They saw themselves and God in a new way—in freedom. At the center of the revelation of God in the New Testament is the experience of being set free—free from sin, often free from illness or possession by spirits, free from the power of fate, free from the threat of a meaningless existence. In Jesus Christ the first Christians experienced the very presence of God. They did not know completely what this meant, and they did not have categories completely adequate to express the revelation of God in Jesus. The reality of God is more than anyone can think or imagine. Nonetheless, the images and narratives and proclamations of the New Testament seek to convey some sense of what this revelation is.

The revelation of God in Jesus led to a new sense of intimacy with God. In ancient Greece, gods were not able to be friends with mortals because they were on a higher plane of existence. Aristotle had taught that friendship demands reciprocity, which is not possible with gods: "For friendship, we maintain, exists only where there can be a return of affection, but friendship towards god does not admit of love being returned, nor at all of loving. For it would be strange if one were to say that he loved Zeus."[69] In the Gospel of John, Jesus tells his followers: "I call you friends because I have made known to you everything that I have learned from my Father" (John 15:15). Later Christians would conclude that the original dialogue is that between the Father and the Son within the Trinity from all eternity. This exchange of love overflows into the world, and Jesus invites his followers to be inserted into the sharing of the Trinity. The reception of revelation transforms followers of Jesus into friends of God and sharers in the divine mystery.

One irony in the Gospel of John is that the followers of Jesus cannot fully receive the revelation as long as he is with them. As long as Jesus is right in front of the disciples, they do not truly understand who he is. Only after he has departed will the Spirit of truth, the Paraclete, come to enlighten them. It is the Spirit that guides the disciples after Jesus is gone so that they can come to recognize who Jesus is. In this recognition they come to know God the Father and themselves in a new way. The recognition changes their whole lives.

In the Gospel of John, the revelation in Jesus Christ comes through signs. The first half of the Gospel of John (chapters 1-12) presents itself as a book of signs, from the miracle at Cana through the healing of the royal official's son, the feeding of the multitudes, the healing of the blind man, to the raising of Lazarus.[70] Strange things happen in the accounts of these signs, for they are not simply external signposts that point somewhere else. All of them are symbols of transformation. The signs of revelation in the Gospel of John are events that break into people's lives, turn their lives around, and leave them different than they were before. Such signs initiate a person into a deeper reality.

Signs are ambiguous. They do not state their meaning directly but demand that we participate in the creation of meaning. They confront us with a choice; they tease our minds and provoke different reactions. In the Gospel of John, some people see and believe and find life, but others see the exact same events and want to put Jesus to death precisely because of these signs. Signs are a matter of life and death: if you understand and believe, you live; if you do not, you die. Signs take place in a special time that interrupts the flow of human lives.

According to the Gospel of Luke, the ability to see and hear the revelation of God is not given equally to everyone. Jesus sets forth the principle that those who have will receive more, while those who have not will lose even the little that they think they have (Luke 8:18; cf. Matt 13:12; 25:29). This is a wisdom principle that has many possible applications. To an entrepreneur, it describes the principle of wealth accumulation: the rich will get more money, and the poor will lose what little they have. To the realistic politician, it is the principle of *Realpolitik*. Those who have power will get more; those who do not have power will lose the little they have. But in the context of the Gospel of Luke, Jesus is referring to the ability to hear the Word of God. Those who have the ability to hear the Word of God, to receive revelation, will receive still greater ability. Those who do not have this ability will lose even the little they think they have.

Hearing the Word of God ushers us into a new horizon, where all our usual notions of having and not having are turned upside down. Again and again Jesus calls us to leave all we have and to follow him. Often, the more things people have, the less they can hear. The more things humans cling to and grasp after, the more obstacles they pile up to hearing the Word of God and allowing it to transform them. Possessions, in whatever form, very quickly become so many illusions that we can secure our own lives. In effect, we then worship them and pray to them for protection and safety.

To hear the Word of God requires that we empty ourselves and open ourselves and allow ourselves to be transformed by what we hear. To hear the Word of God requires a radical openness and honesty. As long as we are listening only to hear what we want to hear, we are using the Word of God to confirm our own presuppositions. As long as we are seeking God only for our purposes and goals, we are seeking our own purposes and goals and missing God. As long as we turn to God seeking our own comfort, assurance, and success, we are seeking our comfort and assurance and success and missing God. To hear the Word of God, we must empty ourselves. In grasping we close ourselves off, but in losing we gain.

Jesus tells his followers that all will be revealed. There is nothing hidden that will not be exposed (Luke 8:17). The light of the Word of God shines into our lives, into the darkness we inhabit. As long as we have things to hide, we are possessed by our secrets and remain trapped. We cling to the darkness for safety and comfort. When we fling away all the secrets we have, light pours in. In having nothing, we are set free. When Jesus confronted people with their secrets, they did not experience the shame they feared; instead they found forgiveness and freedom. As long as they cling to the darkness of secrecy, they hold themselves prisoners. In trusting the light, they find pardon and peace.

IMAGES OF REVELATION

The New Testament applies the images of revelation of the Hebrew Bible and the Septuagint to Jesus, but each one is transformed and broken open. In the Gospel of Matthew, Jesus is the new Moses who announces the terms of the new covenant. The Sermon on the Mount is the counterpart to Moses' discourse to the people of Israel before they enter the Promised Land in Deuteronomy. Throughout the Gospels, Jesus acts in many ways like the prophets of Israel, challenging the established authorities. Like earlier prophets who performed symbolic actions to communicate their message, Jesus performs symbolic actions in the healing of the sick and the possessed, in his meals with tax collectors and prostitutes, in his entry into Jerusalem and his attack on those buying and selling in the temple. Like the prophet Elijah, who had healed the sick and raised the dead, Jesus appears as the wonder-working prophet who has these powers, and some people even wonder if Jesus is Elijah (e.g., Mark 6:15). The outward healings are the concrete signs that the reign of God is at hand, reinforcing the revelatory message. The power of God is breaking into this world. Jesus appears as the eschatological prophet, the prophet of the end-time.[71] One of the most important models used to interpret the revelation of God in Jesus was the Suffering Servant of Second Isaiah (e.g., Matt 12:16-21). In Jesus, God enters into the suffering of violence and degradation, but through his humiliation comes healing.

Another important model for interpreting Jesus came from the wisdom tradition. Jesus repeatedly used images of creation, such as the farmer who watches the seed sprout and grow, the housewife cleaning her house, the farmer who finds buried treasure, the lilies of the field and the birds of the air who do not labor for their food or clothing. These sapiential images continue the wisdom tradition's openness to a revelation of God in and through the created world itself, in the processes of everyday life. Revelation need not come through an explicitly supernatural call or vision.

The Gospels remember Jesus as a teacher of wisdom. According to the Gospel of Luke, Jesus presents himself as a teacher of wisdom, a representative of Sophia (7:33-35; see also Matt 11:18-19). The Lukan Jesus is a prophet and apostle of Sophia, the culmination of a series of messengers sent by her (Luke 11:49-51; see also Matt 23:34-36). The corresponding passages in Matthew are slightly different and present Jesus in place of Sophia. Some scholars have argued that Matthew deliberately interprets Jesus as Sophia, but the evidence is ambiguous.[72] Matthew clearly sees Jesus as a wisdom teacher, even though the Gospel does not explicitly identify Jesus and Sophia and does not attribute to Jesus the cosmological role that was central for Sophia.

The Sermon on the Mount is itself a wisdom discourse in which Jesus appeals to the order of creation as the ground for morality. The beatitude was a traditional wisdom saying that pronounced certain people blessed. The wisdom teachings of Jesus treat such traditional sapiential themes as God's providence, the proper use of wealth, donations to the poor, character, humility, choosing the right treasure, living one day at a time, not judging others, the rich fool, the necessity of following one master, and life itself as the highest good. Jesus' parables portray the consequences of wise and foolish behavior: the wise and foolish maidens (Matt 25:1-13), the wise servant (Matt 24:45-51), the wise man who built his house on rock (Matt 7:24-27), and the rich fool who builds barns for his grain (Luke 12:16-21). Many of Jesus' wisdom sayings find parallels in the wisdom literatures of Judaism, Greece, the ancient Near East, and sometimes more distant cultures and religions. While Jesus in the New Testament is not merely a wisdom teacher, the Gospels clearly present him in that role: by one count there are 102 wisdom sayings attributed to Jesus in the Synoptic Gospels.[73] The Sermon on the Mount in particular demonstrates repeated similarities to wisdom traditions in the Hellenistic world.[74]

While many of Jesus' sayings reflect the ordering power of God in the continuities of life, other sayings and parables function as creative disruptions, calling into question established assumptions. To a Jewish audience, Samaritans were not supposed to be good; thus to tell the narrative of a good Samaritan is to overturn the assumptions of the hearers' worldview. These unsettling sayings and stories have been compared to the queries of Qoheleth,[75] or to the sayings of the Christian desert fathers or Zen masters,[76] or to the sayings of the Taoist tradition.[77]

The Epistle of James continues the traditional empirical teaching of wisdom and is filled with sayings on the use of wealth, handling emotions and desires, and proper conduct in community. The Pauline and Deutero-Pauline letters and the Gospel of John, which include an intertwining of sapiential and apocalyptic perspectives, take the momentous step of identifying Jesus Christ as the incarnation of personified Wisdom, Sophia, the ordering power of the universe through whom all things were made and are held together (1 Cor 8:6; Col 1:15-20; John 1:1-18; see also Heb 1:2-3).

Jesus is also presented as an apocalyptic leader who sees Satan fall from heaven and who foretells the coming of the Son of Man before the present generation has passed away. There was a complex relationship between the wisdom and apocalyptic traditions during the first century. Unlike the wisdom of the sages found in the Book of Proverbs, the apocalyptic wisdom represented by the Book of Daniel was not found through reflection on ordinary experience but came only through a special supernatural revelation, often a vision that itself had to be interpreted to be intelligible. At times there was a clear choice between the two traditions. Ben Sira regarded apocalyptic views as dangerous speculations to be avoided (Sir 3:23-24; 34:1-8). Nonetheless, predominantly apocalyptic works could use sapiential themes and vice versa. Where some scholars have sought to identify separate apocalyptic and sapiential layers in the New Testament as earlier or later, more recently the assumption of a chronological sequence has itself come into question, and scholars have argued for a complex intertwining of the two traditions in the New Testament. However one judges the exact relation between wisdom and apocalyptic in the New Testament, it is clear that the images of revelation in both traditions exerted a major influence on New Testament authors.

Jesus is both the sage who calls attention to the presence of God in everyday experience and also the eschatological prophet who announces the reign of God and the apocalyptic seer who foresees the fall of Satan. The intertwining of sapiential and apocalyptic models is evident in Paul. Paul proclaims Christ crucified as "the power of God and the wisdom [Sophia] of God" (1 Cor 1:24). The earlier figure of personified Wisdom in Proverbs appeared in the context of the sages' reflections on the experience of God in the patterns of everyday life. Paul's use of Sophia in 1 Corinthians 1 presupposes an apocalyptic background: transcendent apocalyptic wisdom is not available in ordinary experience and is hidden from all except through special revelation in Jesus Christ. As "the wisdom of God," Jesus Christ is the central, supremely important element in God's secret plan of revelation and salvation. In the same letter Paul also began the tradition of attributing to Christ the cosmological role in creation that had been held by Sophia: "For us there is only one God, the Father from whom all things come and for whom we exist, and one Lord, Jesus Christ, through whom all things come and through whom we exist" (1 Cor 8:6). In Paul's letters there is no opposition of sapiential and apocalyptic imagery. Paul draws upon both sapiential and apocalyptic language and transforms the significance of every image by reinterpreting it in light of Jesus Christ.

The hymn in Colossians 1 developed the cosmic perspective of revelation more extensively, applying the characteristics of Sophia to Christ, in whom all things were created (Col 1:15-20). The cosmic Christ holds all things together and reconciles all things in heaven and on earth; thus Christ is present in all of creation, in all human existence. The implication is clear that all humans, whether they are conscious of Jesus Christ or not, whether they explicitly accept Jesus Christ or not, are offered grace and reconciliation through his life, death, and resurrection.

BIBLICAL PRECEDENTS
FOR INTERRELIGIOUS DIALOGUE

The biblical witness provides many points of contact for dialogue with other religious traditions, but it also makes strong claims for the universal power of the God of Israel and the universal implications of the revelation of God in Jesus Christ. The presentations of revelation in the Bible draw heavily on the images of other religious traditions, but they also transform these images in the act of appropriating them and applying them in new contexts. In relation to other religious traditions, Israel and the early Christian community went through a dynamic process of continuity and development, of critique and appropriation.

The Israelite and the later Jewish wisdom tradition in particular recognizes the knowledge of God in other nations, at least among the wise.

The sages' trust in a universal revelation offered by Wisdom in and through the experience of the world provides a common ground for discussion with the entire human community. Since Sophia's activity extends to all persons and nations, representatives of various sapiential traditions can learn from each other. The ancient wisdom teachers' dialogue with representatives of Egyptian and Babylonian wisdom encourages their contemporary heirs to dialogue with the wisdom traditions of South and East Asia.

While trusting in the gracious approach of Sophia, the biblical sages also insisted on the limits of all human claims of wisdom. They stressed the inscrutability of Yahweh's paths and the difficulty of finding wisdom. The sages' insistence on discerning the proper time for applying proverbs implies a recognition that proverbial insights are partial and time-bound. Thus, in approaching dialogue with other traditions, heirs of the biblical wisdom tradition need not and indeed cannot claim to have definitively grasped the mystery of God. Sophia approaches us, but we never fully comprehend her. Fear of God, which is the beginning of wisdom, means a recognition and acceptance of human limitations. To fear God is to realize that we are not perfectly wise.

The Bible also includes a variety of perspectives which at times conflict with each other. Narratives find revelation in privileged, dramatic moments such as the deliverance at the Sea of Reeds and the theophany at Mt. Sinai and present the significance of these events in mythic terms. The presence of myth throughout the Bible roots it in the most ancient traditions of the human community. Prophets hear the word of Yahweh in the experience of being called to prophesy; the dynamics of their ministry follow patterns that transcend cultures and centuries. Sages hear Sophia calling at the city gates in the texture of everyday experience and provide an opening to dialogue with all the wisdom traditions of the world.

The proclamation of the revelation of God in Jesus Christ draws upon all of these traditions in making the unique claim that the life, death, and resurrection of Jesus manifest the presence of God in this world in a definitive and unsurpassable way. The affirmation that the Logos or Wisdom of God is incarnate in Jesus implies a fundamental confidence in the harmony between the intelligibility of the entire cosmos and the revelation of God in Jesus. On the other hand, the surprising and paradoxical sayings of Jesus, Paul's proclamation that the wisdom of God appears as folly or scandal to human beings, and the plurality of portraits of Jesus within the New Testament itself all warn against any naïve sense of having comprehended the meaning of this revelation.

The intelligibility and incomprehensibility of the revelation of God in Jesus Christ paradoxically intertwine in the New Testament itself. The paradoxical, world-questioning sayings of Jesus himself call into question any pretension to have finally comprehended God and the cosmos. These sayings set up a tension at the heart of the revelation of God which can open hearers to the widely different experiences of other religious traditions.

3

The Divine Warrior and the Crucified God

REVELATION AND VIOLENCE IN THE BIBLE

The Christian Bible proclaims God as the divine warrior, leading Israel to victory over its foes on the battlefield, and also as entering the world as incarnate love, suffering violence without retaliation, and dying on the cross. The central revelatory narratives in the history of Israel and the birth of Christianity, the Exodus and conquest of the Promised Land and the death and resurrection of Jesus, present rather different relationships between revelation and violence. Revelation comes in the Exodus and conquest narratives as deliverance from destruction and victory over Israel's foes; revelation also comes in the refusal of Jesus to retaliate with force, in his shameful death on the cross, in his resurrection, and in apocalyptic hopes for a divine warrior to end oppression and right the wrongs of history. Military victory and the unjust suffering of the innocent both serve to make the divine presence known. The later Christian tradition would develop theologies of holy war, just war, and pacifism, all inspired by biblical texts.[1]

In the ancient Near East, deities revealed their power in the military victories of their respective peoples. The gods acted in history, and their empires' conquests were the visible evidence of their might. In many ways early Israel shared the religious worldview of the neighboring cultures. In one of the central images of their faith, the people of Israel proclaimed Yahweh as the "man of war," the divine warrior whose right hand had shattered his enemies and cast them into the sea (Exod 15:3-7). Later Yahweh led the people of Israel into the Promised Land, giving them victory over their foes in wars that were remembered as sacred events. Within the biblical witness, however, a remarkable transformation occurs: alongside the portrait of the divine warrior there emerges the portrait of a God who suffers from the violence of this world, who wills peace and who enters the world as nonviolent, incarnate love. The latter image does not simply displace the former, however, for the divine warrior appears in the Book of Revelation and would have a long career in Christian history as well. The history of the Christian reception of revelation reflects the ambiguity of the biblical heritage itself.

EXODUS AND THE DIVINE WARRIOR

The narrative of the Exodus and the journey through the wilderness into the Promised Land shaped the consciousness of the people of Israel regarding God more than any other. God, aware of the sufferings of the Hebrew slaves, calls Moses from the burning bush and instructs him to go to Pharaoh and to lead the people of Israel out of slavery into a land of milk and honey. In recent decades, Gustavo Gutiérrez, George Pixley, and other interpreters have seen the Exodus account as a call to liberation, the intervention of a just and gracious God on behalf of an oppressed people. Gutiérrez believes that God acted in history, and he stresses the concrete political-economic theme: God acted for the liberation of slaves. "The liberation of Israel is a political action. It is the breaking away from a situation of despoliation and misery and the beginning of the construction of a just and fraternal society. It is the suppression of disorder and the creation of a new order."[2] Revelation here means freedom from slavery and oppression and the challenge to build a more egalitarian society. Gutiérrez protests against any separation of the concrete political-economic liberation from the religious meaning of the event: "The Exodus is the long march towards the promised land in which Israel can establish a society free from misery and alienation. Throughout the whole process, the religious event is not set apart."[3] Gutiérrez's interpretation set the tone for many other interpreters who stressed the analogy between the liberation of Hebrew slaves and a variety of liberation movements in the contemporary world.[4]

In the context of liberation theology, revelation opens up the vision of a just society, free from the inequities of Egypt. Whatever violence is exerted is necessary and justified in a situation of overwhelming, systematic oppression. Sometimes the institutional violence of slavery can be broken only by force. The liberationist interpretation of the Exodus has been one of the most persuasive in recent decades, giving hope and support to contemporary efforts to secure justice.

The relation of divine revelation to violence in the Exodus and conquest narratives is, however, complex and ambiguous. In the course of the drama, there are forms of divine violence that are not simply responses to oppression. After the dramatic call at the burning bush, as Moses makes the journey back to Egypt to fulfill his mission, Yahweh enters the scene again, this time not as the God of benevolence and compassion, but rather as a mortal threat. Yahweh tries to kill Moses (Exod 4:24-26). Divine violence threatens God's own messenger without warning or explanation. The One Moses trusted turns on him to slay him. Fortunately, Moses' wife, Zipporah, thinks quickly and knows what to do. She circumcises their baby boy with a flint, takes the foreskin and touches it to Moses' body, thereby communicating to Moses the effect of the circumcision. The moment of terror passes: Yahweh releases Moses and allows him to go free. What experiences may have lain behind the story are impossible to know, but the memory remained, enshrined in the Book of Exodus for generations to come. Circumcision, according to this account, wards off divine terror and protects Israelites from the violence of Yahweh. The blood of circumcision offers a protection against the terrors of the divine attack in the night. It is an image of the fears that lie deeply hidden in the origins of religious traditions, fears that reach so far back into the mists of the past that it is difficult to know how to interpret them.

The struggle between Moses and the Pharaoh culminates in violence. According to the biblical narrative, Yahweh asserts control of the situation and demonstrates divine power through the actions of Moses. The power of God is made clear in the plagues. The conflict escalates through the series of plagues, culminating in the death of the firstborn sons of the Egyptians. In the climax, the power of Yahweh is revealed in the deaths of firstborn children, themselves innocent of the deeds of their fathers (Exod 12:29-30).

In the famous scene of deliverance in Exodus 14-15, Yahweh splits the sea in two to allow the Israelites to pass over and then destroys the Egyptians. As we saw in the preceding chapter, the deliverance at the Sea of Reeds was interpreted in mythic terms to disclose the pattern of God's action and establish a paradigm for later generations.

After defeating the enemy, Yahweh goes in a triumphal march up to his abode on his holy mountain, striking terror into the hearts of other nations (Exod 15:13-18). The power of God is revealed in the deliverance of the Israelites, the destruction of the Egyptians, and the terror of other nations. The revelation of the power of Yahweh as the divine warrior establishes one model for the holy war or "Yahweh war," one of the most important elements of the early biblical tradition. While the holy war is profoundly problematic to many contemporary interpreters and thus is often passed over in silence, scholars have held that Israel itself originated in warfare and have noted that the name "Israel" means "El does battle."[5] In the tradition of the holy war, which was common throughout the ancient Near East, earthly battles are viewed as only one dimension of the conflict. While Israel marches out to fight its earthly opponents, Yahweh similarly goes to war (cf. Judg 5:19-20; Isa 24:21).[6] Hymns repeatedly celebrate the power of God in war (Deut 33:2-3; Num 10:35-36; Ps 24; Isa 35; Hab 3:3-60).

The concrete provisions of the holy war were gruesome. According to

Moses, Yahweh commands the people of Israel not to make treaties with the inhabitants of the land and promises that with God's help the Israelites can destroy them all (Deut 7:1-24). Yahweh is to be at war with Amalek in every generation (Exod 17:14-16), and the Israelites are ordered to blot out the very memory of Amalek under heaven (Deut 25:17-19). The Book of Joshua recounts the destruction of the entire population of Jericho, except for Rahab and her household, at the command of Yahweh (6:17-21). The promises of land include the conquest and extermination of other peoples.

The violence of the Exodus and conquest narratives does not fit neatly into a contemporary liberationist perspective. Gutiérrez's own vision of a society free from oppression and misery is rather different from the concrete details of the Book of the Covenant in Exodus 20:22-23:33, which explicitly accepts slavery as in accord with the will of God. As historian Donald B. Redford noted, a number of the commands allegedly revealed by God to early Israel are barbaric:

> Alien groups whose actions or even presence were deemed in opposition to Israel are consigned to genocidal slaughter at the behest of Yahweh (Exod. 17:14; Num. 31; 1 Sam. 15:3); even fraternization with foreigners brings the plague (Num. 25:9, 18); anyone who dissents Yahweh burns up (Num. 11:1-3; 16:35); anyone who complains he strikes with plague (Num 11:33; 14:37; 16:49), or sends poisonous snakes after (Num. 21:6). Aberrant cultic practices, even though indulged in innocently, bring death (Exod. 32:35; Num. 15:37-40).[7]

Where Gutiérrez and Pixley praise the Exodus as a liberation from tyranny, Redford is more jaundiced: "An honest reading of the account of Exodus and Numbers cannot help but reveal that the tyranny Israel was freed from, namely that of Pharaoh, was mild indeed in comparison to the tyranny of Yahweh to which they were about to submit themselves."[8] While Redford's own assertion is itself something of an overstatement, he calls attention to a serious problem for contemporary theological appropriations. The biblical heritage not only supports contemporary notions of liberation; it also justifies slavery and calls for the extermination of entire populations.

INTERPRETING ISRAEL'S ATTITUDES TOWARD WAR

Early Israel's attitudes toward war were complex and conflicting. Susan Niditch has identified in the Hebrew Bible seven different models of waging war:[9]

1. One model demanded the utter destruction of the enemy, male and female, child and adult, as a sacrifice to God. The killers themselves do

not bear responsibility because it is the will of God that the foe be put to death (e.g., Deut 2:34-35; 3:6-7; Josh 6:17-21; 8:2, 24-28; 10:28-40; 11:14). In this perspective, the death of the enemy is not a matter of just retribution but of pleasing God through human offerings.

2. Another ideology of war called for the annihilation of enemies as sinners condemned by divine justice (Deut 13:12-18; 20:10-18). Here the reason for the slaughter is the requirement of justice in accordance with the perspectives of the authors of the Book of Deuteronomy.

3. The Priestly tradition of Israel insisted on the elimination of the enemy because they were unclean. According to Moses in Numbers 31, all males of the enemy nation should be killed, whatever their age; but girls who are virgins are to be spared because they can be purified, become ritually clean, and be incorporated into the people of Israel.

4. The bardic tradition glorified war as beautiful and noble, celebrating the heroism and courage of the warriors (1 Sam 17:1-54; 2 Sam 2:12-16; 2 Kgs 6:22-23; 2 Chr 28). For this tradition, war is a game that must be played according to the rules to win honor. There is the beginning of a code of just war emerging in this tradition, as wars are waged for just causes (Gen 14; 1 Sam 30), and prisoners are allowed to return home (2 Kgs 6:22-23; 2 Chr 28:9-11).

5. Still another model of war focused on the underdog who plays the trickster, using subterfuge and deceit to win against a superior foe (Gen 34; Judg 3:12-20; 4-5; 14-15; 19-21; Esth 8-9). Here deception is a matter of course, as in the case of guerrilla warfare.

6. The ideology of expediency sees all means as necessary and justified in war. This is similar to the ideology of the underdog, but it assumes the perspective of the powerful who use brute force to accomplish their goals. Niditch compares this ideology to William Tecumseh Sherman's strategy: "War is hell."[10] Sometimes this ideology is implicitly critiqued by the biblical narrative itself when it fails, as in the case of Abimelech (Judg 9:45-57); but elsewhere, as in the case of David, ruthlessness brings success (2 Sam 5:6-8; 8:2). 1 and 2 Chronicles and Amos also offer critiques of the ideology of expediency.

7. Finally, there was also the ideology of nonparticipation by the Israelites themselves (Exod 14-15). They stand on the sidelines while God fights the battle for them so that God may have all the glory. Here Israel relies solely on the help of God, as in the prototypical victory of Yahweh over the Egyptian army at the Sea of Reeds.

The violence demanded by God in the Hebrew Bible presents a problem for Jewish and Christian interpreters alike. The later rabbinic tradition itself expressed reservations regarding exulting over the destruction of the Egyptians. According to later Jewish tradition, as the angels began to sing for joy after the deliverance of Israel at the Red Sea, God told them: "The work of my hands has drowned in the sea and shall you chant songs?"[11]

Walter Brueggemann has wrestled with the problem of revelation and violence and has sought to find a way to accept the war narrative in Joshua 11 as revelation. The text presents the victory of Israel, led by Joshua, over a coalition of kings with great armies and a huge number of horses and chariots. Brueggemann begins by noting that the interpretation of scriptures is always an ongoing process in which the interpreters play an active role: "We not only accept meanings offered, but we construct meanings which we advocate."[12] In this process, Brueggemann turns both to sociological methods of examining the socioeconomic context and also to literary methods of exploring what visions of possibility are opened up by the text. This approach allows Brueggemann to distinguish between what ancient Israel understood as revelation and what contemporary Christian interpreters may understand.

Brueggemann understands early Israel to be an egalitarian society and the opposing monarchies to be oppressive concentrations of power that are threatened by the socioeconomic alternative Israel represents. The kings have horses and chariots, symbols of power, wealth, and oppression, while Israel has none. Even though the military situation is unfavorable to Israel, Yahweh tells Joshua not to fear and directs him to destroy the chariots and hamstring the horses. Brueggemann comments: "The disclosure is that Yahweh gave permission for Joshua and Israel to act for their justice and liberation against an oppressive adversary. . . . What is revealed is that Yahweh is allied with the marginalized, oppressed peasants against the monopoly of the city-state."[13] Brueggemann sees three elements coming together in the revelatory experience: (1) the memory of the liberation from slavery in the Exodus, (2) the present hopes of the Israelite peasants confronted by overwhelming military force, and (3) Yahweh's speech, which authorizes Joshua to act but does not promise any explicit divine action. The power of God comes in the word of hope, not in direct outward military assistance. This revelation does not simply come down from heaven in an intrusive fashion; it rises from the hopes and dreams of the Israelites and receives confirmation in the words of Yahweh to Joshua. Brueggemann finds the God of Israel squarely opposed to domination and passionately supporting liberation and egalitarian structures. In this context, the violence by an oppressed community against the weapons of power of the enemy kings is justified.

One difficulty with Brueggemann's interpretation is that he sees the God of Israel only and always on the side of the oppressed, and he passes over the clear commands of Yahweh in other passages to kill all members of the enemy group.[14] In the climax of Joshua 11, the Israelites do indeed put the enemy peoples to the sword, and it is clear that they are following orders that Yahweh had given to Moses and Moses had given to Joshua (Josh 11:15). Brueggemann limits the revelatory discourse to the one verse in this chapter that Yahweh speaks to Joshua (11:6), and he gives no importance to the broader context of the holy war, which was believed to be commanded by God's will. Brueggemann accepts the passage as revelatory at the price of tailoring it to fit a contemporary liberationist perspective.

In Brueggemann's more recent work, he understands Yahweh as the divine warrior in Israel generally on the model of just wars: as defensive and protective of life for an embattled, oppressed community that was repeatedly threatened by more powerful foes. Brueggemann also sees God's activity as lying on the edge of violence and not as central to it. He does, however, acknowledge a further dimension of fierceness in biblical portraits of Yahweh as a warrior and he admits the problems that this poses for normative theology. In addition to the measured violence that defends justice, there is something more strange and frightening: "an undomesticated quality of Yahweh allows a play of violence, on occasion, that cannot be contained in any sense of justice. That potential violence can break out at any time, because Yahweh is not finally accountable to any other agent, not even to Yahweh's partner Israel to whom fidelity has been pledged."[15]

Another, more directly critical approach to the ideology of the holy war was proposed by Martin Buber, who commented on the prophet Samuel's demand, in the name of God, that Saul kill not only the captured leader of the Amalekites, but all the Amalekites, including infants and children (1 Sam 15:3). Buber insisted: "Samuel has misunderstood God."[16] In reflecting upon the religious basis for this criticism, Buber concluded: "an observant Jew of this nature, when he has to choose between God and the Bible, chooses God. . . . [I]n the work of the throats and pens out of which the text of the Old Testament has arisen, misunderstanding has again and again attached itself to understanding, the manufactured has been mixed with the received. . . . Nothing can make me believe in a God who punishes Saul because he has not murdered his enemy."[17]

For Buber, there emerges from the biblical witness an understanding of God that shapes the judgment of believers. In light of this overall sensibility, it is necessary to reflect critically on passages within the Bible itself, even to the point of deeming them not revelatory of God's will. More recently, Jon Levenson has described some of the conquest narratives with the command to annihilate entire populations as "a genocidal Blitzkrieg"; while noting that the events most likely did not take place according to the biblical account, Levenson comments that even though the murderous *Blitzkrieg* is not a historical event but a later creation of Deuteronomic historians, "it is not a pleasant ideal to contemplate."[18]

Recent Christian teaching on war and peace often implicitly rejects Moses' and Joshua's and Samuel's violent demands for the holy war without reflecting explicitly on the assumptions or implications of rejecting biblical teachings. For example, the discussion of nuclear war in the American Catholic bishops' pastoral letter *The Gift of Peace* and Pope John Paul II's eloquent affirmation of the sacredness of all human life in *The Gospel of Life* pass over in silence the biblical demands for the complete extermination of Israel's opponents.[19] Joseph Cardinal Ratzinger cites both "the absence of error in the inspired sacred texts" and "the doctrine on the grave immorality of direct and voluntary killing of an innocent human being" side by side as examples of infallible teachings. He does not, however, explain how Samuel's clear and direct demand, in the name of God, that Amalekite infants be put to death (1 Sam 15:3), or the similar command of Moses, also in the name of God, to kill all male Midianite children and all female Midianites who are not virgins (Num 31), or the order of Joshua to kill all the inhabitants of Ai according to divine will (Josh 8), is to be reconciled with John Paul II's unambiguous defense of innocent human life.[20] In practice, most Jews and Christians select some perspectives from the Bible as revelatory of the will of God and tacitly reject others. Choosing God over the Bible remains a challenge for Jews and Christians today.

JONAH AND NAHUM

The tradition of the holy war had a long history of effects, both within Israel itself and in later Christianity. It was not without criticism within the biblical tradition itself, however. The books of Jonah and Nahum reveal sharply different perspectives on revelation and violence. The background of both is the power of the Assyrian Empire, with its capital in Nineveh. The Assyrians were notorious for being ruthless in battle and merciless in victory. The Ninevites effectively worshiped the gods of power and violence that dominate so much of human history. Their gods were more powerful than anyone else's, at least for a time. Because they could "prove" their claim in battle, it was in its own way a very effective empirical theology. It is not surprising that in the narrative Jonah has no desire to preach to them. When the reluctant Jonah finally does go to Nineveh, his preaching is an abbreviated form of what another prophet, Nahum, had proclaimed: Let Nineveh be utterly destroyed; let the wrath of God come down and destroy them. Nahum had offered a vivid description of the bloody destruction of the city of blood:

> Galloping horse, jolting chariot, charging cavalry,
> flashing swords, gleaming spears,
> a mass of wounded, hosts of dead, countless
>   corpses,
> they stumble over corpses. (Nah 3:2-3)

Nahum saw in the hoped-for destruction of Nineveh the hand of Yahweh. Nahum invoked the will of God as the justification for violence. In effect, the Ninevites deserved to die, and thus it was good for the conquerors to kill them. It is the myth of redemptive violence, not from the side of the imperial conquerors but from the side of the little nation in danger of being overrun.

The Book of Jonah reverses this scenario. At the preaching of Jonah, the Ninevites abandon their gods of power and war. They repent, turn to the God of Israel, and are forgiven. This is one of the most ironic moments in the entire Bible. According to the fictional narrative, Jonah does one day's work and becomes the most successful prophet in the history of Israel. The Ninevites even put sackcloth and ashes on their animals. The people of Nineveh, the very epitome of evil, are forgiven by God. Jonah, after this astonishing triumph, goes off to pout, clinging to the god of war and demanding that God fulfill the promise of destruction. At the end of the book, the Ninevites have converted from the god of war, but Jonah apparently has not. Jonah still wants blood and laments that God will not carry out the threat. God mockingly reminds Jonah that the Ninevites are children of God as well. At the end of the book, Jonah is sitting on a hill outside the city, being questioned by God, looking rather ridiculous. The juxtaposition of the books of Nahum and Jonah in the Bible presents both sacred violence and the renunciation of violence as part of the heritage of Israel.

THE PATHOS OF GOD AND THE VISION OF PEACE

There also emerges from the Hebrew Bible itself a witness to God's own suffering from the violence of this world and a prophetic vision of a more peaceful community of nations. Commenting on the lamentations of Jeremiah, Abraham Joshua Heschel says: "Israel's distress was more than a human tragedy. With Israel's distress came the affliction of God, His displacement, His homelessness in the land, in the world. And the prophet's prayer, 'O save us,' involved not only the fate of a people. It involved God in relation to the people."[21] Heschel stresses that God's pathos is the center of the prophets' revelatory message. Prophecy reveals God's intimate involvement in the life of the people of Israel, and thus the sufferings of Israel affect God. The marriage of Hosea is "a mirror of the divine pathos"; Hosea's sorrow "echoed the sorrow of God."[22] Second Isaiah teaches us that "Israel's suffering is God's grief."[23] God shares in the sufferings of Israel and accompanies Israel, alternately challenging and denouncing the people for their injustice and supporting and comforting them with visions of new possibilities.

The pathos of God manifests itself in God's active concern for the world, especially for the defeated and the poor. The prophets of Israel protested against reliance on military might and stressed God's care for the victims of history. The prophets did often see God acting in military actions. Isaiah looked forward to God leading Israel to victory over the Philistines, the Edomites, Moabites, and Ammonites (Isa 11:12-14);

Jeremiah saw the hand of God in the victories of Israel's enemy, Babylon (Jer 21:3-7; 34:1). Nonetheless, prophets also repeatedly denounced the use of force. Heschel comments that the prophets of Israel "proclaimed that might is not supreme, that the sword is an abomination, that violence is obscene."[24] Isaiah proposed a moving vision of peace, of beating swords into plowshares and spears into pruning hooks (Isa 2:4), which still challenges the Jewish and Christian communities. Heschel asserts: "The prophets were the first men in history to regard a nation's reliance upon force as evil. Hosea condemned militarism as idolatrous" (Hos 5:13; 8:9-10, 14; 10:13).[25] Alongside the image of the divine warrior and hopes for Israel's victories in battle, the Hebrew Bible also presents the hope for a world in which the wolf shall live with the lamb, nations will live in peace, and the poor and oppressed will find justice (Isa 11:1-9).

THE REIGN OF GOD SUFFERS VIOLENCE: REVELATION AND VIOLENCE IN THE NEW TESTAMENT

First-century Palestine was filled with violence.[26] There was the systemic violence of Roman imperial rule, the violence of Herod the Great's terror even toward members of his own immediate family, the violence of the Zealots who would take up arms to drive the Romans out, the violence of the Romans crucifying those who challenged or threatened Roman power. Palestine was an occupied territory with a series of corrupt and vicious kings and governors who ruled with the help of foreign soldiers under the reign of a foreign emperor. Peasants before, during, and after the time of Jesus were in a state of constant political turmoil. Taxes were oppressive, designed to transfer wealth either to the Roman Empire or to King Herod and the temple in Jerusalem. It was difficult for all except the very wealthy to accumulate wealth, and so most lived in financial insecurity. There was constant unrest, including spontaneous, unorganized movements, violent political strikes and riots, and local rebellions; but until later in the century, in the 60s, there was no widespread, organized resistance. The Romans crushed mercilessly those who disturbed the peace of the empire. Pontius Pilate had many, many Jews crucified without a second thought. The New Testament assumes a horizon shaped by violence; but it mentions only a few specific acts of political violence, as in the case of the Galileans whom Pilate had killed and whose blood was mingled with their sacrifices (Luke 13:1) and the deaths of John the Baptist and Jesus.

In the New Testament, the powers and principalities who rule this world appear as sources of violence and, indeed, the very presence of evil. While the ancients believed that these powers were intelligent spirits, Walter Wink recently has interpreted the powers and principalities as concrete symbols for the spirituality of institutions and the collective dimension of human existence.[27] The powers and principalities are, as it were, the personalities of institutions. These powers are strengthened and supported by individual decisions, but they seem to transcend the power of individuals. When corrupted by sinful patterns, they become demonic and enslave entire societies in destructive patterns of thought and behavior. Before them we are weak. From them we need to be saved. Paul writes that the powers of this world crucified the Lord of glory because they did not recognize the wisdom of God and thus did not know who he was; to Christians, however, his identity is revealed, and with it the path to salvation (1 Cor 2:8-10).

Wink stresses, however, that the powers and principalities are created by God and thus are not intrinsically evil. As the personalities of institutions, they need to be called to conversion. While the influence of any single individual may appear minimal before such powers, Wink proposes a model of nonviolent action modeled on Jesus and notes the repeated success of nonviolent action in recent history. Wink sees the heart of the revelation in Jesus' teaching of a "third way" that avoids violence but refuses to accept injustice.

JOHN THE BAPTIST

According to Mark and Matthew, Jesus began his public teaching in the context of Herod's violence, shortly after John the Baptist had been arrested (Mark 1:14; Matt 4:12-17). While there are many angles from which one can approach the account of John's death, René Girard's interpretation is a good example of the power of his mimetic theory to provide a framework for reading narratives of desire and violence. Girard considers the story of the death of John the Baptist (Matt 14:1-12; Mark 6:17-29) to be one of the clearest revelations of the patterns of mimesis and violence in all literature; indeed, he finds mimetic desire and scapegoating shaping every turn of the story.

The conflict arises from sibling rivalry. Herod has taken his half-brother's wife. Two brothers, both of whom are named Herod in historical accounts outside the New Testament, want the same woman and thus become mimetic rivals and enemies. Girard notes that it was not against the law in Israel to have your brother's wife. In earlier Israel the law stipulated that if your brother died without an heir, you had to take your brother's wife. The problem is wanting the same wife when the brother is alive.[28]

In the background is an unstable family divided by competing rivalries and jealousies. Even the names, two Herods and a Herodias, suggest a near identity of desires. As long as Herodias is desired by two half-brothers, Girard notes that she wields great power over King Herod.

Once she is married, however, a new triangle is formed, one that is less advantageous to her: Herod, Herodias, and John the Baptist. In this new triangle, John the Baptist appears as the obstacle, the *skandalon* or stumbling block, who denies the desire. Herod feels the attraction of John's words and refuses to have him killed. There seems to be no way out. Even in prison, John is still a powerful figure, and Herodias is publicly humiliated. The *skandalon*, the obstacle, opposes desire, renders it impossible, and thereby continues it. The scandal is the obstacle that attracts and repels at the same time.

Herodias's response to the situation involves creating still another triangle: Herodias's daughter, who is unnamed in the Gospels and is usually named Salome because of a reference by Josephus, comes on stage to dance. In the Gospel narrative the daughter has no name and no desire apart from what her mother gives her. She is a double, a mirror image, of her mother, only younger and more pliable. This child is a classic example of the younger person being corrupted by the older model, recalling Jesus' warnings about corrupting the innocent children (Matt 18:5-7).

Girard stresses the role of dancing. Even though the text states only that she danced, this dance has taken on a life of its own in Western art and music. There are countless paintings of Salome, and Richard Strauss wrote a famous opera filled with sex and violence, climaxing in the lurid Dance of the Seven Veils. The brevity of the text does not stop Girard from imagining the scene. The setting is a ritual banquet to celebrate Herod's birthday. The leaders of the community and the army are there, celebrating the order of the kingdom, personified in Herod's continued reign. The birthday of a king is a public ritual celebration of order. But something happens. The dance casts a spell, catching everyone up in the movement of desire and evoking the power of primitive rituals which often lead to death. Primitive sacrificial rituals are in the background as Girard claims that the dance leads inevitably toward the sacrifice of someone. According to Girard, in one way or another art continually returns to this dynamic of desire and death to simulate the primordial crisis and its resolution. This process is, of course, dangerous because it seeks a victim. "If the dancer does not control the desires, the public immediately turns on her, there is no one else to become the sacrificial victim. Like a lion-tamer, the master of ritual unleashes monsters that will devour him unless he remains in control through constantly renewed efforts."[29]

Herod himself is caught up in this excitement, extravagantly offering the girl half his kingdom. The offer is way beyond measure. As Girard notes, to give her half the kingdom would make the daughter Herod's double. Herod swears an oath, a ritual gesture invoking the gods, in front of the assembled leaders. He is as one possessed and offers to dispossess himself. In possession we are not simply alienated, for an

alienated person retains a self that observes. In possession we are outside of ourselves altogether, caught up in a process beyond ourselves as
in a trance. Herod begs Salome to accept his homage and be, in effect,
his master, possessing him. There is no objective reason for this at all.
Herod has lost himself. His dilemma comes from the play of desire that
seeks to be freed from itself by finding an idol in Salome.

Girard notes that the resolution demands a scapegoat. Someone must
die. Herod did not see this coming, but he fears what his guests will
think. The ultimate power is the opinion of the assembly of guests, in
whom the primitive crowd and the ruling class meld together—in a way
anticipatory of what will happen later on in the passion narrative. Like
the reluctant Pilate of the passion narrative, Herod worries about what
people will think. His power comes from what others think of him, and
so he orders the death of John the Baptist. Herodias knows how to
manipulate and steer the process, but she does not invent it. According
to Girard, it would be a mistake to blame any one particularly malevo-
lent individual. This is the age-old drama. When the prophet brings the
truth of desire out of hiding, he must die. Thus Girard argues: "The unani-
mous mimeticism of the scapegoat is the true ruler of human society."[30]

In one sense, this narrative is like all the primordial myths and rituals: mimetic desire enthralls a crowd, and someone must die. The difference is in the point of view. Herod is no hero, and order is not really
restored. The Gospel of Mark tells us that he did not even believe that
John the Baptist was really dead, because he thought that Jesus was John
come back from the dead to haunt him (Mark 6:16). It is hard to be
more certain of someone's death than by cutting off the person's head,
but even this does not succeed in bringing Herod peace of mind. Girard
comments: "But the text itself does not carry out what it reveals; it sees
nothing divine in the mimeticism that gathers men together."[31] Instead
of reinforcing the process one more time, the Gospel presents the death
as an attack on the reign of God. The reign of God suffers violence, but
does not oppose violence with violence. Instead of continuing the cycle
of violence, the Gospel unveils the pattern of mimetic desire and scapegoating in solidarity with the victim, thereby setting in motion the long,
slow process of the dissolution of the scapegoat mechanism. Once the
process has been revealed, Girard asserts, it will in the long run lose its
efficacy. Girard's reading of the death of John the Baptist is evocative
and persuasive.

JESUS AND VIOLENCE

In the Sermon on the Mount Jesus teaches his followers to love their
enemies and pray for their persecutors (Matt 5:44). Jesus seeks to break
the cycle of violence imitating violence by challenging his hearers not to

retaliate for injuries suffered. Instead of responding in kind, we are to imitate the all-inclusive love of God, who sends sun and rain upon the just and the unjust alike (Matt 5:45). Jesus broadens the range of the term "neighbor" so that even enemies are to be included as the objects of love.[32] The golden rule (Matt 7:12) forbids retaliation and judging others (Matt 7:1-5).

In the Gospels, Jesus enters into situations where the drama of mimetic desire, violence, and scapegoating is being acted out; but he refuses to play along. Often Girard's mimetic theory helps to analyze the dynamics of the situation. For example, elements of the surrogate victim mechanism shape the story of the adulterous woman (John 8:2-11), but the usual violent conclusion is prevented. The crowd has captured the woman, but they did not bring the man. He must have been there too, but apparently was able to or was allowed to escape. In first-century Palestine, adultery was only a crime against a man: a man could not commit adultery against his wife—only against another man by having relations with the other man's wife. The crowd surrounds the woman, threatening to kill her. It is a highly charged scene of sex and violence. As the men look on the woman, they can project all their anger and guilt and lust on her as they pick up stones.

Where the crowd publicly shames her in the name of morality and righteousness, Jesus reminds everyone present, especially the men who want to stone her, of our common sinfulness. Jesus is bringing out into the open the bias of a society that condemns the woman to death while allowing her male partner to escape unharmed. It is not only a personal act of forgiveness of one woman; it is an exposing of the scapegoat mechanism itself, the pattern of a male-dominated society blaming women one-sidedly for sexual misconduct and using women as scapegoats so that men can feel virtuous and righteous. Jesus moves into a highly charged situation and reminds the crowd that we all are sinners.

The Gospels retell the drama of scapegoating, but reveal its demand for violence as a fraud. Acknowledging that all of history is dominated by violence, Jesus says:

> Therefore I send you prophets and wise men and scribes, some of whom you will kill and crucify, and some you will scourge in your synagogues and persecute from town to town, that upon you may come all the righteous blood shed on earth, from the blood of innocent Abel to the blood of Zechariah the Son of Barachiah, whom you murdered between the sanctuary and the altar. Truly, I say to you, all this will come upon this generation. (Matt 23:34-36).

Violence reigns from the beginning of the Bible to the end of Second Chronicles, the last book of the Hebrew Bible. The present generation sums it all up. There is a solidarity in persecution: The sons repeat the acts of the fathers without being aware of it. They think they are different, but they do the same things. The same process of scapegoating would be repeated in later centuries when Christians would blame the entire later Jewish community for having killed Jesus, and then would commit acts of violence against them. Denying our own guilt and insisting that we are different renders us tragically like the earlier generations who committed violence in the name of God.

Early Christianity remembered Jesus as condemning violence and urged Christians to make peace and to suffer violence without retaliation.[33] Jesus' entry into Jerusalem on a colt (Mark 11:1-10) rejects the expectation of a military Messiah entering the city of David with horses and chariots and turns instead to the hope of Zechariah for the king to come, "humble and riding on a donkey, on a colt, the foal of a donkey. He will banish chariots from Ephraim and horses from Jerusalem: the bow of war will be banished" (Zech 9:9-10).[34] While two of Jesus' followers are reported to have carried arms on the night of his arrest (Luke 22:38, 49), Jesus himself rejected the option of violent resistance.

The call to peace in the New Testament is strong. As in the case of the Hebrew Bible, however, the evidence is complex and conflicting and not all texts fit neatly into a pacifist or a Girardian model. Michel Desjardins has pointed out that there are other aspects of the New Testament witness that are not easily harmonized with the call to peace and instead accept, condone, or expect certain forms of violence. Jesus, John the Baptist, and early Christianity accepted soldiers.[35] When Roman soldiers turned to John the Baptist for advice, he told them not to extort money and to be content with their wages (John 3:1-4); he did not demand that they find another occupation. Jesus praised the Roman centurion in Capernaum for his faith in Jesus' authority and power to heal (Luke 7:1-10), with no criticism of his military role. The Acts of the Apostles presents the conversion of the Roman centurion Cornelius to Christianity without any expectation that he abandon military service (10:1-48). Thus military service was not seen as evil in and of itself.

The teaching of Jesus on loving one's enemies did not mean that Jesus himself was averse to controversy. Indeed, the command to love one's enemies implies that one has enemies. Richard Horsley notes that the Synoptic Gospels portray Jesus himself as in sharp conflict with the Jewish authorities: "It should thus be clear that the synoptic Gospels do not portray Jesus as 'innocent' and innocuous."[36]

Desjardins notes that apocalyptic passages in the New Testament anticipate a violent climax to the war between good and evil and look forward to the coming of the divine warrior (e.g., Rev 19:11-20:3).[37] According to apocalyptic writers, God will intervene with force to end the rule of evil in this world. Christians will be vindicated, and those who have rejected God will suffer dire torments. Apocalyptic literature claimed to reveal the outcome of the battle, promising victory to

Christians. Thus, Desjardins notes, the peacemaking efforts of the New Testament presuppose an apocalyptic context in which the violence of God will intervene to resolve the injustices of history: "superimposed on these sanctuaries of 'peace' was an awesomely violent context."[38] The Book of Revelation draws upon the ancient tradition of the Israelite holy war to present Jesus as the divine warrior who does battle for his people (19:11-21). Adela Yarbro Collins comments: "The mythic pattern of combat, which is used often in the Jewish Bible to portray Yahweh as the divine warrior, is the basic principle of composition in the Apocalypse. Thus the struggle with Rome was interpreted by John as a holy war."[39]

Other New Testament texts cite the earlier Israelite accounts of the holy war as signs of God's power and favor. In the speech delivered immediately before his martyrdom, Stephen recalls the ancient holy war conquest of Palestine as an example of God's gracious deeds (Acts 7:45). In the Acts of the Apostles, Paul recalls God's destruction of the nations of Canaan (Acts 13:19). Divine violence even threatens the early Christians themselves if they displease God. When Ananias and Sapphira lie about their contribution to the Christian community, God strikes them dead (Acts 5:1-11). The parables of Jesus themselves sometimes present violent events as symbols of the reign of God, as in the case of the guests who did not come to the wedding banquet (Matt 22:2-10). The parable escalates beyond all reasonable expectation toward a violent conflict. Some of the invited guests do not simply decline the invitation; they mistreat the servants bearing the invitation and kill them. The king, in response, commands his servants to destroy the murderous invitees. The early church found in this narrative a model for understanding the destruction of the city of Jerusalem in 70 C.E. within the history of revelation: God's messengers bearing a divine invitation were mistreated or killed, and so the invitees suffered destruction. The divine violence of revelation history as presented by the parable offered the church a precedent for later Christian abuse of Jews. Thus even the memories of the teaching of Jesus himself became in the reception of revelation an occasion for violent abuse of others.

JESUS' RELATIONS TO "THE JEWS": THE QUESTION OF ANTI-JUDAISM IN THE NEW TESTAMENT

Much of the most violent language of the New Testament involves the description of Jewish opponents of Jesus. The context for this language is the problematic relation between the early Christian movement, which was largely Jewish in the first century, and the majority of Jews, who did not accept Jesus. The language that Jesus uses toward his Jewish opponents in the Gospels often seems to violate his own command to love one's enemies. Many passages in the New Testament were interpreted by the later Christian tradition as condemning the entire Jewish people for rejecting the revelation of God offered to them. John the Baptist excoriates the scribes and Pharisees as a "brood of vipers" (Matt 3:7). Jesus himself also attacks the scribes and the Pharisees in vehement language, as hypocrites, blind guides, and murderers (e.g., Matt 23:13-32). In the Gospel of Matthew, the crowd that calls for the death of Jesus exclaims: "Let his blood be on us and on our children!" (Matt 27:25). The Gospel of John contains much of the harshest language, condemning "*hoi Ioudaioi,*" which is often translated as "the Jews," but which often refers more specifically to the Judean leadership of the temple.

The history of later Christian interpretation of revelation often understood these texts as condemning the entire Jewish people in every generation for the execution of Jesus, and a number of scholars have charged that the New Testament itself is anti-Jewish or anti-Semitic.[40] Other scholars, however, have pointed out that the New Testament texts were written by Jews who did not have a clear sense of attacking members of another religion.[41] The term "anti-Semitism" comes from nineteenth-century Germany, where it was used to make hatred of the Jews seem more respectable by grounding it in a pseudo-biological theory of racism. There is nothing like this in the ancient world, and thus the term is misleading when applied to the first century.

Jesus spoke and New Testament authors wrote from within the tradition of Hebrew prophetic criticism. The harsh language of Jesus and John the Baptist is reminiscent of the prophets' own forceful attacks on the Jewish people; thus it is faithful to the Jewish tradition of prophetic self-criticism. Raymond Brown has argued that the early Christian presentations of the death of Jesus should not be seen as "anti-Jewish" because the Jewish authorities, Jesus, and his disciples were all Jews; and the description of the innocent victim being condemned recalls the sufferings of Jeremiah, the travail of the Suffering Servant in Isaiah 52-53, the cries of the Psalmist (Ps 22), and the murder of the just man in the Wisdom of Solomon (Wis 2:17-21).[42] The entire conflict is an inner-Jewish dispute, not a polemic against Jews as a people.

Coming from first-century Jews who had accepted Jesus as the Messiah, these criticisms are not anti-Jewish or anti-Semitic in the sense of condemning the entire people as a nation or as a race. Indeed, the New Testament criticisms of scribes and Pharisees use the same type of rhetoric as other Jewish groups used for each other during this period.[43] When later centuries of Christians read these texts, however, they usually understood them to be condemning the Jewish people as a whole. Celebrations of Holy Week, inspired by the reading of the passion narratives, often became occasions for violence against Jewish communities.

Girard interprets the attacks on Jewish leaders in light of his analysis of religious attempts to cover up violence. Jesus in the Gospel of John accuses the Jews of having the devil as their father (John 8:43-44). Like other texts, this has classically been interpreted in anti-Jewish ways, but Girard argues that this is to miss the meaning. The point is not that the Jews are uniquely diabolical, but that the type of religious leadership represented by Jesus' opponents in the Gospel of John goes back to the primeval scapegoat mechanism. There is a triple correspondence between Satan, the original homicide, and the lie. Biblical scholars have related the charge that Satan was a murderer from the beginning to the killing of Abel by Cain.[44] The Bible finds violence at the foundation of history and culture, presenting the first murderer as the founder of the first city (Gen 4:17). For Girard, "To be a son of Satan is to inherit the lie. What lie? The lie that covers homicide."[45] The "children of Satan" continue the process of murder and deception, killing the prophets and then honoring them after their death until the end of time. We always see this in other people and never in ourselves, and thus we continue the cycle. To take this accusation as simply about the Jews misses the entire point. In this sense "Satan" is not a literal, fallen angel or an extraterrestrial spirit. "Satan" is a symbolic way of naming the entire process of mimetic rivalry leading to violence and scapegoating. Satan is the prince of this world because this process of violence and deception dominates human life. The name "Satan" is a symbol for the source of rivalry and for all the forms of deceptive order that structure our lives. According to Girard, Satan is a liar and a homicide from the beginning, the source of falsehood that dominates all human culture and thought except for biblical revelation and its aftermath.

For Girard, when Jesus tells the scribes and the Pharisees that they build the tombs of the prophets whom their fathers killed, he is revealing the entire process of mimetic violence. The murder is covered up by the building of a tomb (Luke 11:47-48), and religion actively participates in and continues the cover-up. For Girard, the "Pharisees" in the Gospel criticisms represent the process of displacing violence into cultural institutions. The image of the tomb also applies to the individual. There is a corpse inside of us that is rotting: "Alas for you, because you are like the unmarked tombs that people walk on without knowing it!" (Luke 11:44). The "Pharisees" not only conceal the murder in a tomb; they conceal the tomb. The double concealment suggests the way that murder is hidden first in sacrificial rituals and then later on in postritual institutions that continue the original murder in ever more subtle and concealed forms.[46] According to Girard, religious practices coming from human initiative always involve forms of "good violence" that seek to end "bad violence"; divine revelation, by contrast, uncovers the founding violence of culture and condemns it.

Girard's interpretation strains to fit the New Testament polemics against Jewish leaders into his system and thereby justify them. The result, however, requires accepting the entire Girardian analysis of violence and culture, which, as we have seen, is problematic. Later Christian treatment of the Jewish community is a classic example of the scapegoating mechanism dominating an entire culture. The attempt to exonerate New Testament texts from all responsibility, however, does not resolve the problem. The New Testament's rhetoric of vilification of scribes, Pharisees, and, especially in the Gospel of John, of "the Jews," remains problematic. Contemporary interpreters can understand these passages as reflecting the fierce polemical rhetoric of the time, but the history of effects makes clear the tragic potential for violence in these texts. As in the case of the texts of the holy war in ancient Israel, Christians need to exercise a critical discernment in interpreting the New Testament's treatment of Jewish opponents of Jesus.

In a remarkable example of this type of critical discernment, Joseph Cardinal Bernardin, in a speech at Hebrew University in Jerusalem on March 23, 1995, referred to the teaching of the Gospel of John that "the Jews" are children of the devil:

> Father [Raymond E.] Brown maintains that this teaching of John about the Jews, which resulted from the historical conflict between Church and synagogue in the latter part of the first century C.E., can no longer be taught as authentic doctrine or used as catechesis by contemporary Christianity. This is the key pastoral point. Christians today must come to see that such teachings, while an acknowledged part of their biblical heritage, can no longer be regarded as definitive teaching in light of our improved understanding of developments in the relationship between early Christianity and the Jewish community of the time. As Brown says in his book, *The Community of the Beloved Disciple,* "It would be incredible for a twentieth-century Christian to share or justify the Johannine contention that 'the Jews' are the children of the Devil, an affirmation which is placed on the lips of Jesus (John 8:44)."[47]

THE DEATH AND RESURRECTION OF JESUS

The death and resurrection of Jesus confront us with the terrible cruelty of human violence and present to us God's response. The crucifixion of Jesus was, from the perspective of the Roman and Jewish authorities, the regular way to handle someone who was causing trouble. The Jewish leaders in Jerusalem were more interested in keeping the peace with Rome and maintaining their own power than in hearing prophetic criticism. When Jesus was preaching in the hills in Galilee, he could be tolerated as a minor nuisance, but when Jesus directly challenged their authority in the temple, they decided he had to be removed.

In one way or another it is a tale that has been told over and over again in human history. Caiaphas, the high priest, put it with brutal clarity in the Gospel of John: "You do not seem to have grasped the situation at all; you fail to see that it is to your advantage that one man should die for the people, rather than that the whole nation should perish" (John 11:49-50). The system of domination needs to eliminate certain individuals to protect itself. From time immemorial, mobs and governments and societies and even religious leaders have believed that violence was an answer to their problems. They thought that violence would bring order and peace. If only we get rid of a certain troublemaker, if only we exclude a certain group, if only we get rid of those people, things will be okay. Exclusion and violence become bonding forces in society. Thus groups have made some persons scapegoats for the sake of preserving social order.

According to the usual calculations of human power, the execution should have been the end of the story of Jesus—one more religious reformer eliminated to maintain a corrupt status quo. Power and violence always want to have the last word, but they always call forth more of the same. But this was not simply one more religious reformer. For Christians, what happened in Jesus was that God entered into the cycle of violence in order to break it and offer us a way out. The system of domination is not closed. In Jesus, God proclaims that we do not have to live this way, dominated by unending cycles of anger, hatred, fear, and violence. The reign of God is not like the reign of human violence and does not play by its rules. That is why Jesus goes to his death without fighting back. When a disciple draws a sword, Jesus warns that those who live by the sword will die by the sword (Matt 26:52). Violence calls forth more violence, and Jesus wants to offer us another way of living and loving. The ancient demand for scapegoats is based on a lie. The true God does not demand victims and even accepts being put to death as a victim to awaken us. A nonviolent God enters into history and dies the death of the innocent.

In the passion narratives, Jesus appears in the same ritual that dominates life on this planet. In the traditions of the Saturnalia, Roman soldiers would crown a false king and then punish him.[48] Dio Chrysostom described the ritual of the mock king of the Sacaea: "They take one of the prisoners condemned to death and seat him upon the king's throne, and give him the king's raiment, and let him lord it and drink and run riot and use the king's concubines during these days, and no man prevents him from doing just what he likes. But afterwards they strip and scourge and crucify him."[49] In the classic pattern, the victim receives all the violence of the community and is condemned as genuinely guilty. Because the guilt seems real, it is never doubted, and the process of scapegoating is never apparent. The victim bears the weight of all the contradictory meanings that are projected; and thus peace follows, for a time.

In the Gospels there is a complete deconstruction of the primitive system. The drama is played out in full awareness. The evangelists are not taken in by projection for a moment. God is not on the side of the crowd or the Jewish leaders or Pilate. The victim is the Son of God. The demand that the victim must die is an illusion of the persecutors. In the Gospel narratives' portrayals of the decision to crucify Jesus, the crowds function as the real power, determining even Pilate's decision. "This crowd is the group in dissolution, the community is literally dispersed and cannot reform except at the expense of the victim, of the scapegoat."[50] This is the way God reveals God's presence in the world: "a non-violent deity can only signal his existence by having himself driven out by violence—by demonstrating that he is not able to establish himself in the Kingdom of Violence."[51]

In principle, the powers that govern this world have been unmasked and their power is weakened. They did not realize what was going on. "None of the rulers of this age understood this; for if they had, they would not have crucified the Lord of glory" (1 Cor 2:8). There was a certain, limited healing effect from Jesus' death in the older sense of scapegoating: "And Herod and Pilate became friends with each other that very day, for before this they had been at enmity with each other" (Luke 23:11-12). For the most part, however, the older order is not restored by the crucifixion. Instead, the reign of the gods of violence is undermined.

When Peter preached to the crowds in Jerusalem in the Acts of the Apostles, he tried to help them see that they—and we—are the ones who put to death the author of life (Acts 3:13-14). Every generation contributes its own share to the age-old patterns. Christian artists in Europe recognized the connection between their own time and the Gospels when they painted the crucifixion as a public execution, where people would pack up meals and take the children out to watch someone being executed.

The resurrection is not more of the same old cycle—it is a new chance for the entire human race, both in this world and the next. The resurrection of Jesus is the sheer power of absolute love bringing forth life from amidst the ruins of history. Human systems have done their worst. They have put to death the author of life, and God still loves us. The author of life will not stay dead. He bursts back into history and reaches out to each of us with an invitation. The old cycle of sin and death, of violence and shame has been defeated. After sin comes forgiveness, after domination comes freedom, after violence comes healing, after shame comes acceptance, after death comes life. Even from the cross Jesus prayed to God to forgive his executioners because they did not know what they were doing (Luke 23:34). According to the Gospel of John, Jesus' first word to the group of disciples after the resurrection was "Peace" (John 20:20).

The resurrection opens up for us a fundamental trust in the power of

God beyond anything in this world. If we are united to Christ, we do not have to be afraid of any power in this world. We do not have to accept the assumptions of domination. The resurrection tells us that violence is not as final as it pretends to be, that the executioner does not have the last word and will not triumph forever over his victim. The resurrection tells us that God loves us more than we can possibly know or understand. The peace of Christ envelopes even the cruelest suffering and death.

In dying, Jesus entered into the cycle of violence that dominates so much of world history and broke through its power. The powers and principalities that rule this world through violence have been overcome, even though in practice their might is still great. Often we believe that we either have to flee the power of violence and evil or we have to fight it with its own weapons. Either way we lose. By fleeing, we abandon the field to evil; by resisting with the same tools of violence, we become like the powers we are opposing. Jesus opens up a third way.[52]

In this world of brutality and violence, Christians proclaim the resurrection and all that it brings: the forgiveness of sins, the healing of the soul, peace, a season of refreshment. And yet the cycles of violence obviously continue. Jesus gave us an example of facing oppression in his own meeting with Pontius Pilate. He did not fight violently; he did not summon legions of angels to destroy Pilate. Neither did he simply accept Pilate's authority. He quietly undermined the assumptions of the whole Roman system, calling Pilate himself into question (John 19:11). This set the pattern for Christian resistance to the Roman Empire for the next three hundred years. Christians accepted persecution, even martyrdom without fighting back, but they undermined the whole Roman system of violent domination, bringing it to the point where many educated Romans did not believe in it any more.

The death and resurrection of Jesus unleashed the Christian movement into the world, and the world has never again been the same. But the death and resurrection of Jesus are not only outward events with political overtones; they are also the contours of the most intimate movements of our own spirit. Paul tells us that each Christian has to go through the experience of dying with Christ (Rom 6:3-4). In some way we have to enter into his death so that we can rise with him. This affects our most intimate awareness of ourselves.

THE EXPERIENCE OF PAUL:
THE IRONY OF REVELATION

Of all the events in the history of Christianity, from the first coming down of the Holy Spirit upon the apostles to the present, none has been more influential than the revelation of Jesus Christ to the apostle Paul. Not only Christian theology and the church but the Western world and

its very language for understanding human existence have been decisively shaped by this man's experience and writings.

As a young man, Saul was very, very bright. He had received a first-
rate education, trained in the fullness of the Law of Moses by Gamaliel,
and he also had a very sophisticated knowledge of the techniques of
rhetoric, the art of public speaking and persuasion. Saul was one of the
most powerful communicators of all time. According to the Acts of the
Apostles, he was also well connected, with access to the Jewish high
priest himself (Acts 9:2).

Saul was very, very sure of himself. He knew what was right and what
was wrong. He knew what the Law of Moses taught, and what the Law
forbade. He prided himself on being an upright Pharisee and a staunch
defender of God's will (Phil 3:6). He knew that the novelties of the followers of Jesus were a violation of the Law. It all seemed so terribly
wrong.

For the young Saul, a strong, clear logic of identity based on exclusion led to violence. Thus with the authorization of the highest Jewish
religious authority, he set out to end the problem of Christianity through
force. The young Saul represents one of the greatest dangers of religion.
Certainty of God's will leads to intolerance, to threats of violence, to
murder. We always face the danger of mistaking our idea of God for
God, and then we can use our idea of God as a weapon to attack those
who disagree. It is so easy to become self-righteous when we mistake our
cause for God's cause, and then we go out on a seek-and-destroy mission, like Saul. Violence becomes sacralized, cloaked with the justification of God's will. One of the most effective tools to break this spell is
irony. Irony in one sense is a combination of circumstances that is the
opposite of what might be expected.

What Saul encountered was the most ironic turnaround of his life;
indeed, the entire narrative is dominated by irony. When he was confronted by Jesus on the road to Damascus (Acts 9:3-6), all his clear
categories collapsed. The staunch defender of God learned that he was
attacking God. The one who was enforcing the fullness of the Law was
attacking the author of the Law. It is ironic that the religious leader
was actually attacking the God whose cause he pretended to defend.
Saul, who was so clear-sighted, became blind as soon as he began to
see, so that he could learn the meaning of sight. It was only in the collapse of all his certitudes, in the collapse of the logic of exclusion and
violence, in the death of his old self, that Saul became the apostle and
learned who he really was, and who he was called to be. It is ironic
that the self-confident Saul should turn as a blind man to accept
instruction from a man he sought to capture and kill (Acts 9:13-19).
Jesus is supposed to have conquered death and ascended to glory at the
right hand of the Father. It is ironic that Jesus is still suffering right
here on earth in the persecution of his followers.

Irony can be the first face of revelation and grace. Irony undermines our certitude, helps us see how ridiculous we can be. Irony reminds us of the relativity of all our assertions, all our claims, all our achievements. Irony reminds us of the untruth present in every truth. Irony is the power of negation within every affirmation. Irony undermines our single-minded fanaticism and allows us to laugh at ourselves. Irony frees us from the awesome responsibility of playing god and allows us to be rather silly creatures.

But irony alone cannot save us, for it carries its own dangers. Irony can express a false conversion, from fanaticism to cynicism. Irony in another sense is saying one thing and meaning another. This irony is a way of playing safe, of keeping the claims of others at a distance. In an ironic mood, we can mock every certainty and escape into irresponsibility. We can undermine everyone else's perspective and congratulate ourselves on how witty we are. We can engage in an unending game of hiding, never meaning what we say or saying what we mean. Ironically, we play roles in which we do not believe, which we do not fully embrace. Postmodern Western culture is dominated by irony, a culture skeptical of every ideal, wary of any ultimate religious claims, uncertain of its own foundation. Is there a way beyond fanaticism and irony, a way beyond the incessant cycle of intolerance and cynicism, beyond the tragedy of history? The account of Paul's experience of revelation suggests that the way is the love that chooses to be present even at the cost of suffering, a love that is not deterred by threats, a love that nothing in this world can deter, that no murderous threat can scare. Jesus, risen and ascended, chooses to suffer in the lives of his followers. The power greater than fanaticism and cynicism is the redemptive, suffering love of God. The revelation of Jesus Christ to Saul is Saul's initiation into this mystery.

In seeing the Risen Lord, Paul learned first that the victim was innocent. Paul had to learn to see the presence of God in Jesus Christ and in the very people he was persecuting. In seeing the Risen Lord, Paul learned that even though he had been attacking Jesus, Jesus was not angry with him and was calling him to be a disciple.

The effects of this moment would shape the rest of Paul's life. In the encounter with the Risen Lord, Paul found the central challenge of his life: to share with others the revelation that he had experienced himself. He saw everything in a new light. The rigid demand to follow all the ritual prescriptions of the law collapsed. He saw in the people he was judging and persecuting the face of God. In the last place on earth he expected to find God—in those he despised—God appeared. For Paul, this was not a conversion to another religion. Judaism and Christianity had not yet been separated into two different religions. For Paul, to accept Jesus as the Lord and Messiah was the proper culmination of the Jewish tradition. He did not stop being a Jew to become a Christian.

There were many questions of Christian identity to be sorted out, and struggles over the logic of identity would dominate much of his life. Paul himself as an apostle would have to confront other people who had a very clear and rigid logic of identity that led to excluding other people. In the Letter to the Galatians, his fiercest attacks would be against Jewish-Christian opponents who were binding Christian people by the Law of Moses because that was the way Jews had always done it.

Paul, who had been so strict, learned to see all things in a different light. It was not that he lost his concern for identity, but he discovered a different logic of identity based on self-emptying, modeled on Jesus. He would write to the church in Philippi: "Let the same mind be in you that was in Christ Jesus, who, though he was in the form of God, did not regard equality with God as something to be grasped at, but emptied himself, taking the form of a slave, being born in human likeness" (Phil 2:5-7). The self-emptying of Christ set the model for Paul's mature identity. To grasp at equality with God would be to repeat the sin of Adam and Eve, who were made in the image of God but could not accept their condition. They tried to ascend to divine status in the wrong way, and thus descended. Jesus, by emptying himself, by not entering into rivalry with God, humbled himself to the point of dying on the cross, and thus ascended in the proper way to God.

This meant that Paul had to learn the flexibility that comes from inscribing his understanding within a broader context of not grasping and not clinging. In the face of rigidity on every side, he later wrote to the Corinthians that to the Jews he became as a Jew; to those under the Law, he became as one under the Law; to those not under the Law as one not under the Law; he became all things to all people (1 Cor 9:19-23). Paul had to learn to see life from different perspectives, to appreciate the value of different situations. He taught people to rejoice as if not rejoicing; to mourn as if not mourning; to possess all things as if not possessing them because the form of this world is passing away (1 Cor 7:29-31). To be in the world "as if not" allows us to affirm our ideals without absolutizing them, to risk our own lives without mistaking ourselves for messiahs; thus is irony set free from cynicism and is redeemed. In the world opened up by this revelation, we can laugh at ourselves and our silly pretensions.

For all that, Paul remained a most uncomfortable figure; he was usually in conflict with someone or other, and also in conflict with himself. The experience of revelation and his conversion on the road to Damascus were the end of his struggles but the beginning of a new phase in his life. Revelation and conversion were not simply one dramatic moment in his life—they were the beginning of a process that lasted a lifetime. The acceptance of revelation is not final or complete in this world. The state of final peace comes only in heaven. Over twenty years after his conversion, Paul wrote to the church in Rome the anguished lines: "The good I will I do not do. The evil I will not, that I do. But if what I do is against my will, it is not I who do it, but sin dwelling in me" (Rom 7:19-20). Even after twenty years of leadership in the Christian community, Paul is still struggling. Here, toward the end of his life, Paul admits that he does not fully understand himself. At least on one level, his life is out of control. Looking at himself, he finds another power dwelling within him, another law at war with the law of his mind, another power that he does not control—the body of death, which drives him to sin despite his best intentions.

Paul experienced his own life as a battlefield on which he was at war with himself. The wisdom of Paul is not to deny the reality and the difficulty of the struggle. Victory does not come by pretending that we are perfect, that we have got it all together. Wisdom comes not from turning away from our own compulsions and sins but from acknowledging them and presenting them to God. For Paul, we know ourselves most truly only when we recognize this other power of sin and death dwelling within us. At the heart of who we are is an inscrutable mystery of sin and grace that we can never completely figure out, even after receiving God's revelation in Christ. This is Paul's challenge to any Christian triumphalism. If we are tempted to think we have finally arrived, Paul reminds us that we are forgiven sinners. We are a relationship to ourselves and to God that we never quite get right. For Paul, this is the end of the optimism of the Greeks, who believed that to know the good was the same as doing the good.

After twenty years as an apostle, Paul still cries out: "What a wretched man I am! Who can free me from this body of death?" (Rom 7:24). He answers his question by shifting to a different way of speaking. The line of introspective questioning and analysis that he has been pursuing leads to a dead end. This is a sharp warning that the introspective turn, however necessary and helpful it can be, is not the final highway to truth. Constant worrying over ourselves can lead us ever further into a labyrinth or a hall of mirrors.

Paul abruptly cuts off his line of thinking and turns to the presence of God, the one who has been with us all along. Who will save him from the body of death? "Thanks be to God through Jesus Christ our Lord!" (Rom 7:24). The Greek word translated as "thanks" is *charis*, the same word as "grace." Paul, confronted by the dilemma of his own failures, lets out an acclamation of praise and thanksgiving to God. The acclamation is like a guttural shout welling up from the depths of Christian experience. Yes, we are in a mess that we have created and from which we cannot extricate ourselves. In this world, left to our own devices, there is no hope for us. The only thing to do is to thank God. Like Jonah in the belly of the fish, Paul does not pray out of despair, but lets out a wholly incongruous shout of praise. This acclamation of praise inserts the entire line of self-questioning into another level of mystery, that of God's free offer of grace in Jesus.

As we listen to Paul in his own letters, he tells us about the aftermath of his reception of revelation. He did not lose his feisty nature or his strong convictions, but the path of violence faded into the past. Angry as Paul could be, he would no longer resort to physical threats to eliminate opponents. He also became more aware of the relativity of all things in this world and of the limits of our own understanding. Instead of founding his identity on the logic of exclusion and violence, he embraced a more paradoxical logic of identity through self-emptying. This went to the point that his own ego-self could disappear, and he could write: "It is no longer I who live but Christ who lives in me" (Gal 2:20). The upshot of his experience of revelation was that the path of violence gave way to the path of persuasion. The raw struggle for power was replaced by a gentler logic based on a different source of power in love.

To become a Christian is to learn to see through the patterns of violence and imitate the path of Jesus. Paul's experience became prototypical for Christians. The one who breathes murderous threats against his victims thinks he is doing God's will, but in his confrontation with Jesus he realizes he is persecuting Jesus, the Son of God. The encounter with the Risen Lord opens Paul's eyes to the violence in his own religious beliefs, to the violence in his own life, and to the presence of God in the victims. The mimesis of rivalry will be replaced by the mimesis of Christ, centered on *agapē*, selfless love. *Agapē* is point by point the opposite of mimetic rivalry. The cross makes possible the generous mimesis of Christ as the renunciation of the conflictual mimesis that dominates the world. Faith accepts God as creator and refuses to play the game of mimetic rivalry with God. In this surrender we are freed from the incessant rounds of fighting and scapegoating, from the works of the Law and life according to the flesh. The process of divine self-emptying sets the model for human self-emptying. As Jesus accepted being a surrogate victim, so Paul has become one of the scapegoats of the world: "We have become like the scapegoats [*perikatharmata*] of the world, the noxious waste of all things, until now" (1 Cor 4:13). In this self-emptying, modeled on that of Jesus, Paul finds the basis for generosity and love.

BIBLICAL PERSPECTIVES ON VIOLENCE

Biblical understandings of revelation closely intertwine with violence, but they do so in starkly contrasting ways. On the one hand, in the tradition of the holy war the Bible sacralizes violence as directly willed and sometimes as directly exercised by God. God's power is revealed in the destruction of the enemy, in victory on the battlefield. The image of God as the divine warrior who leads armies to victory over their foes would set in motion a long tradition of later holy wars, reaching through the Crusades down to the practice of ethnic cleansing in the late twentieth century, which has sometimes been done in the name of protecting a "Christian" Europe against a perceived Muslim threat. The fierce attacks on the Jewish opponents of Jesus in the New Testament vilify them in ways that would warp all later Christian history.

On the other hand, the Bible also takes the side of the victims of history, exposes the patterns of scapegoating, and presents God as revealed in the nonviolent example and death of Jesus. In entering into and identifying with the innocent suffering of history, God does not demand victims; God accepts being the victim. This heritage also set in motion a long tradition of concern for the oppressed, of skepticism regarding imperial might and of searching for peace. There is no easy way to harmonize the various teachings of the Bible on violence. For Christians, the teaching, witness, and example of Jesus himself are central in assessing other perspectives. The ambiguous heritage of the Bible's support for violence places a special demand on Christian interpreters today: to be aware of the historical tragedies that have flowed from biblical polemics and warfare and to recognize the tradition of nonviolent peacemaking that also appears.

4

Revelation and Other Religions
in the Early and Medieval Church

The awareness of other religions is not new to Christianity. At every moment of its history, Christianity has faced other religious traditions and has responded in a variety of ways, both constructive and destructive. While an exhaustive study of the full range of these encounters is beyond the scope of the present work, a brief survey of some central aspects of the patristic and medieval encounter with other religions can offer important examples and instruction for contemporary encounters.

In the middle to late second century, a major crisis broke out over the meaning of revelation. The central question was how to relate the revelation that happened in the person and event of Jesus Christ to other sources of knowledge about God. Is this a completely new revelation of a God humans had never previously heard of? Is the God of Jesus Christ the same God that the people of Israel worshiped? If so, how does this revelation relate to the revelation given to Moses and the people of Israel on Mt. Sinai? How does this revelation relate to the order of creation and to Greek philosophy and religion? A variety of movements and communities challenged the church by proposing different responses to these questions. Enveloping this debate was the presence of Hellenistic philosophy and Greco-Roman religions with their own traditions and rites. The early church was faced with various options that radically excluded other religions from the truth. In response, early church writers often adopted a strategy of selective, critical inclusion, incorporating insights from other traditions, especially Greek philosophy, into Christian theology.

GNOSTICISM

The Gnostic movement placed tremendous importance on a secret revelation that promised to free humans from a world of suffering. The

83

term "Gnostic" has been used in different ways, sometimes being applied to movements during and before the time of Jesus. There are, however, no explicitly Gnostic texts known to have been written before 130 C.E. All the great Gnostic leaders and systems that we know from the Gnostic library discovered at Nag Hammadi, Egypt, and from early church fathers such as Irenaeus of Lyons, are from the second century C.E. Among the many versions of Gnosticism, there are general themes that most held in common.[1] In recent discussions Gnostics have sometimes been seen as mystics who celebrate the oneness of all reality because of certain Gnostic sayings of Jesus: "Split a piece of wood and I am there. Lift up the stone, and you will find Me there" (Gospel of Thomas 77).[2] However, second-century Gnostics saw creation itself as a fall from goodness.[3] For them, the good God of Jesus Christ did not create this world. There were various cosmogonies, some of which presented a lesser god as creating the world out of conceit and then boasting about it. This god was sometimes identified with Yahweh of the Old Testament. For all Gnostics, this world is a prison. Thus the purpose of the Gnostics is to escape from the evil world in which they are imprisoned to a better transcendent world. Gnostics see humans as trapped in bodies, not knowing who we really are; we have forgotten the divine element within us.

According to the Gnostics, we can escape and find our true identity through gnosis,[†] a secret revelation, a special knowledge that cannot be learned elsewhere. Through self-knowledge, we can ascend beyond the powers of this world into our true home above. Thus Gnostics call people to awake from their slumber (cf. Eph 5:14) to learn who they really are. According to the Gospel of Truth (22:3-19), true Gnostics know their origin and their destination.[4] In most Gnostic systems, Christ is the revealer of the secret, the bearer of the special message of salvation. Gnostics could not admit that the revealer actually suffered violence. Some, like Basilides, said that Simon of Cyrene was the one who was crucified, while Jesus took the form of Simon and watched the crucifixion from a safe distance. Jesus escaped unharmed, ascending to the heavens and mocking the powers of this world.

The gnosis that Jesus brings is a special revelation that allows humans to escape from being trapped in a world of violence and deception. The revelation is a reminder of one's origin in the heavenly world, a promise of redemption, and instruction on how to live in light of this revelation.[5] Gnostics claimed to have secret traditions, including resurrection appearances of Jesus and extra books of the Bible known only to a few. The Gospel of Mary presents a tradition of special postresurrection appearances of Jesus to Mary Magdalene. In these Mary receives a private revelation from Jesus himself, and Peter has to ask her to instruct him and the other disciples about what she knows. After hearing the revelation, however, Peter is upset and wonders: "Did he [Jesus] really speak privately with a woman (and) not openly to us? Are we to turn about and all listen to her? Did he prefer her to us?" (17:18-22).[6]

Gnostics used the accounts of secret revelations to interpret the earlier scriptures in a highly allegorical manner. In this process, the Gnostics developed the first systematic interpretation of the scriptures. By reading their own systems into earlier texts, they forced the church to consider the issue of biblical interpretation more systematically. The sociological result of living in a fallen world was that Gnostics retreated from the violence of society. Since the world is totally fallen, there is no reason to participate in it. For Gnostics, the wise response is to withdraw. This entailed a radical rejection of the Greco-Roman valuation of the cosmos as an ordered whole that is in harmony. For the Gnostics, the order of this world is imposed by evil, tyrannical forces who keep humans in ignorance and subjection. The "cosmos," which had been highly praised by Stoics, became a negative concept for Gnostic discourse. The order of the cosmos itself is a form of violence and deception, and humans are called not to play any constructive role within it, but to wake up and escape.

The mainstream Christian church's response set the framework for theologies of revelation for centuries: the revelation given in Jesus Christ builds on the knowledge of God already available in creation and does not contradict it. The God of creation and the God revealed in Jesus Christ are one and the same. Irenaeus of Lyons affirmed: "To say that the world is a product of fall and ignorance is the greatest blasphemy" (*Against the Heresies* 2.3.2).[7] Since this world is good, the church can engage culture and society critically but constructively. The wisdom tradition of ancient Israel, the Hellenistic Jewish wisdom tradition, and the wisdom Christology of the New Testament provided a basis for acknowledging the presence of God in all creation and in all cultures. The Gospel of John and the Epistle to the Colossians had applied the language of personified Wisdom to Jesus Christ, presenting him as the one through whom all things were created and hold together in being. Even though Gnostics used the language of Wisdom, or Sophia, they would not admit that the same divine Wisdom that created the world also appeared in Jesus Christ. In sharp contrast to the Gnostics, the biblical wisdom tradition provided a precedent to the early church for affirming the goodness of creation, the presence of wisdom in other cultures, and for engaging Hellenistic society constructively.

In response to the Gnostics, Irenaeus presents Christ as the creative and revelatory Word of God, the power of God in creation, who became incarnate and who recapitulates all the stages of humanity's existence. The Word reveals God to humans and humans to God (*Against the Heresies* 4.20.6). The Word makes it possible for humans to know the unseen Father: "for the Father is the invisible of the Son, the Son the visible of the Father" (*Against the Heresies* 4.6.5). In contrast to the Gnostics' denial of Christ's sufferings, Irenaeus insisted strongly on the suffering of Christ as the Son of God. Jesus entered into the violence of human history, praying on the cross that God would forgive his persecutors: "If he did not really suffer there was no grace" for the executioners whom he forgave (*Against the Heresies* 3.18.6). Irenaeus offered a unified vision of the entire human drama from creation through the fall to redemption to the eschatological fulfillment in the coming reign of God on earth.[8] The revelation of God came by the Word of God entering into every aspect of human life and summing up all of human history. By becoming what we are, Jesus Christ makes us what he himself is (*Against the Heresies* 5, Preface).

To counter the Gnostics' bifurcation of creation and redemption and their claim of a secret revelation, Justin Martyr proposed a Logos Christology that acknowledges that all people can know the Logos, even if they have not known the Logos incarnate in Jesus Christ. Socrates did, and thus lived in accordance with the Logos of God without explicitly knowing Jesus. The incarnate Logos is identical with the Logos through whom all things were made.

Justin's vision of creation and revelation would be very influential in relating to people outside the church. Because Jesus Christ is the incarnation of the Logos which is everywhere, Christians have something in common with the wise of all cultures. Everything that is true comes from the Logos. Thus people who have never heard of Jesus Christ can have a real knowledge of the truth, and Christians do not have to shrink from acknowledging this. Christians can use Greek philosophy and education and literature even while rejecting the Greek gods.

Other responses to the Gnostics came from Clement of Alexandria and Origen, who developed a sophisticated orthodox Christian understanding of gnosis.[9] Paul had used the word "gnosis" in a positive sense in 1 Corinthians 8 and 2 Corinthians 10:5; and thus, Clement and Origen reasoned, there must be a proper meaning for it. Christian gnosis for them was the revelation of God given to the soul in baptism, and it was also a further, deeper penetration into the meaning of Christian revelation. Gnosis brings the Christian a reflective grasp of what is at stake in revelation. For both Clement and Origen, this reflection involved a discerning use of Greek philosophy.

MARCION OF PONTUS

The Marcionites were similar in some ways to the Gnostics, but there were also important differences. Marcion was born in Pontus in Asia Minor (northern Turkey, on the southern shore of the Black Sea), the son of a Christian bishop. He came to Rome about 140 C.E., shortly after the bitter Jewish revolt against the Romans led by Bar Kochba in 132-135.

The Jews defeated an entire Roman legion, but then were destroyed themselves. After crushing the Jewish resistance, the Romans refounded Jerusalem as a Hellenistic city and named it Aelia Capitolina. Jews were forbidden to go there for centuries. Marcion's anti-Jewish teaching and his initial success may have been related to the wave of anti-Jewish sentiment after the revolt.

Marcion argued that the God of the Old Testament is just, but the God of Jesus Christ is good.[10] Pitting justice against goodness, he argued that a lesser god, the demiurge of Plato's *Timaeus,* fashioned this world. This lesser god, who appears in the Old Testament, should not be confused with the highest God, the God of Jesus Christ, who was completely unknown prior to Jesus. Thus Marcion rejected the Jewish claim of receiving revelation from the one God, and he denied that the Old Testament was a normative body of writings for Christians. This strategy solved the problem of the warlike portraits of Yahweh in the Hebrew Bible by denying their relevance for Christian understandings of revelation. Marcion took the Bible literally, in contrast to the Gnostics' spiritual interpretation. A literal reading of Paul convinced Marcion that the old Law had come to an end and thus there was no reason for Christians to accept the Hebrew Bible or the Septuagint as scripture. Claiming to be following the teaching of Paul, Marcion created the first canon or list of authoritative Christian books: he included an edited version of the Gospel of Luke and of the letters of Paul, removing what he claimed were interpolations.

Marcion challenged the church to reflect on the limits of scripture and on the question of how Christians are related to Judaism. The church responded by accepting the Septuagint as its own First Testament but did not take the Mosaic Law literally. The church developed its own more moderate style of allegorical interpretation, which would last through the Middle Ages. Lists of accepted books of the Bible begin to appear in the late second century, such as the Muratorian canon, which was proposed in Rome about 200 C.E.

MONTANIST PROPHECY

Another question concerned whether revelation was still taking place in the present or not. Christians had to face the question: After Jesus has ascended into heaven, does God still speak through prophets? Montanus was a Christian prophet who began preaching in Phrygia, which also was in Asia Minor, south of Pontus, about 150 C.E. Montanus continued the tradition of prophecy in the strong sense of a present revelation received from God. He was like the Hebrew prophets in claiming that God was speaking through him. He spoke in ecstasy, claiming to be a mouthpiece of the Holy Spirit. Thus, like the Hebrew prophets, he would speak in the name of God, proclaiming: "Man, like a lyre, I pluck"; and "It is I, the Lord God Almighty, who am present in a man" (Epiphanius, *Heresies* 48.4.1; 11.1).[11] Montanus predicted that the heavenly Jerusalem would descend upon a little town in Asia Minor called Ardabau. A number of women prophesied with him, such as Priscilla and Maximilla. Priscilla saw Christ come in the form of a woman in a shining robe and predicted the descent of Jerusalem on that spot. Maximilla said she was compelled, willing or not, to learn knowledge of God (ibid. 48.12.4). She prophesied that after her, the end would come soon. When history continued, many took this as a disproof of her divine calling.

The Montanists were rigorously exclusivist, regarding other Christians and all members of other traditions as excluded from God's grace and destined for damnation. The renewal of prophecy also posed a challenge to the hierarchy of bishops. Montanist prophets claimed direct authority from God on the basis of new revelation. Prophets did not need to establish their credentials through scripture or tradition. Because a prophet spoke in the name of God, he or she could claim greater authority than bishops. Church leaders such as Apollinaris, bishop of Hierapolis, opposed Montanus, convening synods of bishops in Asia Minor from the 160s through the 190s. Eleutherus, bishop of Rome, condemned the Montanist movement. Irenaeus of Lyons, however, did not condemn Montanus but feared rather that the anti-Montanists were themselves driving prophetic voices out of the church. Nonetheless, by the end of the second century, Montanism in Asia Minor was crushed. Meanwhile, Montanism spread to North Africa, where Tertullian joined them in the early third century, ca. 212. Montanism was the last effort of prophecy as a crucial force in the Catholic Church. In opposing Montanus and his followers, the church held that the definitive revelation of God in Jesus Christ is to be interpreted by bishops. A bishop claimed authority by interpreting the scriptures in light of the apostolic tradition. His authority was not to be challenged by wandering prophets claiming a new message from God.

Taken together, the various movements of Gnosticism, Marcion, and Montanus constituted a comprehensive challenge to the understanding of revelation. Each movement excluded others from access to the truth. Gnosticism raised the questions of the relation of revelation to creation, of the interpretation of the scriptures, and of a secret tradition that passes on a revelation not known by others. Marcion raised questions regarding the relation of revelation to creation, the canon of the scriptures, and the church's relation to Judaism. Montanus protested against any attempt to correlate Christian revelation with the life of the Greco-Roman world, and he raised the question of continuing prophecy, ongoing revelation, and the source of authority in the church. All three groups were radically alienated from Roman society. Revelation, according to these understandings, calls Christians out of the world into small groups in which there is little basis for public engagement of the world.

To understand revelation in response to these movements, the Church established a triadic relation of the canon of the scriptures, the apostolic tradition, and the bishops as the leaders of a community of interpreters. Revelation is understood to have been given in the past, both in the history of Israel and in Jesus Christ. Christians receive this revelation in the present through scripture and the apostolic tradition. Bishops are the authoritative interpreters for the community. This established the basic structure of Catholic and Orthodox understandings of revelation and ecclesiology to the present day.

RELATIONS TO HELLENISTIC RELIGIONS AND PHILOSOPHY

In relating to Hellenistic society, Justin Martyr proposed Christian revelation as the true philosophy, the answer to the search of the ancient philosophers. He hailed Socrates as a model and stressed that Christians are like the Platonists. Everything good about Hellenistic culture was affirmed and accepted and related to the Logos. Justin and other apologists stressed the possibilities of integrating Christian revelation into Hellenistic thought and culture. He defended Christians against false accusation and stressed that Christians pray for the emperor.

Clement of Alexandria also argued that the Logos enlightens all people: "No one is a Cimmerian [in Greek mythology this people lived far in the north where it was always dark] in respect of the Word" (*Exhortation to the Greeks* 9.72).[12] Clement exhorted the Greeks: "But there was of old implanted in man a certain fellowship with heaven, which, though darkened through ignorance, yet at times leaps suddenly out of the darkness and shines forth," and he proceeded to quote verses of Euripides as examples (ibid. 2.21). Thus all people know something of God, and pagan philosophy can be instructive. Philosophy was given by God to the Greeks as a preparation for the gospel. Human reason is itself a gift of God and can know something of God from reflecting on the universe itself. Moreover, the Logos has inspired some Greeks in a manner analogous to the Hebrew prophets: "[T]he Greeks spoke as they were moved" (Clement of Alexandria, *Miscellanies* 6.7.55.4).[13] God guides some leaders from other nations with a special inspiration so that they can help the multitudes.

The inclusiveness of Clement is balanced by a sharp critical judgment. Clement is fierce in his polemics against the licentiousness and the violence of the Greek gods and goddesses: "[Y]our gods are inhuman and man-hating daemons, who not only exult over the insanity of men but go so far as to enjoy human slaughter" (*Exhortation to the Greeks* 3.36). Clement warns against the immoral example of the Greek deities: "Cease the song, Homer. There is no beauty in that; it teaches adultery" (ibid. 4.52). Clement understands the Psalmist to be condemning the Greco-Roman gods: "[W]ith the utmost plainness and brevity the prophetic word refutes the custom of idolatry, when it says, 'All the gods of the nations are images of daemons'" (ibid. 4.54).[14]

Origen had a detailed knowledge of the Greek philosophy of his time and used it to construct the first systematic presentation of Christian faith. The affirmation of the continuity between creation and revelation set up the foundation for Christian humanism and for dialogue with all humans. Like Clement, Origen combined a trust in the universal working of the Logos of God with a polemic against the violence and idolatry of other religions. Responding to the pagan polemicist Celsus, who argued that each nation should follow its own customs of worship, Origen drew out the consequences of accepting all traditional religions because they are old and established: "It follows from his view that the Scythians do no wrong when they indulge in cannibalism according to the traditional customs" (*Against Celsus* 5.36).[15] An uncritical pluralism† would lead to accepting cannibalism. In contrast to the open-minded, uncritical multiculturalism of Celsus, Origen stresses that it is precisely the violence of concrete religion itself that forbids acceptance of all religious customs. If custom is king, as Celsus urges, then there is no basis for rejecting the practice of child sacrifice.

When Celsus mocks the claim of the Jews to be chosen by God, Origen defends the claim by pointing to their manner of life. Their rejection of idols and the ethical ideals that they proclaimed and lived distinguished them from other nations (*Against Celsus* 5.42-43).[16] Origen also proposed a critical appropriation of elements of other religions and cultures based on their coherence with the revelation of God in Jesus Christ. He praised Plato and used Platonic thought extensively in constructing his own system of Christian theology.

CHRISTIANITY AND JUDAISM

The most tragic relation of all was that of Christianity to Judaism. From the beginning of the Christian movement, many Jews rejected the claims of followers of Jesus, and a fierce debate ensued, which periodically led to physical violence. Jews maintained that the Messiah would usher in the messianic age. This age was to be a time of peace and justice, when all the nations would worship the God of Israel. The Messiah would bring a clear, visible change to the conditions of this world. Many Jews looked at the ongoing horrors of history, for example, the destruction of Jerusalem in 70 C.E. and again in 135 C.E., and denied that the messianic age had come. The continuing violence of history proved that the Messiah had not yet come. Some Jews, such as Philo of Alexandria, had already developed elaborate allegorical interpretations of the Torah to harmonize with Plato and Hellenistic thought. But in dialogue with Christian allegorists who found Jesus Christ hidden throughout the Jewish scriptures, later Jews argued that the Hebrew Bible did not refer to Jesus. The most fundamental reason for the Jewish refusal of Christian revelation was that Jews refused to accept that God has a son or that the Son of God suffered and died: "It is not permitted a human mouth to say, 'The Holy One—blessed be he—has a son.' If God could not look on in anguish while Abraham sacrificed his son, would he then have suffered his own son to be killed, without destroying the entire world?"[17]

Some Christians simply added Christian practice onto observance of the Jewish Law in various forms of Jewish Christianity. These Jewish Christians continued to observe the Jewish Law and also accepted Jesus as Messiah. The difficulty with the term "Jewish Christians" is that all Christian groups except the Marcionites were reading the Septuagint as scripture, and thus all preserved elements of the Jewish tradition in Christianity. All Christians were continuing at least some of the Jewish tradition, and thus the term "Jewish Christianity" is ambiguous because it risks including too much. Irenaeus (*Against the Heresies* 1.26) and Origen (*Against Celsus* 2.1) talk of people who still observed the Jewish Law and accepted Jesus as the Messiah, but not as the Son of God. They were often called Ebionites (Poor Ones). Jewish Christians, in the strict sense of that name, insisted on the observance of the full Torah and had a low Christology, seeing Jesus as prophet and Messiah, but not as pre-existent Son of God.

Other Christians engaged in intense polemics against Judaism as a false religion that was to be rejected as a whole. Despite Paul's affirmation that the covenant with the Jews was irrevocable (Rom 11:29), many Christians saw Judaism as completely superseded by the new revelation of God in Jesus and as having no positive relevance for the present. The *Epistle of Barnabas* argues that the covenant at Mt. Sinai belongs to Christians because the Jews broke it as soon as they had received it (4.7). The *Epistle of Barnabas* comes possibly from Alexandria, ca. 130-140, and was written possibly by a Jew who rejected his past, for he knows much about the Jewish scriptures and Jewish exegesis. According to Barnabas, an evil angel seduced the Jews into their legal practices. Moses spoke in the spirit, and the Jews should have observed the commandments in a spiritual sense. They should have known better than to take the commandments literally. "Moses received the covenant, but the people were not worthy" (14.4). According to Barnabas, Christians, by contrast, receive it in the right sense. Moses and Jesus were messengers of true revelation, but the Jews did not receive either one properly, and thus the Jews are not the recipients of the covenant. The *Epistle to Diogne-*

tus views Jewish sacrifices as on the same level as pagan idolatry (3.5) and rejects Sabbath observance as ridiculous superstition (4.1-2).

Another strategy that would have a long history was to reinterpret Judaism in a relation of fulfillment and correction. What was foreshadowed in the Law is fulfilled and corrected in Christ, but the Law must be understood in its spiritual sense. No Christians in the second century argued both that the Old Testament is inspired and also that the Old Testament is to be read literally. Marcion said Christians should read the Old Testament literally but he rejected it as scripture. Most Christians, except the Marcionites, interpreted the Old Testament allegorically in light of Jesus Christ. Thus reinterpretation became a major theme of early Christian writings. Christians claimed that the promise made to Abraham is fulfilled in Jesus Christ.

Justin's *Dialogue with Trypho* is the earliest surviving Christian apology directed to the Jews. Justin wrote this after his *Apologies* addressed to the Roman emperor. The setting is a two-day discussion with a learned rabbi, probably Rabbi Tarphon, who was well known as an opponent of Jewish Christians. Justin recounts the story of his personal journey through different schools of philosophy and of his eventual conversion to Christianity. He argues that the Mosaic Law was only temporal, whereas Christianity is the eternal law for all humankind. For Justin, Christians are now the true chosen people of God. Justin repeatedly cites passages that speak of the rejection of Israel and the election of the heathens. According to Justin, the Law was given to the Jews because of their perversity and sin. It was not a preparation for Christianity but a punishment for the stubbornness of the Israelites. The commandments of the Law were meant symbolically as guides to moral living, but the Jews took them literally and thereby missed their significance. For example, unleavened bread was to be a symbol of doing away with evil deeds, not a literal food (*Dialogue* 14.3).

By the second century, Christians were reading New Testament criticisms of Jewish leaders as indictments of the entire Jewish people; and the foundation was being laid for centuries of Christian anti-Judaism. Justin Martyr taught that the covenant with the Jews had been abrogated by the new covenant, and he charged that all Jews, including those of later generations, were responsible for the death of Jesus (*Dialogue* 11, 17). Where Paul had invoked the divine promises to Abraham as including both Jews and Gentiles (Rom 11), Justin understood the Jews to be excluded from God's promises (*Dialogue* 119.3-6). In effect, for Justin, Christians are the true children of Abraham, while the Jews are disinherited.[18] In the early third century, Origen voiced the belief that the Jews had to suffer more than any other people because of their rejection of Jesus (*Against Celsus* 2.8). These beliefs were repeated century after century and shaped the Christian mentality toward the Jews throughout the Middle Ages and into the twentieth century. In light of this widespread understanding of Christian revelation as superseding Jewish practice, one can understand the protest of conservative bishops at Vatican II that revising the church's view of Jews after Christ would be to reject the teaching of scripture and tradition.

Indeed, even after Vatican II, negative patristic attitudes toward the Jews continued to be echoed by the prominent French theologian and later cardinal Henri de Lubac. De Lubac, writing in 1967 after his extensive studies in patristic and medieval modes of biblical interpretation, could still continue the ancient tradition derived from Justin Martyr and others of degrading, displacing, and disinheriting the Jews:

> The Church, born from the side of Christ on Calvary, drawing life from faith in his resurrection, and animated by the Spirit received at Pentecost, henceforward takes the place of Israel. The church is Abraham's posterity, and alone possesses his inheritance, for "no one can receive the inheritance of Abraham except those whose thinking will be completely conformed to the faith of Abraham with full awareness of all its mysteries." . . . The church takes over from the Synagogue, which, now blind and sterile, is no longer anything but her librarian: "*Codicem portat Judaeus, unde credat Christianus*" (The Jew bears the book from which the Christian draws his faith). "Your books," St. Justin early remarked to Tryphon, the Jew, "or rather, ours: for it is we who follow them; while you, on the other hand, even as you read them, do not understand their meaning. . . . It is we who are the true race of Israel, the spiritual one."[19]

With the victory of the emperor Constantine (d. 336) in the early fourth century, the church gained new power in society, but with it came the abuse of power. The tone of the fathers is often bitterly anti-Jewish, and this became more pronounced after Constantine. John Chrysostom, the "golden-tongued" preacher, is one of the fiercest. Many Christians in Antioch in Chrysostom's time found Jewish customs and practices attractive and sought to combine them with Christian observance. Chrysostom saw this as a threat to Christian identity and responded with a virulent rhetoric of abuse that portrayed Jews as the most miserable of all people, as wolves who threaten the flock of Christ (*Sermons against the Jews* 4.1). The synagogue is a place of drunken parties where prostitutes and thieves gather (ibid. 1.1-2). John Chrysostom attacked Judaizing Christians and Jews in vitriolic terms that are an embarrassment and a scandal today.[20] Chrysostom was later honored as a doctor of the Catholic Church and is still proclaimed as the patron saint of preachers.

This rhetoric of abuse injected a vicious tone into Christian understandings of revelation, which would contribute to a long and tragic history of Christian anti-Judaism. Even though John Chrysostom did not stir up his people to direct physical violence against the Jews, his bitter rhetoric called forth powerful emotions that harbored the potential for later violence. Relations with Jews became worse as Christianity became accepted as the established religion of the empire. A Christian mob, encouraged by their bishop, destroyed a synagogue in Callinicum in 388. The Christian Roman Emperor Theodosius wanted to rebuild it from church funds as the law demanded; but Ambrose of Milan, who was later proclaimed a doctor of the Catholic Church, insisted that this should not be done; and he threatened the emperor with excommunication if he followed Roman law on the matter.[21]

The vitriolic rhetoric of the early church poisoned the atmosphere of Europe and helped set up a long series of tragedies. From the fourth century on, Catholic councils and synods repeatedly issued formal decrees that restricted Jewish life and practice. Even when popes defended Jewish rights in the Middle Ages and early modern period, they never proposed that Jews were to be accorded equal rights with Christians. Jews were to be preserved, but in misery as witness to the divinely willed punishment for their crimes.

AUGUSTINE

For the later centuries in the West, the most influential theologian of the early church was Augustine. The young Augustine was immersed in the world of Neoplatonic philosophy and saw revelation as summoning humans to rise from the world of matter and sense appearances to a purified understanding of the true and the good. The early Augustine, wrestling with the dualism of the Manicheans, stressed the freedom of the will and the goodness of this world, including everything God created.

Augustine developed a very powerful method of interpretation of scripture in *De Doctrina Christiana* (variously translated as *On Christian Doctrine* or *Teaching Christianity*). This handbook for preachers and teachers showed how to interpret the Bible, and it became one of the most influential books of the Middle Ages. For Augustine, the basic hermeneutical rule was *caritas*,[†] charity, the self-giving love modeled on Jesus Christ. According to Augustine, this is the central lesson of Christian revelation. The opponent of *caritas* throughout history is *cupiditas*,[†] the distorted love that makes something finite into an absolute and thereby becomes fragmented and self-destructive. Augustine set forth the principle of the two loves as the key to interpreting the meaning of revelation, both in personal experience and in the history of the world. Scripture teaches nothing but *caritas;* scripture condemns nothing but *cupiditas* (*On Christian Doctrine* 3.10.15).

God is love, and so the content of the revelation is love. Despite the incomprehensibility of the divine reality and the limits of our understanding, divine love itself empowers us to accept the revelation. Augustine assumed that many biblical passages were allegorical and were to be interpreted symbolically. The central message always related to love, however. The basic rule looked to the divine intention in revelation as the key to the meaning of the whole of scripture and its parts. Even if a reader finds a meaning that the human author did not intend, as long as it coheres with *caritas*, it is true, because the divine author, the Holy Spirit, intended it. The basic problem in human existence is *cupiditas*, the love that elevates some finite reality to deity and thus creates an idol. This has a thousand variations, but the central dynamic is the same. All the condemnations in scripture concern *cupiditas* in one form or another.

Augustine developed a powerful theory of signs in relation to this principle. Signs point to realities. We cannot comprehend the divine reality, but signs, established by God, can point to it. We cannot understand the signs unless we understand the reality. Otherwise, it is like talking to a deaf person about music or to a blind person about color. We cannot understand revelation without understanding the signs, and we cannot understand the signs unless we understand the object of revelation, God. This seems to be an impossible situation, but the reality intended by the signs is God, who is love; and God's love enters our world, transforms our minds, and allows us to understand revelation. Love makes the circle productive, allows us to see God as love, and calls us to conversion. For Augustine, interpreting biblical revelation is always a call to love.

Augustine's engagement with Hellenistic culture and religion followed from his analysis of the two loves that build two cities. His great, sprawling work *The City of God* traces the paths of the two cities: the city of God follows the path of *caritas* and knows that its true homeland is elsewhere; the city of this world follows the path of *cupiditas*, grasping at finite realities that cannot save. Augustine assumed that from the beginning of history, people outside of Israel could be saved through some special revelation of which we have no record (*City of God* 18.47), but he was less hopeful for those outside the church in his own day. In a strong polemic against traditional Roman and Greek religions, Augustine continued the biblical rejection of gods of other nations as idols. The pagan gods were demons, or they were human beings who had been mistakenly elevated to divine status (*City of God*, books 8-9).[22] Demons, for Augustine, were the fallen angels, the evil powers whom the New Testament describes as ruling this world. Their influence was evident not only in the public cults but also in astrology, fortune-telling, and other superstitions. The struggle between Christianity and the traditional religions of Greece and Rome was part of the ongoing battle between the two cities, and Augustine vigorously defended Christianity against Roman attacks that it was responsible for the fall of Rome. During his lifetime, Augustine saw many statues of gods overthrown, the traditional temples abandoned and destroyed, and Hellenistic religions go into a decline from which they would never recover. Augustine concluded, according to F. Van der Meer, that "[p]aganism had outlived its usefulness and was perishing of its own rottenness."[23]

Nonetheless, he respected the wisdom of Greek philosophers and used much of the thought and language of Plotinus and Porphyry to structure the narrative of his own soul's journey. The Platonists, he affirmed, knew the Logos even though they did not know the Logos incarnate (*Confessions* 7.9.14). Augustine assumed that God could be known by all humans.

The thought of Augustine would be of decisive importance for Western Christianity throughout the Middle Ages and beyond. Augustine's influence would spread throughout Latin Christianity, shaping the process through which the Christian scriptures replaced the Greco-Roman traditions as the classic texts of European culture. About two hundred years after his death, however, another religious movement would arise that would sweep through all of North Africa, changing its religious heritage permanently.

CHRISTIANITY AND ISLAM

The greatest external challenge to Christian understandings of revelation during the Middle Ages came from Islam. The rise of Islam in the seventh century posed a major threat to Christian civilization that lasted for about a millennium.[24] After the swift conquests of the first century of Muslim history, much of the heartland of early Christianity became Muslim through a gradual process of conversion. The energies of Christians would be directed toward direct military struggle against Islam in the Crusades, and the minds of theologians would be challenged by philosophical and theological works coming from the Muslim world.

Islam traces its origin to the appearance of the *Qurʾan* during the month of Ramadan in about the year 610 C.E. For Muslims, the *Qurʾan* itself is the revelation of God, the final and fullest revelation that God has given to humans.[25] There can be no questioning its authority.

Muhammad was about forty years old when he received the first revelation from God, and the messages continued for about twenty-two years.[26] Muhammad would go to a cave outside of Mecca and contemplate. One night, he felt someone come and say, "Recite" or "Read." Muhammad's answer was ambiguous: "I do not know how to recite [or read]." The word *iqra*, translated as "recite" or "read," comes from the same root as "*Qurʾan*," which can itself be translated as "recitation." From this response, Muslims have traditionally concluded that Muhammad was illiterate and that thus the reception of the *Qurʾan* itself was a miracle. Modern Western scholars often believe that since Muhammad was a trader, he could read and write. The other possible meaning of Muhammad's question is: "What shall I read [recite]?" Then the angel Gabriel instructed him to recite the first four verses of Sura 96. According to Muslim tradition, these were the first verses revealed:

> Recite in the name of your Lord
> who created man from clots of blood!
> Recite! Your Lord is the Most Bountiful One
> who by the pen taught man
> what he did not know. (96:1-4)[27]

"Clots of blood" is a reference to the embryo in the womb. After this Muhammad woke up. The voice had come in his sleep. He then saw the whole sky covered by the agency of revelation, which is also called "Spirit" or "spiritual messenger" in the *Qur'an*. Frightened, Muhammad ran home to his wife, Khadija, who consoled him and was the first person to accept Islam. Muhammad was filled with fear, doubt, and bewilderment. He may have feared that he was being possessed by a jinn, or spirit.

The second person to accept Islam was Ali, a cousin of Muhammad. Muhammad preached to his relatives and close friends for about two years. One of his wife's cousins, Waraqah, was a Christian, and he told Muhammad that his revelations were similar to those that Moses had received. Muhammad came to believe that the messages all came from one divine source, which he called the Preserve Tablet, where all truth is hidden. This is the Hidden Book, or the Mother of All Books, the source of all revelation and divine guidance to humans (*Qur'an* 56:78; 43:4; 13:39). Every people receives divine guidance. The *Qur'an* rejected the Jewish idea of God electing a special people. According to the *Qur'an,* God elects all peoples and sends them messengers of revelation (40:78; 4:164).

At the center of Islam is submission to the one God who created humanity with definite responsibilities. God created the universe as an ordered whole and presides over the universe's workings. All of nature is naturally submissive to God's will and thus is Muslim. *Islama* means to surrender oneself and be at peace, to be an integral whole. "Muslim" is the active participle, "surrendering." Humans have a choice because God put into human nature the capacity both to be evil and to be good. There is little direct talk about God or God's nature in the *Qur'an*. The revelation to Muhammad is more concerned with transforming life on this earth in preparation for the final judgment. God's nature is essentially mercy, but mercy and justice always go together. Two of the titles that are most common are Al-Rabb, the Lord, and Al Rahman, the Merciful. The central virtues to which God calls humans are intention, attentiveness, striving (*jihad*), and gratitude leading to praise of God. The greater *jihad* is the struggle with oneself. The lesser *jihad* is the struggle with outward foes.

Three themes are at the center of the revelation in the *Qur³an*: the rejection of idols; the criticism of social injustice, especially the gap between the wealthy and the poor; and the coming Day of Judgment. The *Qur³an* is very critical of social injustice. A society where the poor cannot live is irresponsible. "Have you thought of him that denies the Last Judgement? It is he who turns away the orphan and does not urge others to feed the poor. Woe to those who pray but are heedless in their prayer; who make a show of piety and give no alms to the destitute" (107). The criteria on the Day of Judgment will include helping the poor. The *Qur³an* praises the righteous "who though they hold it dear, give sustenance to the poor man, the orphan, and the captive, saying: 'We feed you for Allah's sake only; we seek of you neither recompense nor thanks; for we fear from Him a day of anguish and woe'" (76:4-10).

Of the major world religions, Islam is the only one born after the rise of Christianity, and the only one besides Christianity itself with a divinely revealed interpretation of Jesus and Mary. The *Qur³an*'s view of Jesus establishes the central difference between Muslim and Christian revelation, for the *Qur³an* explicitly rejects the high christological and trinitarian claims of Christian theology.[28] The *Qur³an* rejects any notions of begetting within God or of divine incarnation into this world. For Muslims, the *Qur³an* is the directly revealed Word of God and is not to be contextualized or relativized in any way. Because the *Qur³an* appeared from divine power, Muslims are to accept it, not to interpret it or criticize it. Where for Christians the central revelation of God is the person of Jesus Christ, to whom the New Testament bears witness, for Muslims the *Qur³an* itself is the revelation.

The *Qur³an* has a very high regard for Jesus, Mary, and other major figures of the Jewish and Christian scriptures. The *Qur³an* acknowledges that God gave both the Torah and the gospel "for the guidance of men and the distinction between right and wrong" (3:1). While the Torah and the gospel of Jesus were genuine revelations from God, most Jews and Christians have misinterpreted them, and Christians in particular have erred in proclaiming Jesus to be the eternal Son of God and in interpreting God as triune. For the *Qur³an*, God does not beget and is not begotten. Jesus was a prophet who did not claim to be divine. His message was true, but Christians have distorted. it.

The *Qur³an* presents Islam as the one true path of following God's will, outside of which there is no salvation (3:85). It cites Abraham as an example of Islam (3:64). Since the heart of Islam is surrender of one's will to God, anyone who makes this surrender is literally a Muslim. This call for submission to God, according to the *Qur³an*, is the central message of both the Torah and the gospel of Jesus. The small number of

Jews and Christians who do submit themselves totally to God are true believers or Muslims (3:110, 197-99).

The *Qur'an* sees most of the Jewish people as having broken the covenant that God had made with them, and it accuses the Jews of having "perverted the words of the Scriptures and forgotten much of what they were enjoined" (5:13), but it also urges Muslims to pardon the Jews (5:13) and call them to observe the Torah that they have received (5:68).

While the *Qur'an* regards Jesus as the Messiah sent by God, it sees most of his followers as unbelievers. The *Qur'an* recounts the angel's words to Mary: "Allah bids you rejoice in a Word from Him. His name is the Messiah, Jesus the son of Mary. He shall be noble in this world and in the next, and shall be favoured by Allah" (3:41). For the *Qur'an*, Jesus was a true prophet sent by God to confirm what had already been revealed in the Torah (5:46), but those who hail Jesus as God are unbelievers. "Unbelievers are those who declare: 'Allah is the Messiah, the son of Mary'" (5:17). "Jesus was no more than a mere mortal whom We favoured and made an example to the Israelites" (43:60). The *Qur'an* warns Muslims to beware of contacts with Jews and Christians: "Believers, do not seek the friendship of infidels and those who were given the Book before you, who have made of your religion a jest and a pastime" (5:57).

On a more positive note, the *Qur'an* also offers a basic principle for interreligious relationships: "We have ordained a law and assigned a path for each of you. Had Allah pleased, He could have made you one nation: but it is His wish to prove you by that which He has bestowed upon you. Vie with each other in good works, for to Allah you shall all return and He will declare to you what you have disagreed about" (5:48).

MUSLIM–CHRISTIAN ENCOUNTERS

Historically, Islam is the most formidable rival Christianity ever faced, at least before the rise of modern secularism. No other religion or movement has captured as many centers of early Christian life as Islam has done. Serious internal Christian divisions had preceded the rise of Islam by over a century and a half. The Church of the East, which was the Christian church in the Persian Empire and which spread in time across the Silk Road into China, did not accept the Council of Ephesus in 431 and was condemned, somewhat inaccurately, by Catholic and Byzantine Orthodox Christians for being "Nestorian."[29] The Oriental Orthodox Churches, traditionally but inaccurately called the "Monophysites," refused to accept the christological language of the Council of Chalcedon in 451.[30] This tradition held that there is only one divine nature in Jesus Christ. Many Christians in the Middle East were disaffected from Byzantine Orthodox and Roman Catholic leadership after these condemnations.

The faith of Islam was much simpler than the complex christological and trinitarian formulas of Catholic and Orthodox Christianity, and this contributed to its appeal to many. Over time, Islam converted many Christians. In the early Middle Ages, however, Muslim rulers were usually not eager to convert Christians because Jews and Christians, as people of the Book, had a special status in Islamic society and had to pay an extra tax. Conversion to Islam would mean a loss of revenue for Muslim governors.

There was a stark contrast in the beginnings of the two movements. Christianity began in weakness, with the central revelation of God coming in the life of Jesus, his death on the cross, and his resurrection. Christians were a small, persecuted minority for nearly three hundred years. Islam, by contrast, began with a series of early military and political victories. After moving to Medina in the *hejira,* or migration, of 622, Muhammad led his followers in battle three times, and they defeated their foes in Medina. Later he returned to Mecca in triumph, where he ended his life ruling over the city and surrounding area with only slight opposition. Soon after his death, Muslim armies swept through the Persian and Byzantine Empires, which were already exhausted from fighting each other. Within a century, Muslim armies had conquered the eastern and southern rims of the Mediterranean and much of Persia. The will of God seemed manifest in their dramatic military victories.

For hundreds of years, Muslims were frequently on the offensive against Christians. Christians did succeed in turning back Muslim forces from France and eventually drove them out of Spain, though the *Reconquista* took seven hundred years. Christians enjoyed some early and dramatic successes in the Crusades, but a resurgent Islam was eventually able to drive the Crusader kingdoms onto the defensive. In 1453 Ottoman Turks conquered Constantinople; and after that, Turkish armies besieged Vienna in 1527 and in 1683. For a millennium, Europe was threatened.

Bede the Venerable (ca. 673-735) in the West and John of Damascus (ca. 675-ca. 749) in the East set the tone for medieval Christian views of Islam. By the year 1000, most Christian writers viewed Islam not as a new revelation but as a Christian heresy, the last and greatest of the heresies, the only one that had not been adequately answered. In accord with the Muslim tradition itself, Christians viewed the Saracens as the descendants of Abraham through Ishmael; but Christians emphasized the status of Ishmael's mother, Hagar, as a slave and strongly rejected the claim of Islam to be the true religion of Abraham. Some Christians, such as Paul Alvarus (active 840-860) in Muslim Spain, interpreted the Muslim threat in apocalyptic terms as foretold by the book of Daniel: Islam was the last of the enemies to rise up against the Most High, a foe who would rule for three and a half periods of time. Alvarus also tried to demonstrate that Muhammad was a forerunner of the Antichrist.

In the Muslim-ruled parts of Spain, Christians had certain protections under Muslim law, but they had to face the hostility of the Muslim population. There were periodic outbursts of contempt, especially at clergy, and there were some persecutions. Christians lived in segregated areas called *dhimmis*, and there were numerous restrictions on Christian life. Many Christian churches were transformed into mosques, but Christians were allowed to worship openly in the remaining churches. The Muslim rulers controlled the appointment of bishops; it was forbidden for Muslims to become Christian under penalty of death; and the children of mixed marriages had to be Muslims. Some tried to live a double life, professing Islam in public and practicing their Christian faith at home. When secret Christians were discovered, they were usually put to death. Some Christians actively sought out martyrdom; but the Muslim rulers themselves generally discouraged this, preferring quiet but relentless pressure, which was often successful in making converts to Islam over time.

Amid the struggles, there were moments of positive appreciation and dialogue. The nun Hrosvitha of Gandersheim (ca. 935-ca.1002) bears witness that admiration of Muslim culture was strong as the year 1000 approached. She described Muslim Cordoba as the most splendid of cities:

> In the western parts of the globe, there shone forth a fair ornament, a venerable city, haughty because of its unwonted might in war, a city well cultured, which the Spanish race held in possession, rich and known by the famous name Cordoba, illustrious because of its charms and also renowned for all resources, especially abounding in the seven streams of knowledge, and ever famous for continual victories (*Passio S. Pelagii* vv. 12-18).[31]

In the decades following the year 1000, Christian scholars would increasingly turn to Muslim sections of Spain in search of manuscripts, translations, and learning. Muslim scholars offered Christians priceless knowledge of the ancient world, which was crucial in the intellectual revival of medieval Europe. Impressed by the jewels of Islamic culture, many medieval Christians saw the East as a place of utopian bliss, a world of wealth and wonder, the source of civilization and culture.

As Spanish Christian rulers progressively pushed back the borders of Islam, they granted their new Muslim subjects freedoms and restrictions similar to those of Christians under Muslim rule. Muslims could practice their religion and retain their mosques; but they were an inferior class, forced to live in separate areas and to pay special taxes to church and state. Under such conditions, Islam declined, some Muslims moved to North Africa, and some became Christian.

JEWISH–CHRISTIAN RELATIONS
IN THE MIDDLE AGES

Christian relations with Jews in the Middle Ages were marred by ancient prejudices and animosities. In the early Middle Ages, Jews usually suffered from discrimination in law and occasionally from attempts at forced conversion despite repeated papal prohibitions on the latter practice. Pope Gregory I warned that anyone who is baptized by force "dies the worse for having been born again" (*Epistle* 1.47) and urged that Jews be drawn "by kindness, tenderness, admonishings and persuasion" (*Epistle* 1.35). Jews were generally forbidden to hold public office or to exercise any form of authority over Christians, though the law of the Carolingian Empire gave greater rights to Jews and removed many of the old restrictions on Jewish life. Charles the Bald (reigned 840-877) defended equal rights for Jews and even reduced the taxes on Jewish merchants.

In many places in the ninth century, Jewish communities prospered and spread despite the restrictions. Intermarriage between Christians and Jews was frequent; and some Christians, notably Deacon Bodo, confessor to Louis the Pious, even converted to Judaism. In response, however, St. Agobard (779-840), archbishop of Lyons, fiercely attacked the Jews and the emperor's favorable treatment of them, charging that Jews were cursed in every place and every activity. In the early tenth century, Archbishop Frederick of Mayence sought advice from Pope Leo VII on whether he should force the Jews in his area to choose either baptism or exile. Pope Leo forbade forced baptism, but he did urge repeated preaching. If attempts to convert the Jews failed, the pope advised, the Jews should be expelled.

There were annual ritual expressions of the belief that Jews were responsible for the death of Jesus; indeed, the celebration of Good Friday often became an occasion for violence against the Jews in the early Middle Ages. In the ninth century, in Toulouse the custom began of striking a Jew on the face on each Good Friday as punishment for the crucifixion of Jesus. In Beziers, France, Christians would listen to a sermon by the bishop on Palm Sunday and would then proceed to stone the houses of Jews; this custom lasted until 1160.

There were other ominous signs of anti-Jewish sentiment as the year 1000 drew closer. The abbot Adso of Montier-en-Der wrote the *Letter on the Antichrist* about 950.[32] He presented the Antichrist as a Jew who would have himself circumcised, would come to Jerusalem where Jews would flock to him, and would slay all Christians whom he could not convert. The Antichrist was to rebuild the temple in Jerusalem, attack the places where Jesus lived, and would claim to be himself the son of God. The association of the Antichrist with the Jews would have a long and vicious history, especially in Germany.[33] Throughout the tenth century, however, there were no outbreaks of popular violence against the Jews. It was a time of relative calm before the fierce anti-Jewish violence of the Crusades, beginning in the late eleventh century. As the next chapter will discuss, the rhetoric of the holy war against the Muslims brought forth unprecedented levels of physical violence against Jewish communities in Europe.

Most medieval Christians viewed the Jews as marked by the curse of Cain, condemned to wander the earth as outcasts until the time of their conversion to Christianity. Pope Innocent III expressed this perspective:

> The Lord made Cain a wanderer and a fugitive over the earth, but set a mark upon him, making his head to shake, lest any finding him should slay him. Thus the Jews, against whom the blood of Jesus Christ calls out, although they ought not to be killed, lest the Christian people forget the Divine Law, yet as wanderers ought they to remain upon the earth, until their countenance be filled with shame and they seek the name of Jesus Christ the Lord.[34]

In the later Middle Ages Jews would be the scapegoats for virtually all the ills befalling European society. Jews were often accused of being sorcerers and magicians and of poisoning people. During the Black Death in the fourteenth century, Jews were frequently accused of poisoning the wells, which led to widespread attacks upon them.[35]

THE CHURCH OF THE EAST AND ISLAM

Farther to the east, other Christians were a minority within Muslim territory in central Asia. The Christian church that began in the Persian Empire was known as the Church of the East; in the West it was often called the "Nestorian" church because it honored the patriarch Nestorius as a teacher of the faith. Nestorius himself, however, was the patriarch of Constantinople and was not even a member of the Church of the East. For centuries, Christians in Central and East Asia had been persecuted by the Zoroastrian Persian Empire and were effectively cut off from contact with the church in the former Roman Empire.

The spread of Islam and the rapid Arab conquests posed new challenges and opportunities for the Church of the East. Through the

Umayyad caliphate (661-750), Christians generally prospered, enjoying greater freedom than under the Persians; but under the Abbasid caliphate (750-1258) conditions began to change. In the ninth century, there was greater social and religious discrimination against Christians, but the tenth century brought internal troubles to the caliphate, and the dynasty's weakness meant more freedom for Christians and Jews.

There were many bright moments of serious intellectual exchange. In or around 781, the learned patriarch Timothy I (patriarch of the Church of the East from 779 to 823) engaged in a debate with the caliph Mahdi that was notable for its openness and gentility. Each partner maintained his own beliefs, and the Christian patriarch generously praised Muhammad for teaching the doctrine of the one God and for walking in the path of the prophets. Even though the debate was held in Muslim territory, remarkably, there was no clear winner. The exchange has been described as "the high point in Muslim and Christian relationships in the whole history of the Muslim conquest."[36]

The attitude of openness represented by the patriarch and the caliph was a major factor shaping world intellectual history, including later Western Christian learning. For about a century, from 750 to 850, scholars of the Church of the East played a critical role in making accessible the Greek classics to Muslim scholars, classics that later Western European scholars were to receive in turn from Muslims in Spain.

Such openness to dialogue was not always possible, however. Under Caliph Mutawakkil (reigned 841-861) Muslim attitudes became more rigid, and religious dissent within Islam was suppressed by force. Religions of the book were, in principle, exempt from persecution. There were, however, periodic popular outbursts of violence, such as the attacks on Christians near Jerusalem and in Damascus in 923/24. Such violent assaults were usually short-lived. Far more dangerous to the Church of the East was the long-term pressure and the restrictedness of life in the *dhimmi*. In the late tenth century, the caliph held the power to appoint the patriarch of the Church of the East. During the period from 850 to 1000, the Church of the East began to decline, probably at least as much because of inward corruption as because of outward pressure.

THE CHURCH OF THE EAST IN CHINA

Most Christians in Europe in the Middle Ages had little or no awareness of Hinduism or Buddhism or the other religions of South and East Asia. While Clement of Alexandria had been aware of Buddhists in early-third-century Alexandria, for the most part Buddhism faded from direct Christian consciousness in Europe. Nonetheless, the life of Siddhartha Gautama, who became Shakyamuni Buddha, was transformed into the medieval legend of Josaphat, a young prince who encountered a monk named Barlaam, renounced his throne, and sought wisdom in ascetic practice. Christians across Europe unknowingly honored the life of Buddha in the tale of Josaphat.[37]

During the centuries when European Christians were largely cut off from contact with Asia, the Church of the East was experiencing both success and failure in China. A missionary, Bishop Alopen, followed the Silk Road through Afghanistan into China, arriving in the capital, Chang'an, in 635, where he was welcomed warmly by Emperor T'ai-tsung. Christianity thrived throughout the T'ang dynasty, and relations with other religions were often cordial. When Buddhist missionaries in the eighth century needed help in translating their scriptures into Chinese, they received assistance from Bishop Adam (or Ching-ching) of the Church of the East.

In the late ninth century, however, there were terrible persecutions of Christians in China. For reasons we do not fully understand, the Church of the East appears to have died out completely in China sometime before the year 1000, only to return again in later centuries. In 987 a Christian monk in Baghdad told an Arab that he had traveled to China seven years earlier only to find that "the native Christians had perished in one way or another; the church which they had used had been destroyed, and there was only one [or: not one] Christian left in the land."[38] The Church of the East would flourish again during the early Mongol period in the thirteenth century. When Franciscan missioners would arrive in China in the late thirteenth century, they would find Christians from the Church of the East in prominent positions at the imperial court.

ATTITUDES TOWARD OTHER RELIGIONS IN THE LATER MIDDLE AGES

The attitudes of many Christians toward members of other religious traditions hardened during the later Middle Ages. The Crusades spawned new levels of hostility toward Jews and Muslims, and the outbreak of the Black Death in the fourteenth century led to new accusations against Jews. Many Christians assumed that non-Christians would be eternally damned. Pope Boniface solemnly defined that it was strictly necessary for salvation that all human beings be subject to the Roman pontiff (*Unam Sanctam*). As noted earlier, the Council of Florence professed and preached that "all those who are outside the catholic church, not only pagans but also Jews or heretics and schismatics, cannot share in eternal life . . . unless they are joined to the catholic church before the end of their lives" (Bull of Union with the Copts, February 4, 1442). It was assumed that the gospel had been preached clearly to all the world, and thus those who rejected Christianity were thought to have brought condemnation upon themselves.

Papal and conciliar teaching did not decide the matter for all Christians, however. Spanish Christians often knew Jews and Muslims firsthand, and at least some did not accept the official declarations of church officials. One Spanish Christian is reported to have said: "The Muslim can be saved in his faith, just as the Christian can in his."[39] Another Christian remarked that "the good Jew and the good Muslim can, if they act correctly, go to heaven just like the good Christian."[40] Diego González was assisted by Jews and Muslims as a poor orphan and later affirmed that Jews could be saved in their faith. He was later burned as a heretic for being too supportive of Jews.[41]

Most medieval Christians were not concerned with dialogue with other religions. Religious dissent was generally dealt with harshly, and other religions usually appeared as bitter opponents. There were, however, a few who experimented with other ways of relating to other religions. John of Segovia, a fifteenth-century Salamancan theologian, sought to improve relations with Muslims by proposing to publish a trilingual edition of the Qur'an and to host a conference where Muslim and Christian theologians could discuss their differences in harmony.

Impressed by his personal contacts with a Muslim theologian and concerned after the fall of Constantinople in 1453, John of Segovia drew up a proposal for a direct dialogue and sent this to Nicholas of Cusa in a long letter of December 2, 1454. At a time when Pope Nicholas V was calling for a new crusade against Islam, John of Segovia noted that warfare is not appropriate for followers of Christ. Where Muhammad had used the sword, Jesus and the apostles had refused to do so, and Christians should follow their example rather than Muhammad's.[42] Moreover, victory in war led only to further hatred and resentment, not to conversions. John was aware that Muslims believed Christians worshiped two gods, and he hoped that such misunderstandings could be cleared up by amicable face-to-face discussions.

John also knew that earlier Christian missions to Islam had failed and that Muslim rulers would not allow Christian missionary activity. He believed that a new format, which he called *contraferentia* (conference or dialogue), should be attempted. His proposal involved three steps. In the first place, Christians and Muslims should establish peaceful relations. Second, broader and deeper cultural ties should lead to mutual understanding and trust. Finally, theologians should meet to discuss doctrinal issues. What is most striking is that John's proposal did not explicitly aim at the conversion of the Muslims to Christianity. He believed his proposal had the backing of natural law and Catholic theology. For John, the starting point of dialogue should be beliefs held in common by Muslims and Christians, and he trusted that even beliefs in the Trinity and Christology could be explained to the satisfaction of Muslim thinkers. Because of the political dangers of making this proposal at a time of papal sponsorship of a new crusade, John sent his ideas to Cardinal Nicholas of Cusa, seeking his assistance. John died before seeing any concrete results, but his ideas may have influenced Nicholas's own thought. Nicholas liked the idea of a *contraferentia* and suggested that Christians be represented by laymen rather than clerics because they would be more acceptable to the Turks.[43]

NICHOLAS OF CUSA

Nicholas of Cusa's approach to Christian revelation in relation to other religions flowed from his attempt to understand God and all created reality in a way that would reconcile all differences in an all-embracing harmony. Nicholas was a pioneer in seeking to understand Islam and in searching for better forms of communication among religions. He proposed a vision of the universe existing in God and of God permeating the universe. He described God as "not-other" than the world. While limited by the horizon of his age, the principles of his theology offer important resources for dialogue with other religious traditions.

Nicholas of Cusa (1401-1464) was involved in a staggering range of activities: he was a jurist and statesman on the highest levels, priest and cardinal, scientist and mathematician, as well as being a philosopher and theologian. In his diplomatic and political and ecclesiastical endeavors, his central goal was unity and reform. He sought unity and reconciliation between Christianity and Islam, between the Catholic Church and the Holy Roman Empire, between Eastern and Western Christians, between science and religion, and among all the religions of the world. His theoretical reflections grew out of his practical concerns and were intended to give them an intellectual foundation in a coherent view of God and the cosmos. At the very center of his life and thought is the ideal of fostering unity without suppressing differences. His goal was reconciliation, harmony, unity in difference.[44] The powers of disunion were in one case after another too strong, and much of his diplomatic work ended in failure. But he left behind as his legacy the agenda of developing a coherent Christian vision that could incorporate the insights of the new sciences and the new literature and that could guide the decisions of church and civil leaders in unifying the human community.

Nicholas's central philosophical and theological insight seems to have come to him in a particular moment, and led him to a new way of thinking that he would unfold for the rest of his life.[45] When he was returning from Greece in late 1437 or early 1438, the idea came to him, he thought from God, that he was "to embrace—in learned ignorance[†] and through a transcending of the incorruptible truths which are humanly knowable—incomprehensible things incomprehensibly" (*On Learned Ignorance*, p. 158). He continues: "But the whole of our human intelligence ought to center on those lofty [matters], so that the intellect may raise itself to that Simplicity where contradictories coincide" (ibid.).

In this brief letter he sets forth his two most famous concepts: *docta ignorantia* and the *coincidentia oppositorum*. To understand these two concepts, we have to consider the relation of thought to the finite and the infinite. Normally, when I think, I think of something definite and distinct from other things, and I compare it with others. I measure it, judge it, and draw some conclusion. I understand its relations to other realities. As Nicholas puts it: "every inquiry is comparative and uses the means of comparative relation" (*On Learned Ignorance*, p. 50). This is the operation of *ratio*, reason. Whenever I transcend one limit, I encounter another. But, as Augustine had noted, we also experience a discontent with the finite. We experience a drive to something beyond. When we think beyond the range of the finite, our thought moves into a very different realm. Nicholas expresses the basic situation: "Hence, the infinite, qua infinite, is unknown; for it escapes all comparative relation" (ibid.). There is no proportion between the finite and the infinite. The finite cannot become infinite, and the infinite cannot become finite.

Nonetheless, despite the gap between finite and infinite, we experience a drive to transcend the finite. We become aware of our own limits. In this awareness, we also may become aware of a further power beyond reason, which Nicholas calls *intellectus*, intellect. Reason cannot grasp the infinite reality of God, but *intellectus* does find a point of contact with God beyond normal logic. Reason remains in a state of ignorance, not knowing the infinite; but the intellect takes up the quest and develops a new kind of logic, a learned ignorance. In this new logic, intellect discovers that the oppositions and contradictions of the finite world coincide in the infinite: *coincidentia oppositorum*. Thus learned ignorance is fundamentally a positive experience. It proceeds *via negativa*,[†] by way of negating, but it is not an agnosticism. Rather, it is a form of speculation that explores the meaning of the *coincidentia oppositorum*.

Nicholas is aware of the long Socratic and biblical sapiential tradition behind this. The height of wisdom is to know that one does not know; and, according to the Book of Ecclesiastes, even Solomon admitted that things are unexplainable in words (Eccl 1:8; *On Learned Ignorance,* p. 50). This awareness of limits must be held in tension with the basic trust that "the desire in us is not in vain, assuredly we desire to know that we do not know" (*On Learned Ignorance,* p. 50). This knowledge of our ignorance is learned ignorance: "The more [a man] knows that he is unknowing, the more learned he will be" (ibid., p. 51).

We understand the infinite by not understanding. The opposites of the finite world coincide in God, but we never comprehend how this *coincidentia* takes place. The central concepts of *intellectus* are not normal concepts: the words "mind," "faith," "truth" take on paradoxical meanings when pushed to express the relation of the finite to the infinite. Even to oppose the infinite and the finite too one-sidedly is a mistake, because if the infinite were simply opposed to the finite, it would be limited by the finite and would itself be finite. In his later work, Cusanus insisted that God is not other than the world: God is not other than not-other.[46] Cusanus is not collapsing the world into God, but he is insisting that God is not a finite reality simply distinct from the world. Radically transcendent and immanent, God enfolds and unfolds the world. Nicholas sees all created realities existing on two levels: enfolded in God and unfolded in creation. In God all things are one with God. In creation all things are interdependent.

Cusanus sees little conflict between Christian faith and the best knowledge of all nations. All nations have worshiped God and have believed God to be the Absolute Maximum (*On Learned Ignorance*, p. 56). He takes it for granted that the best ideas of Pythagoras, Plato, and Proclus agree with Christian revelation. After all, Pythagoras taught that Oneness is trine (ibid., p. 56). Cusanus always assumes the truth of divine revelation in Christ, and he assumes that Christian faith is the one true faith which the wise of all peoples implicitly share. He hoped that once others understood Christian faith, they would embrace it.

Nicholas holds that we can use affirmative names for God only in relation to created things (*On Learned Ignorance*, p. 81). These are radically inadequate for the divine reality itself, but they are fitting because his infinite power expresses itself in relation to created things. Even apart from creation, the perfections of all things and the power to create are eternally in God, and affirmative names give us some sense of these perfections and power.

Nicholas is remarkably generous to the pagans who named God in polytheistic terms. He discusses various divine names and shows how God enfolds all the characteristics and virtues symbolized by the pagan gods. "The pagans named God in various ways in accordance with His relationship to created things. All these names are unfoldings of the enfolding of the one ineffable name" (*On Learned Ignorance*, p. 83). Nicholas expresses a confidence in the ultimate harmony of the best insights of classical mythology and Christian faith. According to Nicholas, the pagans worshiped God in unfolded things, while the Jews worshiped his simplicity. Even though many were mistaken and became idolators, their religious instincts were not completely wrong.

Nicholas balances his discussion of positive names for God with attention to negative theology. We need affirmative theology for worship of God because we need a concrete focus for devotion. But learned ignorance teaches us that God is beyond all names and so we rise to a higher level of names through removal and negation, as both Dionysius and Rabbi Solomon (i.e., the medieval Jewish thinker Moses Maimonides) teach us. Cusanus insists that in negative theology we must negate any naïve, literal interpretation of language about God. This theology does not teach us to know God; it teaches that only God knows God. Neither in this world nor the next can we know God. Negative theology is not so much a higher form of theology with a different subject matter as a hermeneutical reflection on the way we interpret the affirmative way. Learned ignorance teaches us that negations are true and affirmations are inadequate, but some negations are truer than others. Nicholas sometimes speaks of copulative theology as higher than either affirmative or negative theology because it rises to God as the *coincidentia oppositorum* beyond affirming and negating.

Turning to other religious believers, Nicholas chides both Muslims and Jews for thinking Christ or the Messiah could be the maximum and most perfect man without being God. He denies that a man could be maximum without being God. Following the Council of Florence, he denies the possibility of eternal happiness for Jews and Muslims. Given Nicholas's openness to acknowledging truth in other religions, his denial of salvation seems somewhat inconsistent and puzzling. It may well be that the teaching of the Council of Florence that Jews and heretics would be excluded from salvation led Nicholas to exclude members of other religious traditions from the possibility of salvation even though the major current of his thought was more open to and inclusive of other religions.

Shortly after the fall of Constantinople in 1453, Nicholas wrote a dialogue, *On the Peace of Faith* (*De Pace Fidei*), an attempt to understand religious pluralism and respond to it on the basis of his theological vision.[47] As in his earlier work, Nicholas assumes that all humans have an at least indeterminate knowledge of God, and thus all worship the one God in different ways. He posits one essential faith at the root of all religions and sees only the outer manifestations of religions as in conflict. Moreover, he believes that God has sent prophets to every nation to reveal God's will, and thus God is in part responsible for the differences among the world's religions. On this basis he believes that there is an underlying harmony among the world's religions. Since the truth revealed by God is one, the differences in religious practice form a harmony of contrasts. There is one religion in the many rites. In the dialogue a Greek asks God: "If everyone loves wisdom, do they not presuppose the same wisdom?" The Word of God answers that there can only be one wisdom: "If it were possible to have several wisdoms these would have to be from one, for before there is any plurality there must be a unity."[48]

Nicholas does not, however, want to surrender the christocentric focus of his earlier work, and he assumes that all faith converges upon Jesus Christ, finding its fulfillment in him. As Mediator, Christ allows passage between God and humankind. In the dialogue, Nicholas acknowledges the legitimate reasons Jews and Muslims have had for rejecting the Trinity and seeks to overcome these objections through his own explanation of the productive generativity of unity. In the dialogue, the Word of God addresses a Chaldean, an Arab, an Indian, a Jew, a Persian, and representatives of other nations. The dialogue ends with the hope that people of every nation will come to recognize explicitly the one faith that they already implicitly share. Given the oneness of faith, a plurality of rites and cults can flourish.

While Nicholas's confidence in the power of his explanations to convert members of other traditions was naïve and misplaced, his vision of the unity of the religions of the world stood as a sign of hope in a violent world. In *The Vision of God,* Nicholas of Cusa proposed an image of the presence of God that can stand as a sign of hope for a unity among the world's religions beyond all difference. To express the experience of God, Nicholas used the image of a painting in which the eyes appear to be looking on each person around it. Each person believes that the figure is looking in only one direction at that person and no one else. However, the face continually regards all, even as they move in contrary directions.

THE PATRISTIC AND MEDIEVAL HERITAGE

The early church established a framework for the interpretation of revelation which acknowledged God's presence among all peoples while also judging other traditions by the revelation of God in Jesus Christ. In practice, the patristic and medieval heritage oscillated between the recognition of God's truth offered to all humans and the exclusion of all those outside the church from salvation. In appropriating wisdom from other traditions, the church practiced a strategy of critical inclusion, appropriating many insights while rejecting other perspectives and practices as incompatible with Christian faith.

In this heritage there is both great wisdom and also great tragedy. In principle, the early church recognized the presence of God and the offer of truth among all peoples; but in practice this recognition did not always receive due weight. Through most of the patristic and medieval periods, bitter animosities dominated interreligious relationships. Traditional understandings of revelation, based on the scriptures themselves, nurtured Christian hatred of Jews and Muslims for centuries. The ambiguous biblical heritage, which had presented both the holy war and the nonviolence of Jesus, was understood as the basis for systematic discrimination against and persecution of the Jews, and war against the Muslims. Christian overconfidence that the revelation of God in Jesus Christ was perfectly clear to all humans repeatedly led to harsh, damning judgments of those who did not accept Christian claims. Negative theological judgments often led to physical abuse and violence, as we will see in the next chapter. There can be no question of an uncritical acceptance of the tradition.

At times, however, as in late medieval Spain, the sense of at least some of the Catholic faithful was more generous and inclusive than that of the Catholic magisterium itself. Some Catholics who actually knew devout Jews and Muslims had more confidence in their neighbors' knowledge of God and their prospects of salvation than official Catholic teaching allowed. The heritage of early Christians, such as Justin, Clement of Alexandria, and Origen, who saw the presence of God among all peoples remained as a resource for the future.

Nicholas of Cusa is in some ways a tragic figure, a remarkable pioneer in one area after another who sought a greater openness to other religions. But his theology, shaped by the Council of Florence, remains explicitly exclusivistic; and his hopes for interreligious understanding remained unfulfilled. Nonetheless, Nicholas was confident that followers of other religious traditions know God. He insisted that all knowledge of God, including that mediated by biblical revelation, remains a paradoxical learned ignorance, limited by the incomprehensibility of God. Even biblical images of God fail to capture fully the divine reality. These perspectives open a space in which interreligious dialogue can proceed. Moreover, his trust that opposites coincide in God in a way we do not rationally understand provides a provocative image that challenges us still.

5

Revelation and Violence
in the Early and Medieval Church

The significance of the revelation of God given in the history of Israel and in Jesus Christ unfolds in the tradition of the church as succeeding generations approach this revelation and interpret it anew. The patristic and medieval periods saw both profound interpretations and appropriations of Christian revelation and also tragic betrayals of it. The ambiguity of the scriptures themselves, calling for holy wars and proclaiming an end to all wars, gave rise to an ambiguous history of effects.

The early centuries of Christianity saw a series of intense debates over the meaning of revelation in a world filled with violence. Violence against Christians, though for the most part sporadic, was a constant threat because of the ongoing conflict with the Roman Empire.[1] Violence was also endemic in Hellenistic society and religion. Conquest and slavery were backed by the threat of violence. The *pax romana* was guaranteed by military force without and within, and Clement of Alexandria charged that the Greek gods were lovers of violence (*Exhortation to the Greeks* 3.36). The early church's understanding of revelation set the basic framework for the Christian community's response to the violence of Greco-Roman society.

INTERPRETING VIOLENCE IN THE BIBLE

Early church interpreters of the Bible were aware of the sharp contrast between the divine commands of extermination in the wars of conquest and the teaching of Jesus in the Sermon on the Mount. Often this disparity was reconciled through the use of allegory. During the patristic and medieval periods, most Christians assumed that the Bible should be read not only literally but also allegorically. In particular, Old Testament

113

passages were often taken as allegories referring to Christ and events in the New Testament or as symbols of events within the human soul or as a foreshadowing of heaven. The Jewish commentator and philosopher Philo of Alexandria (ca. 22 B.C.E.–ca. 50 C.E.) allegorized the Pentateuch to make it harmonize with Platonic philosophy. During the same period Hellenistic philosophers offered allegorical interpretations of classical Greek literature to make this heritage compatible with later ethical notions. One reason that allegory came to the fore was that interpreters acknowledged the authority of traditional religious texts, but no longer accepted their direct, literal meaning. Greek myths were notoriously filled with immoral tales about the gods and goddesses. Hellenistic interpreters who were embarrassed by the immorality of these tales could interpret them allegorically to find a more suitable lesson. In a similar fashion, Christians could allegorize the violence of the Old Testament. Often passages would be taken out of their original context and interpreted as referring to events centuries later or to inner events within the human soul.

The Christian roots of this style of interpretation begin as early as Paul, who interpreted the rock of Exodus from which the people of Israel drank as Christ (1 Cor 10). Paul thought that the rock followed them around in the desert, and he interpreted it as a symbol of Christ or the Logos. Similarly, he interpreted Hagar and Sarah as allegories of life in slavery and freedom (Gal 4:21-31).

Origen, who was perhaps the most influential theorist of allegory in the early church, argued that even the events in the life of Jesus were not simply historical events but also symbols of other realities in the lives of believers. Thus, Origen notes, Paul can say, "I am crucified with Christ," and "we are buried together with him by baptism" (*Against Celsus* 2.69). The crucifixion, death, and burial of Jesus are not only historical events in the past but also present events in the lives of believers. What happened to Jesus is the paradigm for what happens to Christians in a different way age after age. For Origen, the literal sense was the body of the text, the sense of the narrative, what the letters say. This was appropriate for uneducated persons who think in simple, straightforward ways. In many cases, however, Origen believed that the literal sense is not the message that God intended to communicate to the church. Thus to cling to the literal sense can cause one to miss the meaning. Origen, like other early Christians, believed this was the case with Jewish interpreters who insisted on the literal meaning of the messianic prophecies and thus failed to recognize Jesus as their fulfillment. The second level of meaning was the "psychic" sense, which was the soul of the text, enkindling the souls of Christians who are in the process of being perfected and moving them to live the Christian life more fully. The climax of interpretation was the spiritual sense, which the true Christian Gnostic can penetrate with a deeper understanding of redemption.

To decide whether a passage should be accepted in its literal sense, Origen used the criteria of worthiness to the divine reality and human reason. If a passage asserted something that was not worthy of God or was contrary to human reason, it must not be taken literally. For example, the prohibition of eating vultures, according to Origen, is irrational because no one would want to eat a vulture (*On First Principles* 4.3.2). When God is said to walk in the garden with Adam and Eve, Origen insists that this is not meant literally (ibid. 4.3.1). Thus Origen could maintain that all of scripture has a true spiritual meaning, but not all of it has a bodily meaning. Indeed, Origen thought that a literal reading of some passages led simpler Christians to "believe such things about [God] as would not be believed of the most savage and unjust of men" (ibid. 4.2.1).

This interpretative strategy gave Origen a way to understand the violence of the conquest of Canaan. In the Book of Joshua, Jericho represents this world, which must be destroyed. Its walls are the cult of idols and the artifice of demons. The trumpets of Joshua are figures of the angelic trumpets that will herald the end of time. The military preparations to capture the city of Jericho represent the spiritual struggle for which Christians must prepare themselves. "The battle which you must wage is within yourself" (*Homily on Joshua* 5.2). The true enemy comes from our own heart. For Origen, a literal understanding of wars of conquest would be an unthinkable scandal. The true meaning of the destruction of the peoples already in the Promised Land was Christ's conquest of the human soul. Indeed, a literal interpretation would be profoundly untrue. "Unless those carnal wars [of the Old Testament] were a symbol of spiritual wars, I do not think that the Jewish historical books would ever have been passed down by the Apostles to be read by Christ's followers in their churches" (ibid. 15.1). Thus Origen could reconcile the biblical commands to slaughter one's enemies with Jesus' teaching of nonviolence.

EARLY CHRISTIANS AND MILITARY SERVICE

Early Christians differed over the question of whether violence was ever justified and whether Christians could participate in the military.[2] The teaching of Jesus on nonviolence in the Sermon on the Mount and the example of Jesus in the garden of Gethsemane were decisive for many. Justin Martyr celebrated the military victories of Israel in earlier times (*Dialogue with Trypho* 139), but he told Trypho that Christians have turned away from war and every form of slaughter and, following the instruction of Isaiah, turned their swords into plowshares and their spears into farming tools (ibid. 110.3). Tertullian and Origen understood the Gospel as calling Christians to avoid all forms of military service.

In his response to the pagan critic Celsus, Origen addressed the problem of the divine endorsement of violence in the Old Testament. On the one hand, he argued, violence was necessary for the national survival of ancient Israel. Without the ability to fight and to enforce capital punishment, the Israelites would not have been able to continue as a nation (*Against Celsus* 7.26). As noted earlier, Origen acknowledged the scandalous character of the ancient holy wars and interpreted the warlike commands of the Old Testament as allegorical accounts of inner, spiritual battles against evil. What was central for Origen was that Jesus himself challenged his followers to nonviolence, forbidding killing of any kind (ibid. 3.7-8).

There were, nonetheless, Christians who served in the Roman armies. One famous story told of a miraculous response to Christian soldiers' prayers. In the late second century, a Roman army in present-day Moravia was threatened by drought. There were a number of Christian soldiers in the Twelfth Legion. After the Christians prayed for rain, a shower came to relieve the Roman troops, while a storm caused trouble for the enemy tribe (Eusebius, *Ecclesiastical History* 5.5.3-4). Tertullian refers to Christians in the military in the late second and early third century (*Apology* 37, 42; *On Idolatry* 19). There were Christian soldiers in the armies of Constantine. One of Constantine's soldiers, Pachomius, who would later become a famous Christian monastic, was converted to Christianity by the love of his fellow soldiers who were Christians.[3]

REVELATION AND SOCIAL ENGAGEMENT

In addition to the overt physical violence of military actions, there was also the systematic violence of a social and economic system based on great inequality and slavery. These structures dated from time immemorial. The power of the ruling elite had already been solidified by the time of our earliest written sources from Egypt and Mesopotamia.[4] For the most part, people in traditional Mediterranean and European societies accepted the rule of a few landed aristocrats over the great mass of peasants because no realistic alternative was envisioned—this was thought to be the natural order of society, legitimated by the will of God or the gods. There did emerge from the prophets and sages of Israel and the example of Jesus a more egalitarian vision that challenged the ancient structures of poverty, domination, and exploitation. However, the implications of this vision were never fully developed since most traditional Christian social engagement sought to infuse the structures of society with humanity and charity rather than seeking to combat them directly. Ancient and medieval Western cultures generally had no vision of the dynamics of social transformation of a society as a whole. Instead, smaller religious communities often became the locus for forming new types of relationships.

Perhaps the most powerful witness of the early church to revelation lay in the social dynamics of the early Christian community. The dynamics of revelation shaped new patterns of human relationships. Inspired by the revelation of God in Jesus Christ, the early Christian community was a social movement that provided equality for the marginalized, support for the poor, and a strong sense of mutual concern, especially in times of epidemics.[5] Most of the early Christian fathers believed that private property was a result of the fall and was the root cause of envy and violence, and they demanded that the wealthy share with the poor. The *Didache,* an early church order, instructed: "Do not turn away the needy, but share everything with your brother, and do not say that it is your own" (4.8). John Chrysostom sharply challenged the possession of wealth or, indeed, of anything: "But when one attempts to possess himself of anything, to make it his own, then contention is introduced, as if nature herself were indignant, that when God brings us together in every way, we are eager to divide and separate ourselves by appropriating things, and by using those cold words, 'mine and thine.' Then there is contention and uneasiness" (*Homily 12 on 1 Timothy* 4). Basil the Great similarly questioned the idea of ownership: "Tell me, what is yours? Where did you get it and bring it into the world? It is as if one has taken a seat in the theatre and then drives out all who come later, thinking that what is for everyone is only for him" (*Homily on Luke 12:18*).[6]

While the early community in Jerusalem is described as sharing all goods in common (Acts 2:44-45; 4:32-35), the predominant response of the early church was not to establish a separate communist economic system but rather to keep a common fund for the care of the poor and the sick and to establish refuges and hospices for those in need, including persons not in the Christian community.[7] In response to Jesus' call to serve those in need, early Christian deacons supervised the care of the sick, the poor, and the disabled. Concrete Christian social concern made a striking impact on the surrounding Hellenistic world. The mid-fourth-century emperor Julian, who tried to revive traditional Roman religion in opposition to Christianity, noted that Christian benevolence to strangers was attracting converts and complained: "The impious Galileans support not only their poor, but ours as well, everyone can see that our people lack aid from us."[8] Sociologist Rodney Stark has recently argued: "the linking of a highly *social* ethic with religion" was a new development for the Hellenistic world: "What was new was the notion that more than self-interested exchange relations were possible between humans and the supernatural."[9]

While the treatment of women in early Christianity was ambiguous (compare the principle of full equality in Gal 3:28 with the subordinate status of women in 1 Cor 11:3-12; Eph 5:22-26; and 1 Tim 2:11-12), Christian women had greater respect and higher status than their counterparts in the Greco-Roman world.[10] Early Christians condemned the prevalent practices of abortion and killing of infant girls, which limited the number of women in Greco-Roman society. Recent studies suggest that the respect for the lives of female children and the resulting greater number of Christian women proportionate to the population as a whole was a major factor in the growth of Christianity.[11]

Following the instruction of Paul (Rom 13:1-7), early Christians did not reject imperial authority in itself; indeed Justin Martyr insisted that Christians were the best helpers and allies of the emperor in building up social order (*First Apology* 12). But they did firmly reject the pretensions of the imperial office to divinity and thereby set in motion a prolonged though intermittent conflict that would end only with the conversion of an emperor to the Christian faith.[12]

MARTYRDOM AND PERSECUTION

Early Christians faced repeated, though intermittent, persecutions by the Roman Empire. Roman authorities often treated Christians with tolerance and indulgence, and general persecutions were rare.[13] Nonetheless, the threat of execution was always present. Ignatius of Antioch accepted and even welcomed the prospect of martyrdom as a way of imitating the passion of his God, Jesus Christ (*Epistle to the Romans* 6.3). He urged the Christians in Rome not to use their influence to save him from death (*Epistle to the Romans* 4). Ignatius saw himself as similar to the Hebrew prophets, who suffered for their message (*Epistle to the Magnesians* 8.2). Ignatius also connected fidelity unto death with a proper understanding of Jesus Christ as both divine and human. A Gnostic or a Docetist, he believed, could not undergo a violent death because they did not accept the reality of the incarnation (*Epistle to the Smyrneans* 6.2; 7.1).

Early Christians firmly resisted Roman demands to worship the symbols of the emperor, but they did not oppose violence with violence. Their nonviolent witness would make a powerful impression on Roman society over time. The martyrs of Lyons in 177 C.E., victims of a violent surge of anti-Christian feeling in Gaul, endured terrible sufferings with courage and faith. Blandina is said to have endured torture for so long a time that "even those who were taking turns to torture her in every way from dawn to dusk were weary and exhausted" (Eusebius, *Ecclesiastical History* 5.117).[14] Many pagans, who could not imagine dying such painful deaths for Greek or Roman gods, were deeply impressed. Nonviolent witness even to the point of death was among the most powerful and persuasive forms of proclamation.

Origen placed martyrdom in the context of the battle between Christ and the powers and principalities that rule this world, holding out the hope that the suffering of the martyrs contributes to Christ's victory: "For the martyrs in Christ disarm the principalities and powers with Him, and they share His triumph as fellows of His sufferings, becoming in this way also fellows of the courageous deeds wrought in His sufferings" (*Exhortation to Martyrdom* 40).[15] Using contemporary social scientific theory, Rodney Stark has argued that Christian martyrs made rational choices to remain faithful even at the cost of death and that their witness was among the most powerful factors in the rise of Christianity.[16]

In the context of martyrdom, Origen specifically took up the question of the names of God, noting that some claim that names are "merely conventional and have no relation in nature to the things for which the names stand" (*Exhortation to Martyrdom* 46). Such persons claimed that it makes no difference whether one worships Zeus or Demeter or Apollo or the sun or the moon. Origen opposed this perspective, claiming that knowledge of the power of the names of demons and other unseen spirits makes them appear when they are summoned. Origen concluded that Christians must restrict themselves to the names given to God in the scriptures.

REVELATION, RESPONSIBILITY, AND POWER IN A CHRISTIAN EMPIRE

A great change in the practical impact of Christian interpretations of revelation began with the victory of Constantine and the legalization of Christianity in the Roman Empire in the early fourth century. Before the century was over, the emperor Theodosius had proclaimed Christianity the official religion of the empire. Christian leaders now had the power to shape society to a degree previously unimaginable. Christian Roman emperors presented themselves as the regents of God on earth. The church historian Eusebius saw the dawn of this new relation of church and empire under Constantine to be the virtual realization of the kingdom of Christ on earth (*Life of Constantine* 3). Many, however, from some fourth-century desert monks who rejected the wealth and influence of the imperial church to the radical Reformers in the sixteenth century, have viewed this moment as the tragic corruption of Christian social engagement and the beginning of a long history of Christian violence, buttressed by understandings of revelation.[17] The community who had suffered from discrimination and violence now began to use these weapons against others. With Constantine, there is already the beginning of imperial legislation against Christian heretics and Jews,[18] and persecution of Roman religions would follow under Theodosius.[19]

Ambrose of Milan took important steps in sacralizing violence in the

Christian world. Ambrose viewed the struggle between rival emperors Theodosius and Eugenius as a holy struggle in terms derived from the Hebrew Bible. Ambrose believed that in the decisive battle in September 394, God was fighting on behalf of Theodosius, sending a strong wind that blew back the arrows and spears of Eugenius's army and propelled those of Theodosius's soldiers all the more strongly. Ambrose saw the wind as an act of God protecting Theodosius, just as God had aided Moses and Joshua and David.[20]

Ambrose lobbied strongly against toleration of traditional Roman cults or Jewish synagogues; and, as noted earlier, he explicitly approved the use of violence against the Jewish synagogue in Callinicum as willed by God. The Catholic bishop of the town had incited a crowd of Christians to burn the synagogue down. When Emperor Theodosius sought to enforce Roman law, which demanded that the bishop who had incited the incident be held responsible, Ambrose objected strongly. Ambrose claimed that he himself burned the synagogue, or at least "ordered others to do it, in order that there not be one place in which Christ is denied. If someone counter my confession by saying that I did not set the fire to the synagogue here, I would say that it had already started to burn by divine judgment; hence, there was no further need of my action" (*Letter to Theodosius* 40.8).[21] Lightning had already burned the synagogue in Milan, and Ambrose interpreted this as an act of God. Ambrose protested sternly against any punishment being imposed on the bishop of Callinicum for burning "a place of unbelief, the house of impiety, a receptacle of folly which God himself has rejected"; and he quoted Jeremiah's threat upon the temple in Jerusalem (Jer 7:14) as forbidding the emperor to avenge the destruction of the contemporary temple (Ambrose, *Letter* 40.14).

AUGUSTINE

We have seen that Augustine proposed a powerful method of biblical interpretation centered on two forms of love, self-giving divine love (*caritas*) and self-centered, self-destructive love (*cupiditas*). Augustine's rhetoric of love was eloquent and powerful. Regarding the use of state authority to respond to religious diversity, however, Augustine was a controversial interpreter of revelation, whose influence extended throughout the Middle Ages and beyond.

Augustine proposed the classic Latin analysis of original sin, charting the ways in which we find ourselves caught and corrupted in a web of sin from which we are powerless to escape by our own power. In many ways, the thought of René Girard is firmly in the Augustinian tradition in its naming of universal, systemic patterns of violence and deception. Girard's analysis of mimesis and violence can be understood as a contemporary development of the Augustinian notion of original sin.

Girard's description of mimetic rivalry and its nonviolent overcoming by Jesus can be compared to Augustine's two loves that built two cities. For Augustine, life in this world is a struggle between the human city, dominated by *cupiditas*, a world of desire centered on finite objects, and the city of God, founded on *caritas*, the self-giving love that finds its center in God and its model in Jesus Christ. For both Augustine and Girard, the world of violence and the world of genuine love interpenetrate and struggle back and forth until the end of time.

Girard stresses that our desires are shaped by other people whom we take as models, and he rejects the notion of an autonomous self independent of others. For Girard, we are not so much individuals as "interdividuals." In Girardian terminology, Augustine offers one of the most profound descriptions of the mimetic self that has lost itself by following false models. Throughout the *Confessions*, Augustine is in search of the proper model for his mind and his desires, from his reading of Cicero, to his joining the Manichaeans, to his discovering the Platonists, to his encounter with Ambrose. Each model teaches Augustine how to understand himself and what to desire.

Moreover, in the *Confessions*, Augustine does almost nothing alone. At the age of sixteen, he sins with other youths in stealing fruit from a pear tree. Girard insists that we learn our desires not from the objects themselves but from others who serve as models. Augustine points out that the theft was gratuitous because he and his companions did not need food, and he claims that he would not have done the deed if he were alone: "But as it was it was not the fruit that gave me pleasure, I must have got it from the crime itself, from the thrill of having partners in sin" (*Confessions* 2.8).[22] What Augustine, inspired by the group, really seeks is a liberty falsely modeled on the freedom of God; in effect, he wishes to be like God, but in reaching and grasping for what is forbidden, makes of himself "a barren waste" (*Confessions* 2.9). The theft of the pears follows the example of Adam and Eve in the garden of Eden and thus becomes a paradigm for Augustine's own understanding of how original sin captures us. Later, he converts to Christianity in company with his friend Alypius; and he enjoys the vision of God at Ostia with his mother, Monica. Augustine also offers a moving description of the genuine love that enjoys only God and thereby renounces mimetic rivalry with finite models and obstacles.

There is, however, a contrast between Girard and Augustine regarding the issue of justifying violence. Girard issues a radical plea for nonviolence, insisting that there is no "good" violence. Confronted with the question of whether war can ever be justified, Augustine proposed the theology of the just war that would be accepted for centuries. Augustine argued that the righteous can be forced to oppose the wicked (*City of God* 19.7). The aim of seeking peace is not by itself justification for war, for every belligerent seeks peace through conquest. To be just, wars must be declared by a just authority, involve a just cause, and be waged with right intention. Just causes include defense of one's nation and customs, and recovery of what has been unjustly taken. Right intention means that there is no ulterior motive and that war is the only way of resolving the problem.

At times, Augustine would argue, one has a positive duty to fight to defend one's community. When Boniface, the Roman governor of Africa, wished to retire from military life and political administration and become a monk after the death of his wife, Augustine wrote to him, urging him to follow God's will by continuing to serve as a soldier. Augustine noted that David was praised by God for being a soldier, that Jesus lauded the centurion for his faith, that Cornelius was converted, and that John the Baptist had told Roman soldiers to be content with their pay; he did not tell them to leave the army (*Letter* 189.4).[23] Citing Paul's advice to stay in one's own condition (1 Cor 7:7), Augustine urged Boniface not to retire from military activities but to continue the struggle: "Thus others [monks] fight for you against invisible enemies by praying; you work for them against visible barbarians by fighting" (*Letter* 189.5). Later medieval commentators would teach that a soldier in a just war can kill without sin.[24]

It was also Augustine who established the theology of repression of religious opponents that would dominate a millennium and more of Catholic practice. Augustine's application of the analysis of two loves (the self-giving love centered on God, *caritas,* and the self-destructive love centered on something finite, *cupiditas*) to the history of the world in *The City of God* led him to secularize history. Where Eusebius had celebrated the ideal of a Christian Roman Empire, Augustine was more jaundiced. Great empires are great robbers, and they do not become Christian. This perspective could have led Augustine to deny any religious role to the state. However, when confronted by the Donatist heretics in North Africa, Augustine turned to the power of the state to persecute his opponents, imprisoning them and destroying their churches.[25] He justified the persecution of heretics through an allegorical interpretation of the parable of the wedding banquet. The king in Jesus' parable commanded, referring to the unwilling guests: "Force them to come in" (Luke 14:23). Augustine took this as divine justification for the repression of heretics by force by the Christian emperor. Ironically, Augustine concluded that Christian charity itself demands coercion. Even though Augustine himself did not call for the use of torture or execution and in fact forbade it, he set an important precedent for later Christians who would not always be so restrained. Tragically, Augustinian Christianity has not only been faithful to but has also betrayed the revelation upon which it is founded. The revelation of the God of love who suffers on the cross intermingles with the age-old practices of exclusion and persecution in Augustine and throughout later Christian history.

REVELATION AND SOCIAL ENGAGEMENT
IN THE MIDDLE AGES

As the Roman Emperor moved to Constantinople, central Italy would come more and more under the rule of the bishop of Rome; and the church would increasingly be the major force shaping European society.[26] Church leaders would have power to govern and wage war on an unprecedented scale. As social order disintegrated and violence became widespread in Western Europe, church institutions became the central bulwarks of cultural and social life; and church leaders took their place among the emerging feudal nobility of Europe.

The violence of poverty and radical social inequality continued to be a curse in society throughout the Middle Ages. While the church continued to express concern for the poor and the sick, medieval Christians assumed that the domination of society by a small, landed aristocracy was the will of God. In memory of the parable of Jesus about the poor man Lazarus and the rich man (Luke 16:19-31), each wealthy household or monastery was expected to support a number of paupers, who were believed to be a source of blessing.[27] Pope Innocent III personally displayed generous concern for the poor, at times feeding up to eight thousand individuals each day; but he did not question the hierarchical order of feudal society itself.[28]

In early medieval society there was no clear distinction between the church (*ecclesia*) and the world (*mundus*): emperors and kings were sacred figures who ruled by divine will, and bishops were political rulers installed by kings.[29] From the mid-eleventh century on, some popes, including Gregory VII and Innocent III, struggled against Holy Roman Emperors in a valiant effort to dominate all of European society.[30] Gregory VII's effort to end the investiture of bishops by lay rulers ended in a compromise that turned on the first systematic distinction between the sacred and the secular in Western culture and paved the way for the later secularization of Western culture.[31] In the end the forces of nationalism and the emergence of the modern state, especially in France, proved too strong for either popes or sacred emperors to subdue.

The patristic suspicions of wealth lingered in negative medieval attitudes toward merchants who made profits from buying cheap and selling dear, and profits from interest or from real estate speculation were judged to violate the principles of a Christian economy.[32] Amid the growing wealth and power of the medieval church, the High Middle Ages witnessed a series of attempts to return to the ideal of simplicity and service of the early church. During a time of severe weather and famine from 1194 to 1204, theologians discussed the rights of the poor, affirming the right of the starving person to steal because in time of necessity all things are common. The poor were viewed as the "vicars of

Christ," the ones who represent Christ in this world and who will intercede for the wealthy in the final judgment.[33]

About the same time, a series of movements sought to return to the voluntary poverty of the original *vita apostolica*, the apostolic life. In different ways, the Poor Men of Lyons, the Cathars or Albigensians in southern France, Peter Waldo, Francis of Assisi, and Dominic Guzman all strove to live the ideal of evangelical poverty and simplicity in order to proclaim the gospel. Many, like Francis, not only gave to the poor but sought to live together with the poor in the name of Christ.[34] Perhaps most famous of all, the image of Francis stripping himself of all his clothes and worldly goods in front of his father and the bishop of Assisi captured the imagination of Europe and inspired generations of followers to renounce all possessions and serve the poor.[35] In this symbolic act, Francis was rejecting the frenetic rivalries of early capitalism in Italy and challenging the emerging value system of a new society. The life of Francis of Assisi appears in Girardian terms as a generous mimesis of Christ that renounces the world of mimetic rivalry and identifies with the lepers, the outcasts, and the despised of early-thirteenth-century Italy. Even though bitter struggles over the concrete practice of Francis's ideal of poverty would later tragically shatter the Franciscan order into rival factions, the ideal of Franciscan poverty and service of the poor would remain an important part of the Christian heritage. Perhaps the image of Pope Innocent III embracing Francis of Assisi and giving him official support best captures the different sides of the medieval church's posture in society: On the one hand, the pope shaped the course of nations and disposed of tremendous concrete political and social power; on the other hand, Francis of Assisi lived on the margins of society, sharing what little he had with lepers and beggars. In a certain sense each needed the other, but Pope Innocent III himself dreamt that he needed Francis even more than Francis needed him.

Because patristic and medieval Christians generally accepted the basic social structures of their society, the potential for radical social transformation contained in the Bible and the example of Jesus was never fully exploited. Traditional Christian practice in the patristic and medieval periods sought to alleviate the suffering of the poor, the sick, and the oppressed; but there was little thought of transforming the structures of society themselves to eliminate the root causes of poverty and social inequality.

THE HOLY WAR IN THE MIDDLE AGES

The scriptures had bequeathed to the church an ambiguous heritage, and the medieval Catholic tradition followed both sides of it. On the one hand, the use of sacred violence was explicitly sanctioned by popes, bishops, and inquisitors; and the patterns of exclusion and scapegoating and persecution dominated the relations of Christians and Jews for centuries. On the other hand, the memory of the nonviolent, all-embracing love of Jesus never died, as witnessed by the example of Francis of Assisi and others who turned away from military arms to seek nonviolent forms of Christian service.

The development of the Christian theology of the holy war took place against the backdrop of the threat from Islam. For hundreds of years, Muslims were on the offensive against Christians. With incredible speed, Muslim armies swept through the eastern parts of the Byzantine Empire and through North Africa and Spain. Christians did succeed in turning them back from France and eventually drove them out of Spain over the course of seven hundred years. In the late eleventh century Christians enjoyed some early and dramatic successes in the First Crusade, but a resurgent Islam was eventually able to retake Jerusalem and drive the Crusader kingdoms onto the defensive. In 1453 Ottoman Turks conquered Constantinople, and after that, Turkish armies besieged Vienna in 1527 and in 1683. For about a millennium, Christians in Europe periodically saw Muslims as a military threat.

Muslims had their own theology of war, which was based on the *Qur'an* and an early speech by Abu Bakr, the first caliph selected after the death of Muhammad to succeed him as leader of the community. *Jihad* properly means "struggle," "effort," or "striving"; and the primary struggle is within oneself to do God's will and to extend the Muslim community by peaceful means. *Jihad* also included military warfare in defense of Islam, but it did not include military offensives. The *Qur'an* commands: "Fight for the sake of Allah those that fight against you, but do not attack them first. Allah does not love the aggressors. Kill them wherever you find them. Drive them out of the places from which they drove you. . . . Fight against them until idolatry is no more and Allah's religion reigns supreme. But if they mend their ways, fight none except the evil-doers" (2:190-91, 193).

Abu Bakr set forth the principles for conducting *jihad* in a speech that recounted sayings attributed to Muhammad himself. The sayings commend those who fight and even die in battle:

He who fights so that the word of God may prevail is on the path of God. He who dies fighting on the frontier in the path of God, God protects him from the testing of the tomb. . . . The best thing a Muslim can earn is an arrow in the path of God. . . . Swords are the keys of Paradise. . . . Every prophet has his monasticism, and the monasticism of this community is the Holy War in the path of God.[36]

The sayings forbade looting and mutilation, the killing of women, old men, and children and ordered all booty to be brought to the community.

The Christian theology of the holy war developed gradually in the early Middle Ages. In 853, several years after Saracens had sacked Rome and ravaged St. Peter's, Pope Leo IV urged Frankish soldiers to fight valiantly against the enemies of the church and held out the hope of a reward in heaven for those who died in battle. While this was not a doctrinal statement, it did establish a connection between eternal salvation and death in battle against Muslims. In effect, the struggle was a holy war.[37] Some years later, in 878, Pope John VIII strengthened the connection between salvation and fighting for the church and one's government. John granted an absolution to those who died in battle against the enemies of Christianity, promising them the same reward as the good thief had received from Christ.[38]

The revival of the papacy in the middle of the eleventh century brought with it new attention to the theme of the holy war. Popes themselves were occasionally combatants and often supporters of wars. Pope Leo IX personally led an unsuccessful attack on the Normans in Sicily in 1053. Pope Alexander II offered a commutation of penance to soldiers fighting against the Moors in Spain, and he supported William of Normandy's invasion of England in 1066. Pope Gregory VII repeatedly used the imagery of the holy war, first in hopes of leading a Crusade against the Turks in the Near East and later for his struggle against the Holy Roman Emperor Henry IV.

One of the most influential proclamations of war as the will of God came from Pope Urban II in 1095. The preaching of the First Crusade called forth a renewed theology of the holy war, which went well beyond Augustine's notion of a just war and drew upon precedents in the Hebrew scriptures to sacralize the violent struggle against Muslims. The successes of the Seljuk Turks had hardened many Christians' attitudes against Muslims as enemies. Ironically, in the areas where Christians and Muslims were in closest contact, in Spain, Sicily, southern Italy, and the Byzantine Empire, relations were often more peaceful and tolerant. But the renewed religious fervor in Europe in the late eleventh and early twelfth century led to sharper contrasts being drawn between Muslim and Christian and greater animosities being kindled.

In the new attitudes, war, far from being displeasing to God, came to be seen as the will of God. Baldric, archbishop of Dal in the early twelfth century, reported the dramatic call to arms of Pope Urban II at the Council of Clermont in 1095:

Under Jesus Christ, our Leader, may you struggle for your Jerusalem, in Christian battle-line, most invincible line, even more successfully than did the sons of Jacob of old—struggle, that you may assail and drive out the Turks, more execrable than the Jebusites, who are in this land, and may you deem it a beautiful thing to die for Christ in that city in which He died for us. . . . [T]he possessions of the enemy, too, will be yours, since you will make spoil of their treasures and return victorious to your own; or empurpled with your own blood, you will have gained everlasting glory.[39]

As Pope Urban finished his famous appeal on November 27, 1095, the crowds shouted: "Deus vult" (God wills it). On hearing this response, Pope Urban reportedly turned his eyes to heaven, gratefully remembered the promise of Jesus to be present where two or three are gathered in his name, and commended the shout as a war cry in battle.

The preaching of and preparations for the First Crusade led directly to new violence against the Jews. Already in 1009, when Europe learned that the Fatimid caliph al-Hakim had destroyed the Church of the Holy Sepulchre in Jerusalem, Jews in Orléans, France, were implausibly accused of collusion, and Jewish communities suffered violence. Once the First Crusade had been proclaimed, Crusaders often had to borrow money from Jews to equip themselves for the long journey and eventual battles. It seemed to many a sacrilege that Christian soldiers should go into debt to the people who killed Christ in order to oppose Christ's Muslim enemies. Guibert of Nogent tells us that Crusaders in Rouen stated: "We desire to combat the enemies of God in the East; but we have under our eyes the Jews, a race more inimical to God than all the others. We are doing this whole thing backwards" (*De Vita Sua* 3.5).[40] Attacks on Jews in France followed, and many Jews were offered a choice of forced baptism or death. The French Jews warned their German counterparts to be on the alert. Count Emich of Leisingen unleashed his crusading army on Jews in Spier in May, 1096. The bishop of the town gave the Jews shelter, and only a small number were killed there. Undeterred, the army went on to plunder and kill many Jews in one town after another in the Rhineland. In Worms and Mainz hundreds were killed. Estimates are that up to ten thousand Jews in France and Germany were killed between January and July 1096, in connection with the First Crusade.

Attacks on the Jews would be a repeated feature of the Crusades. When those preparing the Second Crusade turned to attack Jews, Bernard of Clairvaux, the foremost preacher of the Crusade, insisted that Jews should not be persecuted. Nonetheless, Bernard assumed that the dispersion of the Jews among the nations was God's just punishment for their crimes against Jesus. Jewish sufferings witnessed to the redemption of Christians.[41] Nearly two centuries later, in the spring of 1320, the Shepherds' Crusade was making its way through southern France. Frustrated at their lack of progress, the Crusaders turned with fury on Jewish communities in one town after another, especially in Toulouse,

Périgord, and Carcassone. The ideology of the holy war and the crusading zeal of attacking the enemies of Christ was responsible for a severe deterioration in Jewish–Christian relations and led to centuries of further violence against the Jews.

Steven Runciman, a historian of the Crusades, concludes his study with a lament:

> In the long sequence of interaction and fusion between Orient and Occident out of which our civilization has grown, the Crusades were a tragic and destructive episode. The historian, as he gazes back across the centuries, must find his admiration overcast by sorrow at the witness that it bears to the limitations of human nature. There was so much courage and so little honour, so much devotion and so little understanding. High ideals were besmirched by a blind and narrow self-righteousness; and the Holy War itself was nothing more than a long act of intolerance in the name of God, which is the sin against the Holy Ghost.[42]

AN AMBIGUOUS HERITAGE

In regard to violence, scripture and the later Christian tradition together form an ambiguous heritage. The nonviolent example and teaching of Jesus himself inspired generations of early Christians to reject violence and to accept persecution without retaliation, and the memory of the early Christian martyrs inspired centuries of later Christians. There was also, however, the more violent trajectory of the biblical witness in the holy war tradition. In pondering the biblical commands of the holy war, Origen recognized that an uncritical acceptance of the scriptures can lead to erroneous ideas about God, specifically regarding violence; and he used the criterion of what is fitting and proper for God to determine what was to be taken as literal and what as allegory in the scriptures. Augustine used the criterion of *caritas*, self-giving love, to make this determination. Passages that condemn *cupiditas* and teach *caritas* are to be taken as literal; those that appear to violate this rule must have another, allegorical meaning. Thus each author had an interpretative strategy that could reverse the direct, literal sense of the biblical texts that command violence in the name of God. Augustine himself developed the theology of the just war as a limited, responsible use of violence by government authorities in carefully defined cases, and he turned to the arm of the state for physical coercion of heretical Donatists.

As Christianity became the established power in Europe, biblical precedents for sanctioning violence came to the fore; and violence came to be proclaimed not only as just but as a holy obligation. Popes, bish-ops, inquisitors, and Crusaders sanctioned the use of sacred violence in wars and in efforts to eliminate heresy. Patterns of exclusion, scape-goating, and persecution dominated the relations of Jews and Christians for centuries. Wars against Muslims were seen as sacred affairs, willed by God. The tale of violence done in the name of Christian revelation is, of course, much longer than this brief survey has indicated. Nonetheless, the memory of the all-embracing, nonviolent love of Jesus never died, as witnessed by the example of Francis of Assisi and others who turned away from military arms to seek peaceful forms of Christian service.

6

Encountering the Religions
of China and India

The civilizations of Greece, India, and China went through dramatic shifts of religious self-understanding during the same centuries as the flourishing of the prophets and sages of Israel, roughly 800 to 200 B.C.E. The transformations of this period took place in different places around the globe during the same centuries, largely without direct contact. For most of its history, ancient Israel had little or no awareness of the civilizations of India or China, though there may well have been contacts between Babylon and India through the trade routes. Jews during the Hellenistic age were increasingly aware of Greek and Persian thought and culture and may have been aware of India, but they likely had little or no knowledge of what was taking place in China.

Some early Christians, such as Clement of Alexandria, were aware of Buddhists in Alexandria; and there were Christians in India from the early centuries of Christianity; but contacts between early Christians and representatives of Indian religious traditions were, for the most part, minimal. There may have been some influence from Indian thought upon the philosophy of Plotinus (205-270). Plotinus was interested in learning more about Indian thought, and he joined a Roman military expedition to the East. This ended abruptly, however, when Emperor Gordianus III was killed in 244; and Plotinus went to Rome without ever reaching India. To what degree Plotinus was actually aware of and influenced by Indian thought remains a disputed question.[1] If Plotinus was affected by Indian thought, this would be a very important link to later Christian thought throughout the Middle Ages. The Church of the East, which was in contact with the other great religions of Asia, was increasingly cut off from contact with Mediterranean and European Christianity after the fifth century. The classical development of both Latin and Greek Christianity was largely unaware of the traditions in South and East Asia.

Dialogue among the axial religions does take place in the present, however; and some have thought that the present encounters among the world's religions, combined with the rapid networking of global consciousness and life, may be leading us into a new Axial Age.[2] However different religious traditions have been in the past, our futures are increasingly intertwined.

The religious transformations of the period from 800 to 200 B.C.E. differ greatly in the foundations of their religious self-understanding. While Hinduism clearly understood itself to be based on a divine revelation, Buddhism did not. Moreover, Chinese religions did not believe in a transcendent theistic God and thus did not perceive themselves to be founded on a theistic revelation. In different ways, however, the Buddhist and Chinese traditions do proceed from a manifestation of the truth of the cosmos which transforms human life.

Despite the clear and important differences among these transformations of religious cultures, the similarities in the history of development during the same centuries have given rise to much reflection. The German philosopher Karl Jaspers gave the name "the Axial Age" to the transformation of consciousness, religion, and culture that took place in various places between 800 and 200 B.C.E. Jaspers saw this period as the fundamental dividing line in human history. Before it, consciousness had been tribal, collective, ritual, mythical. After it came everything that we know as human culture down to the present. All later developments of civilization, Jaspers argued, took place within the horizons established by the Axial Age. "What is new about this age, in all three areas of the world [China, India, and the West], is that man becomes conscious of Being as a whole, of himself and his limitations. . . . He experiences absoluteness in the depths of selfhood and in the lucidity of transcendence. . . . The step into universality was taken in every sense."[3] The axial traditions gave a new importance to the individual and commanded each human: "Know thyself." There was a new sense of appropriating the true identity of each individual as a pathway to the transcendent.

Jaspers was aware that the content of the various breakthroughs was very different, and his language is clearly derived from the Western philosophical tradition. Nonetheless, he argued, there were common patterns. Greek philosophers, Chinese thinkers, Indian reformers, and Hebrew and Persian prophets all critiqued earlier mythical forms of thought; and all sought more ethical forms of religion. There was a spiritualization of experience, a quest for union with the whole, the One, or with God. "These paths are widely divergent in their conviction and dogma, but common to all of them is man's reaching out beyond himself by growing aware of himself within the whole of Being and the fact that he can tread them only as an individual on his own."[4] Jaspers has been criticized for applying Western notions of transcendence and Being and subjectivity to a Chinese culture whose context and assumptions were very different.[5] Nonetheless, with the proper qualifications, Jaspers's proposal still merits consideration. Benjamin I. Schwartz has recently commented on the continuing pertinence of Jaspers's claim: "Whether one deals with the Upanishads, Buddhism, or Jainism in India, with the rise of biblical Judaism, with the emergence of Greek philosophy or with the emergence of Confucianism, Taoism, and Mohism in China—one finds a kind of standing back and looking beyond; of questioning and reflectivity as well as the emergence of new positive perspectives and visions."[6] Jaspers saw the present awareness of the Axial Age as a challenge to communication across traditional boundaries and as a rebuke to the claim to exclusive possession of the truth by any one community. Using Western terminology, Jaspers saw God as becoming manifest in various fashions and opening up different ways for humans to find God.[7]

Religions with a developed intellectual tradition often have intuitions of the order and justice of the cosmos that can be compared to biblical wisdom: not only the Egyptian *Maat*, but also the *logos* of Greece, the *rta* of early Hinduism, *dharma*[†] in later Hinduism and Buddhism, and the Tao[†] of Confucianism and Taoism. While these traditions obviously differ from one another, the idea that there are analogies and correspondences among their respective notions of cosmic order is not new. In *The Abolition of Man*, C. S. Lewis, arguing against the dangers of ethical relativism, turned to the universal Tao, or the Way, as the ground of all morality. Lewis assumed that the Tao is known variously in a wide variety of traditions, including those named above; Lewis's description of the universal Tao could well be applied to biblical articulations of wisdom: "the Way in which the universe goes on . . . the Way which every man should tread in imitation of that cosmic and supercosmic progression." The Tao provides the basis for affirming objective values that are discovered, not projected, by humans.

There are, however, profound differences between Jewish and Christian understandings of wisdom on the one hand and Hindu, Buddhist, and Chinese understandings of the Way or order of the universe on the other. Each tradition makes universal claims, asserting that its intuitions apply to the entire cosmos. Yet each tradition is irrevocably particular, rooted in a particular history and culture.

CONFUCIANISM

Asian religions have been fluid during their long histories, being constantly immersed in the developing life of their respective cultures. The Western term "religion" can itself be problematic when applied to Asian axial traditions. The Chinese word for religion, *tsung-chiao*, did not exist until the late nineteenth century, when it entered Chinese through Japanese translations of European works. The same was true for the Chinese word for philosophy. China and East Asia in general have not traditionally made a very clear separation between religion and philosophy. Joseph Kitagawa warns that Westerners abstract one aspect of life and call it "religion."[8] They think that the Western mode of dividing human experience into pigeonholes that are separate from each other is universal. Concretely, religions exist as part of a religious-cultural-social-political synthesis.

Many of the usual Western identifying marks for religion, such as belief in a transcendent God, do not apply to East Asian cultures. Nonetheless, the Chinese people have been religious in the sense of being profoundly concerned with harmony with the whole and the proper cultivation of the human person. They have been aware of their relation to immanence and transcendence even though they did not use theistic language. As Tu Wei-Ming comments: "[T]he dichotomy between faith and reason or between rationality and revelation is quite alien to the Confucian mode of thought. . . . [T]he ultimate Confucian concern is self-transformation as a communal act and as a faithful dialogical response to the transcendent."[9]

Because Chinese religions do not traditionally believe in a God that transcends the universe, they do not rely on revelation in the sense of God's word grasping the Hebrew prophets. There is a sense in Chinese thought that what is most important and close to hand in life can be easily overlooked and neglected. What is needed is a disclosive reorientation that allows us to see what was before us all along. The closest analogue in Israel's experience to Chinese religions is the wisdom tradition, with its sense of the ordering power of Lady Wisdom and the necessity of living in harmony with her.

The "Heaven" of Confucius (ca. 551-479 B.C.E.) and other early Chinese thinkers does not speak to humans directly, as Yahweh does to the Hebrew prophets. Nonetheless, Heaven is not simply impersonal either. Even though Heaven is not a transcendent, omnipotent God, Heaven is omniscient, approving or disapproving of human behavior and exercising a protective care over humans, including Confucius himself.[10] The role of Heaven can be compared to that of Lady Wisdom, or Sophia, in Israel. Lady Wisdom was not identified with Yahweh in the Hebrew Bible and thus was not the transcendent God. She was, however, the way in which Yahweh was present in the cosmos. She was aware of human actions and delighted in people's wisdom and lamented their folly (Prov 8).

The sage in ancient China was one who "penetrates" or "passes through" or "hears";[11] the sage was able to understand the ways of Heaven and disclose or manifest these to others. In China, the original Five Confucian Classics (*Book of History, Book of Poems, Book of*

Changes, Spring and Autumn Annals, and *Book of Rites*) and the later Four Books (*Analects of Confucius, Book of Mencius, Great Learning,* and *Doctrine of the Mean*) were collections of these manifestations. Confucius himself speaks about the intention of Heaven which has given him a mission to teach (*Analects* 7:23; 9:5; 14:35). While later efforts to deify Confucius himself found little support and were condemned as heretical, he remained prominent as a human sage with a unique teaching role. The *Analects of Confucius,* which are a compilation of his teachings, were later revered as one of the Four Books that all Confucian students had to study and internalize. In a similar way, in ancient Israel, the wisdom teacher did not receive an extraordinary call like a prophet but was able to penetrate the way of Wisdom in everyday life through careful reflection.

Julia Ching uses the images of yin and yang to sketch the central dynamic of Chinese religions. Confucianism is the active side, the classic articulation of the yang side in moral and social philosophy. This tradition has usually dominated Chinese life during periods of political unity and social order. Taoism is the moment of passivity, the religion of naturalism and quietism. "Taoism tends to be a tradition of the recluses, of persons who prefer to keep their distance from political involvement."[12] But Taoists have participated in court life in China and have at times fought their Confucian and Buddhist rivals. In practice many Chinese have drawn from both traditions in their lives. It has been remarked that Chinese officials are traditionally Confucian while in office and Taoist in retirement. The sage of Israel played a role at court similar to that of the Confucian wise man, and the later Christian desert fathers and mothers made the decision to withdraw from society in a manner analogous to the Taoist recluses.[13]

Confucianism focuses on the transformation of the human person, realizing the true self in harmony with the Tao of the universe. The central concern was the cultivation of *jen,* humanity, also translated as "benevolence" or "inner moral life." Confucius (551-479 B.C.E.) proposed a humanism grounded in the confidence that if humans truly seek humanity, it will present itself to them: "The Master said: Is benevolence [*jen,* humanity] really far away? No sooner do I desire it than it is here" (*Analects* 7:30).[14] Though near to us, the path to humanity is long and the burden is heavy: "Only with death does the road come to an end" (*Analects* 8:7). *Jen* is difficult because the raw material of humanity must be cut and shaped and molded. *Jen* comes from doing what is difficult; yet it is the achievement of what we already are. *Jen* also means a concern for others; in this sense the desire for *jen* means that *jen* is already present.

Jen is achieved through the observance of rites, ceremonies, propriety, and the forms of social interaction, called *li* (*Analects* 12:1). *Li* was developed by studying the Odes, the rites, and music (*Analects* 8:8), possibly referring to the classic works such as the *Book of Poetry* and the *Book of Rites*. Though many scholars have properly stressed the humanistic emphases in Confucius, Herbert Fingarette called attention to the importance of "the magical" in his thought; the magical is the power of ritual and incantation to accomplish one's will without strenuous effort.[15] Paradoxically, one must work hard to learn *li;* yet through *li* all aspects of civilized life become possible. *Li* consists in social forms that shape raw human impulses into holy rite and thereby form a sacred community; it is the pattern for following the path, the Tao of human existence and the cosmos. *Li* requires behavior toward others in accordance with each person's status and rank in society. While Fingarette argues that Confucius's concern is with the properties of the acts of *li* themselves and not with any inner psychological dimension, Benjamin Schwartz maintains that Confucius's innovation consists precisely in his attention to the inner life of individuals.[16]

Li is rooted in the cosmic Tao, which is the all-embracing normative order. The alternative to following the Tao is chaos. The central challenge is not so much deciding between different paths as seeing the true path. The Way itself exerts an attractive power which is the source of the "magical" in Confucius's worldview. Through *li, jen* is realized and becomes easy.

True nobility, for Confucius, was a question not of birth but of personal attainment and character, and thus his perspectives implied a revolution of social values. He lived at a time of social and political strife and chaos. Larger territories were in the process of becoming a unified political power. Confucius lamented that in his own time the Tao did not prevail. Amid the violent conflicts among the feudal states of his time, respect for the Tao had virtually disappeared. It had, however, prevailed in earlier dynasties, and thus there was hope. Confucius proposed his wisdom as a response to the violence of his time.

In a time of turmoil and violence, he proposed a universal vision of a set of values and practices that could become the foundation for order in a renewed Chinese culture. Rooting his vision in the tradition of *li* of the ancients, Confucius laid the basis for future Chinese unity. "He who by reanimating the Old can gain knowledge of the New is indeed fit to be called a teacher" (*Analects* 2:11).[17]

Confucius, like the sages of Israel, stressed the proper time for speech and silence, for action and waiting (*Analects* 8:13; 15:8). Confucius stressed the importance of learning for one's own sake, not simply for the sake of pleasing others. He also insisted that cultivation of oneself will bring benefits to society, but he did not want to reduce cultivation to the status of a means to some further end. In realizing our own humanity, we contribute to our family, our community, our state, and the entire cosmos. Tu Wei-Ming describes this vision as anthropocosmic.[18] Even though for Confucius Heaven does not appear as a personal God who radically transcends the world, Heaven is the ultimate source for creative self-transformation: "[S]ince the Way of Heaven is right here, near at hand, and inseparable from our ordinary daily existence, what we do in the confines of our home is not only anthropologically but also cosmologically significant."[19]

There is no sense of extrinsic punishment for moral wrongdoing in Confucius; falling away from the Tao brings about disorder and suffering of itself. To follow the Tao is natural and is a matter of yielding rather than forcing. Education is crucial in forming humans so that they can walk in the path. The wisdom teachers of Israel also saw the path of wisdom as leading to intrinsic well-being and prosperity. They did not look to external divine interventions for reward and punishment but trusted in the working of Lady Wisdom herself in and through the cosmos. By following the path of Wisdom, the sages were living in harmony with the ordering power of creation itself: "for whoever finds me finds life" (Prov 8:35). Finding Wisdom was its own reward, for she was greater than wealth and power. Tu Wei-ming's description, "anthropocosmic," could well be applied to the vision of the Israelite sages of Lady Wisdom embedded in the cosmos, guiding human life, friendly to humans.

Confucius praises the ruler Shun for governing by nongoverning in terms that will echo through the Taoist tradition: "If there was a ruler who achieved order without taking any action, it was, perhaps Shun. There was nothing for him to do but to hold himself in a respectful posture and to face due south" (*Analects* 15:5). Here the notion of *wu-wei*, non-action or spontaneous, nondeliberative action, appears in terms so close to Taoism that some scholars have suspected that it is a later addition to the *Analects*. While Confucius's vision of the Tao is firmly rooted in the experience of this world, Schwartz sees him as suggesting "an ascent to an ultimate unity which is beyond all words," thus offering an opening to the reality evoked by Taoism.[20]

The Confucian tradition did not produce ecstatic prophets in the sense of Israel. While some scholars have argued that there are broad similarities between Confucian sages and the prophets of Israel,[21] the comparison is somewhat forced.[22] The stronger analogies, rather, are to the wisdom tradition of Israel. The sages of Israel could well accept in their own manner the Confucian ideal of creative self-transformation in relation to one's society and culture. The wisdom tradition of Israel agrees with the Confucian tradition in trusting in the power of Wisdom at work in the universe and in human life, shaping harmony. The Confucian ideal of a regular, balanced existence in harmony with family, community, and cosmos resonates strongly with the Israelite sages' search for life in accord with Wisdom. The Confucian veneration of the everyday world as spiritual can also be compared to the Israelite sages' trust that Lady Wisdom is to be found in ordinary experience. Israelite sages and Confucian scholars sought to serve their royal courts, advising kings on matters of policy.

Confucius made no explicit claim of special divine revelation, but he did have a sense that Heaven had entrusted an important vocation to him and was protecting him. His claim to authority, like that of the sages of Israel, was based on his insight into the patterns in ordinary human experience. As Tu Wei-Ming comments: "The plainness and reality of Confucius' life, however, illustrate the fact that his humanity was not a revealed truth but an expression of self-cultivation, the result of an unceasing effort on the part of an individual human being to shape his own destiny."[23] Self-cultivation for Confucius was itself an accepting of the mission of Heaven and its providential care.

TAOISM

The Taoist tradition has taken two rather different forms in Chinese history, often called philosophical (*Tao Chia*) and religious (*Tao Chiao*). Religious Taoism came to be largely concerned with longevity and immortality.[24] A variety of prescriptions promised good health, long life, and prosperity, often through alchemical or magical means.[25] Religious Taoism claimed to be founded by a revelation of Lao-tzu in 142 C.E. and involved a covenant with a variety of deities who urged their followers to turn away from earlier bloodthirsty gods and prepare for an age of peace. Religious Taoism drew upon many elements of popular Chinese religion.

Philosophical Taoism, which will be the focus of this discussion, is best known in the texts attributed to Lao-tzu, the *Tao-te Ching* (*The Classic of the Way and Its Power*), and the texts attributed to his later follower Chuang-tzu. There has been much speculation about the historical person Lao-tzu, who may have been contemporary with Confucius (ca. 551-479 B.C.E.), and thus with some of the prophets of Israel. "Lao-tzu" literally means "old master." The second-century B.C.E. biographer Ssu-ma Ch'ien tells us that his family name was Li, and his personal name was Erh.[26] It is reported that Confucius met Lao-tzu; but the story may well be apocryphal and little is known of the historical Lao-tzu.

The text of the *Tao-te Ching* is somewhat later, sometimes being dated to the third century B.C.E.; it is a collection of aphorisms with little or no attempt at an orderly arrangement. The work glorifies simplicity, but much of its language is baffling and obscure. The style is very compact and terse. Until recently, no punctuation was used in Chinese writing, and this circumstance adds to the ambiguity of the work. The original text had no chapters or subtitles. Moreover, classical Chinese syntax has many ambiguities, which leads to different readings. Many of the sayings remain enigmatic and open to a variety of interpretations.

The Tao of Confucius is the social and natural order of the universe. The Tao of Lao-tzu is a mystical reality beyond all names, but it can be evoked through allusive language. It is described as *wu*, non-being, but it is the source of all things. The Tao does not exercise conscious providence like the Heaven of Confucius. The Tao is analogous to the Greek word *hodos*, the Way, and also to *logos*, the Word. "Tao" has been used, with some qualifications, in translating the opening of John's Gospel: "In the beginning was the Tao."[27] The Tao is nameless, indeterminate, the first principle from which all things arise and become determined. The Tao is the ancestor of all things, existing before the universe. "The Tao begets One; one begets two; two begets three; three begets all things" (ch. 42).[28] Later on, there would be a Taoist Trinity with different names at different periods. According to one version, the Primal Celestial One controlled the past; the Precious Celestial One controlled the present; and the Way and its Power Celestial One controlled the future. But the Tao is prior to the Taoist Trinity and gives rise to it.

> The Tao is before all else that is:
> There is a thing inherent and natural.
> Which existed before heaven and earth.
> Motionless and fathomless,
> It stands alone and never changes;
> It pervades everywhere and never becomes
>   exhausted.
> It may be regarded as the Mother of the Universe.
> I do not know its name.
> If I am forced to give it a name,
> I call it Tao, and I name it as supreme. . . .
> Man follows the laws of earth;
> Earth follows the laws of heaven;
> Heaven follows the laws of Tao;
> Tao follows the laws of its intrinsic nature.
>   (ch. 25)

Humans discover the Tao by letting go, by contemplating the universe as it is without imposing their own agenda on it. The key term is *wu-wei*, non-action. Julia Ching explains: "It does not signify the absence of action, but rather acting without artificiality, without overaction, without attachment to action itself."[29] To act in this way is to experience power (*te*), and through *te* the Tao becomes particular. The power that the Tao teaches is the wisdom of surviving, especially in time of disorder. It is found in ascetic withdrawal from the world in order to follow nature. Nature is a reliable guide. One image of the life of Tao is water. "The highest goodness is like water. Water is beneficent to all things but does not contend. It stays in places which others despise. Therefore it is near Tao" (ch. 8).

Taoism's perspective on political action is based on the principle: The less government the better. The *Tao-te Ching* appears to support a small, pacifist village state. The ruler should try to undo the problems caused by too many prohibitions and prescriptions, including the ethical teachings of Confucianism. By being perfectly open to the flow of the Tao, the sage-ruler can allow integrity and harmony to pervade the land. The best government is the rule of non-action, keeping the people healthy but ignorant, free from the dangers of the excesses of knowledge. *Wu-wei* allows the weaker party to overcome the stronger, as water overcomes stone (ch. 78). Lao-tzu trusted that the path of passivity and yielding could lead to victory and harmony.[30]

Not exalting the worthy keeps the people from emulation. Not valuing rare things keeps them from theft. Not showing what is desirable keeps their hearts from confusion.
Therefore the Sage rules
By emptying their hearts
Filling their stomachs,
Weakening their ambitions
And strengthening their bones.
He always keeps them from knowing what is evil and desiring what is good; thus he gives the crafty ones no chance to act. He governs by non-action; consequently there is nothing un-governed.
    (ch. 3)

The other major sage of philosophical Taoism is Chuang-tzu, who lived during the Warring States period in the fourth and early third century B.C.E. Chuang-tzu is similar to Lao-tzu in stressing the Tao as the central principle governing the universe and in disliking political life. Nonetheless, there has been debate over whether the Tao that appears in each of these two authors is the same or not. Some have seen Chuang-tzu as developing the worldview of Lao-tzu; others have seen little relationship between them apart from the reverence for the Tao. Much depends on how one interprets the text that is named for each figure, and in both cases the language is deliberately evocative and open to different interpretations.

Chuang-tzu teaches the student to transcend the distinctions between one's own self and the universe. Through perfect union with the Tao, one can find absolute happiness. This is the knowledge of wisdom that transcends the world of distinctions, including the distinction of life and death.[31] All distinctions depend on each other: right and wrong, birth and death. "But where there is birth there must be death; where there is death there must be birth."[32] The recognition that opposites are relative should lead to seeing no differences between the opposites and transcending them in freedom.

In denying distinctions between right and wrong, Chuang-tzu was not rejecting morality altogether, but he was resisting what he saw as an ambitious moralism prevalent in China. He worried that contemporary Confucians were, in the words of a modern commentator, "busybodies who wander about the world deceiving themselves in the belief that they can transform the human world by *yu-wei* [conscious, goal-directed] activity."[33] For Chuang-tzu, union with the Tao leads to a natural spontaneity in which humanity, benevolence, and love flow forth without forced effort. Withdrawal from the world of political ambitions frees one to return to one's origin in the Tao.

For Chuang-tzu, the Taoist sage rises above the tyranny of desires. This mystical knowledge comes from forgetting the knowledge of all things, especially the knowledge of the self. The text speaks of "sitting and forgetting" and of "fasting of the mind." In one sense, emptying the mind is a technique of meditation, allowing thoughts to arise and subside without being caught in them and thereby coming to peace. In another sense, emptying the mind means letting go of ambitions for social, political, and economic success and following the Tao. It is a purification, a relinquishing of false goals. By emptying the senses and the mind one can communicate with the inner reality and be filled with the gods and spirits. Through concentration of the mind, the practitioner is freed from everyday worries and fears of death and attains freedom, peace, and equanimity.[34]

The language of Chuang-tzu would resonate with later Ch'an (Zen) Buddhists in China, who would interpret his sayings in a Buddhist context. Buddhists could interpret and accept in their own context Chuang-tzu's statement: "The Way gathers in emptiness alone. Emptiness is the fasting of the mind" (ch. 4).[35] Taoism and Buddhism would have a long history of mutual influence in China. Taoism was an important factor in the development of Ch'an Buddhism, and Taoists in turn adapted precepts and meditation techniques of Mahayana Buddhism for their own practice.

The Taoist tradition also bears broad similarities to the wisdom tradition of Israel. Chuang-tzu insisted on transcending the relative distinctions we usually make by seeing all things as flowing from the Tao; similarly, Ben Sira urged his hearers to transcend comparisons and evaluations between things: "All the works of the Lord are good, and he will supply every want in due time. You must not say, 'this is worse than that,' for everything will prove its value in its time" (Sir 39:33-34). For Chuang Tzu as for Ben Sira, insight into the nature of things brings freedom from clinging to preferential judgments. Qoheleth, like Lao-tzu and

Chuang-tzu, also had a strong sense of the vanity and emptiness of courtly ambitions. Qoheleth's counsel to enjoy one's present condition, one's spouse, and one's work without worrying about future death can be compared to the advice of Lao-tzu and Chuang-tzu to live spontaneously and naturally, accepting all things, even death, with equanimity.

The Tao of Lao-tzu is not a transcendent creator with a particular will and purpose for creation; it is the ineffable, ultimate source of all things, shaping all things spontaneously and naturally. For Chuang-tzu, the Tao is the absolute origin and end of all things, beyond the distinction between personal and impersonal.[36] Knowledge of the Tao is an experience that transforms one's life, freeing one from the usual expectations of societal values and allowing us to flow freely in accord with our true nature, or the "Uncarved Block" which is our original potential prior to the corruption of culture. Knowledge of the Tao goes beyond the usual categories of discursive reason, and commentators have described it as mystical.[37]

There are even stronger analogies between Taoists and the early Christian desert fathers and mothers, who left the sophisticated world of Hellenistic society to seek simplicity and wisdom in the desert.[38] Their withdrawal, like that of Lao-tzu and Chuang-tzu, was itself a critique of the usual paths of society and became a powerful influence on Hellenistic culture.[39] Like the Taoist sages, the desert fathers and mothers wished neither to rule over others nor to be ruled by usual societal conventions. The Christian contemplatives sought a society of equals where, in Thomas Merton's words, "the only authority under God was the charismatic authority of wisdom, experience and love."[40] The paradoxical stories and sayings of the desert fathers and mothers bear witness to a playful spirit that knows that ultimate reality is beyond univocal comprehension. To find union with the source of our being, the Christian desert hermits taught that we must overcome our usual likes and dislikes and come to know ourselves directly and spontaneously.

The desert fathers and mothers strongly agreed with Lao-tzu and Chuang-tzu that the deliberate striving for wealth, success, and fame is the root of personal and social ills. For both traditions, humility and simplicity are the path to self-knowledge and harmony with our true nature. Some early Christians, like Evagrius Ponticus, taught a form of prayer that emptied the mind of all thoughts, trusting that this practice, done with a trust in God's grace, would lead through a painful upheaval to the manifestation of the image of God within. Chuang-tzu trusted that his own form of emptying the mind would lead to the manifestation of the Uncarved Block, our true nature and potential.

The revelation of God in Jesus Christ freed the Christian desert fathers and mothers from the incessant striving for success; the manifestation of the Tao performed a similar role for Lao-tzu and Chuang-tzu and their followers. In the life and thought of Thomas Merton, who delighted in the sayings of Chuang-tzu, both traditions flow together. Merton commented that the spirit of the way of Chuang-tzu is characterized by traits that resonate across cultures and religions: "a certain taste for simplicity, for humility, for self-effacement, silence, and in general a refusal to take seriously the aggressivity, the ambition, the push, and the self-importance which one must display in order to get along in society. . . . The book of the bible which most obviously resembles the Taoist classics is Ecclesiastes."[41]

John Wu has compared the paradoxes of the spiritual path of Theresa of Lisieux to the way of Lao-tzu. Theresa taught her followers: "To be empty is to be filled. To be poor is to be truly rich. Suffering is a blessing. To come down is to rise. To be little is to be great. Weakness is strength. Life is exile. To die is to live. . . . Do your duty with all your might, but set no store by it. To give all is to give nothing. To choose nothing is to choose all. To cling to the One is to embrace the whole universe."[42] In a very different context, Lao-tzu and Chuang-tzu would agree with Theresa that the way of the weak and the meek leads to the childlike innocence to which we are called. For all three figures, wisdom is found in the spirit of simplicity and humility.

HINDUISM

Hinduism is not a single organized religion with a central authority but rather a family of religious traditions rooted in India. There is no single cult or creed that all Hindus accept, and there are major differences, even outright contradictions, in matters of belief and practice. Hinduism, like Judaism, is a strongly ethnic religion. If there is a unifying thread that runs through the various Hindu traditions, it is recognition of the authority of the Vedas as revelation, though what this means in practice is often disputed.[43] Hinduism historically has been inclusive of many different beliefs, and thus there is no single way of interpreting the Vedic revelation.

Hindus distinguish two different types of scriptures: *shruti*, that which is heard, and *smrti*, that which is remembered. The most sacred religious texts, the Vedas, are *shruti*. These include the Vedic hymns, or Samhitas (1400-1000 B.C.E.), the Brahmanas (1000-700 B.C.E.), the Aranyakas ("Forest Books," 800-600 B.C.E.), and the Upanishads (800-200 B.C.E.).[44] There are four major schools that are based on the places of various figures during ritual sacrifices. The Rig Veda comes from those who recited the hymns and consists of the hymns. The Yajur Veda, containing sacrificial formulas, comes from the priests who performed the ritual actions. The Sama Veda is a collection of chants, many of which are taken from the Rig Veda. The Atharva Veda comes from those who focused on concrete needs of the people, such as healing, and contains magical spells and incantations. The Vedas were originally passed on orally, and so the texts were literally *shruti*, "that which is heard."

According to some schools of traditional Hinduism, the Vedas are eternal. Like the cosmos itself, they have no beginning and no end. Sanskrit is held to be a divine, eternal language. Some Hindu schools have claimed that the texts are without authors, though others see the author of the Vedas as God. The Vedas come into human experience through *rishis*, seers who have purified their consciousness and see the eternal truth of the divine Word (*Vak*). The Word is sometimes personified as a goddess, Speech, who can be identified as Sarasvati, the consort of the god Brahma. But the Word also appears in other texts as impersonal. The sacred Word is filled with divine power and is the universal principle of life, the energy that shapes the cosmos and human life. It has been compared to the Logos in Christianity.[45] The Word revealed herself to the ancient seers, and they expressed the revelation in their hymns.

For many Hindus, this revelation was not a supernatural event, but rather the result of careful discipline through yogic exercises, leading to enlightenment. The Word is present to all humans, but obstructions prevent most humans from perceiving it. Many Hindus have stressed the importance of direct experience to the point of making the role of *shruti* secondary. On this view, the revelation is grounded in spiritual insight, which is open in principle to anyone and is not necessarily mediated through the Vedas.[46] Each practitioner can come to know and confirm the truth of the Vedas through direct personal experience (*anubhava*).[47] The Vedas are a ladder, but once the experience is attained it can be discarded.

This view was proposed by Vivekananda, the inspiring Hindu representative at the Parliament of the World's Religions in 1893, and it has been widely accepted by both Hindu and Western scholars.[48] It has also been severely challenged, however, at least insofar as it is applied to one of India's most important religious thinkers, Shankara (ca. 788-820). Anantanand Rambachan has argued that Shankara does not acknowledge any independent experience or reasoning that can confirm the revelation of *brahman*† that is offered in the Upanishads. Because *brahman* is without qualities, Shankara maintains that it is only through the authority of *shruti* that humans can know ultimate reality.[49] Rambachan comments that, for Shankara, "[b]rahman is the ever-present Self of every human being and, indeed, of everything that exists. As the Self, *brahman* is already attained but incorrectly known. The words of *shruti* constitute, for Shankara, the valid means of knowing *brahman*."[50] For Shankara, according to Rambachan, there is no need for or possibility of deriving the revelation offered in the Vedas from any type of experience. The words of the Vedas themselves are sufficient to remove the erroneous opinions that obstruct true knowledge of the self. In this understanding, revelation comes in the Vedas, not in personal experience.

Sacred texts of the second category, *smrti*, have lesser authority in principle, though in practice they have often played a greater role in the lives of most Hindus. *Smrti*, "that which is remembered," refers to later tradition which interprets *shruti*. These texts serve to present the truth of revelation in a more accessible form for a broad audience, interpreting the eternal moral truth in terms appropriate for a particular age. The precise limits of *smrti* were never defined. Among the works were Sutras (literally, "threads," that is, mnemonic devices), Law Books, and the Puranas (long mythological works about the gods). The two massive epics, the *Mahabharata* and the *Ramayana*, are the most important of these texts; and the *Bhagavad Gita*, which is a section of the *Mahabharata*, has become the most beloved sacred text in later Hinduism, sometimes being included among the Upanishads.

While there is no evidence of belief in rebirth or reincarnation in the Rig Veda, all the later philosophical religious traditions of India's Axial Age—Hinduism, Buddhism, and Jainism—believe in karma[†] and rebirth. Karma is the law of cause and effect that dominates human life. Every act will bring a consequence; as we sow, so shall we reap, whether in this lifetime or another. This ineluctable link between act and consequence is the working of dharma, which is the cosmic law governing all events and beings. "As a man acts, as he behaves, so does he become. Whoso does good, becomes good: whoso does evil he becomes evil."[51] Rebirth was regarded as suffering; and liberation, *moksha*, meant freedom from the cycle of birth and death and oneness with the Absolute. The classical Indian religious paths were rigorously practical, focusing on the path to liberation. The goal of the Upanishads was to offer the saving knowledge that would bring release from the cycle of birth and death.

Of the hymns found in the Rig Veda, one of the most influential on the later course of Indian civilization is the account of the sacrifice of the cosmic giant Purusha (*Rig Veda* 10.90). The creation of the world came from the dismemberment of the primeval male, Purusha, who is the victim in a Vedic sacrifice. From the members of his body the gods fashioned the four social classes: the mouth became the Brahmins, the arms became the warrior caste, the thighs became the people, and the feet became the servants. Purusha is both the victim whom the gods sacrificed and also the divinity to whom the sacrifice was offered, both the subject and the object of the sacrifice. This hymn set the model for early Hindu rituals and visions of society: cosmic and social order is born from a sacrifice, and humans must imitate this order to survive.[52]

THE UPANISHADS

Of the Vedic texts, the Upanishads have generally had the greatest influence on later Indian thought. They came to be called "Vedanta," the end of the Veda. "Upanishad" in Sanskrit means "connection" or "equivalence."[53] The Upanishads assume that there are hierarchical connections in the universe and seek to convey knowledge of the highest reality. These connections, however, are hidden, and the knowledge that is offered by the Upanishads is a secret knowledge. By recognizing the hidden connections, a person becomes one with the reality recognized. This belief sets up a tremendous interest in identifying things with other things. For example, the opening of the *Brihadaranyaka* Upanishad identifies the parts of the body of a sacrificial horse with the elements of the universe: The head is the dawn, the sight is the sun, the breath is the wind, and the mouth is fire. The body is the year, and the back is the sky. R. C. Zaehner comments: "The idea behind these fantastic identifications is that the sacrificer, by gaining control of the sacrificial horse, thereby gains control of the whole cosmic process, and by *knowing* this process he *becomes* it."[54] The sacrifice corresponds to the parts of the universe, and, as we have seen, the primordial sacrifice, according to the Rig Veda, was that of *Purusha*, the primal man. Thus, by understanding the sacrifice, humans come see themselves as identical with the all.

There are dominant themes in the Upanishads, but there is no single doctrine or philosophical position, and later Hindu scholars have found support for a variety of conflicting views in them. One reason for the multiple interpretations is that the language of the Upanishads delights in paradox, if not contradiction. The logic of "*Neti, neti*," "Not this, not that," runs throughout. Language cannot literally describe *brahman*, ultimate reality, and so the language that is used evokes a sense of what cannot be said. The Upanishads demythologize the gods of the earlier Rig Veda. The earlier polytheism yields to a sense that all the gods are reducible to one underlying reality. Amid the wide variety of later Hindu paths, the principle of the Rig Veda was widely held: "God is one but humans call him by many names."

The central message of the Upanishads is often taken to be the identification of the self and ultimate reality, of *atman*[†] and *brahman*. *Atman* is the reflexive pronoun in Sanskrit and refers to the individual self, which came to be identified with the universal Self. *Atman* can never be fully defined and described, however; for the negative logic of *neti, neti*, "not this, not that," applies here as well. The self can be described primarily by negating possible attributes. The sage Yajnavalkya explains: "About this self (*atman*), one can say 'not—, not—.' He is ungraspable, for he cannot be grasped. He is undecaying, for he is not subject to decay. He has nothing sticking to him, for he does not stick to anything. He is not bound, yet he neither trembles in fear nor suffers injury" (*Brihadaranyaka* Upanishad 3.9.27; p. 51). While the self cannot be defined, it became clear to the teachers in the Upanishads that it cannot be identified with the body. When properly known, it is not bound by corporeal limitations.

Brahman originally meant "sacred word" or "sacred power" and came to mean "the sacred in general, that is to say, the eternal and time-less reality that sustains the transient universe."[55] *Brahman* cannot be captured in the usual structure of language which distinguishes subjects from objects; but we experience *brahman* as the very power that enables us to talk, to think, to see. It is "not this—, not that—." *Brahman* is the power that allows even the Vedic gods to function. The *Kena* Upanishad presents a rather humorous narrative of the Vedic gods learning the power of *brahman*. *Brahman* has won a victory for the gods, but the gods do not recognize their dependence on *brahman* and congratulate themselves instead. *Brahman* manifests itself to them without the gods being able to recognize it. They send Agni, the god of fire, to interrogate the strange appearance. Agni boasts about being able to burn up every-thing in the universe; but when *brahman* challenges the god of fire to burn a blade of grass, Agni cannot do so. Next Vayu, the god of wind, approaches and boasts of being able to blow everything on earth away. But when *brahman* challenges the god of wind to blow away a blade of grass, Vayu is powerless to do so. When Indra, the king of the Vedic gods, approaches, *brahman* vanishes; and a woman name Uma, repre-senting divine wisdom, appears instead. Uma instructs Indra as to the identity of *brahman* (*Kena* Upanishad 3:1-4:2).

The *Isha* Upanishad is sometimes taken to be the heart of the Upan-ishads. *Isha* means "Lord" or "God," whom the Upanishad proclaims as pervading the universe: "This whole world is to be dwelt in by the Lord, whatever living being there is in the world" (*Isha* Upanishad 1; p. 248). The critical turning point is to see all beings in one's self: "When a man sees all beings within his very self, and his self within all beings, It will not seek to hide from him" (*Isha* Upanishad 6; p. 249). If one understands all things in the self and the self in all things, then there are no ultimate dichotomies. "When in the self of a discerning man his very self has become all beings, What bewilderment, what sorrow can there be, regarding that self of him who sees this oneness" (*Isha* Upanishad 7; p. 249). The ultimate is beyond knowledge and ignorance, beyond becom-ing and non-becoming.

The *Isha* Upanishad ends with a hymn to Agni, the god of fire, invok-ing his aid as a guide to final bliss. He, like the Greek god Hermes, knows all ways. And yet he is already within us. The role of the sun and fire is very important and recurs throughout the Upanishads. Fire is one way of imagining the relation of the microcosm to the macrocosm. The universal fire, Agni, which is the universe itself, is imagined as an open mouth. Every human possesses the universal fire, which is part of the universe, a spark of the sun within us. Thus we can recognize our self in the whole.

The Upanishads reflect on and transform the meaning of the earlier Vedic sacrifices. In a traditional sacrifice there was one upper-caste

Brahmin who did not perform any outward action but sat and meditated on the sacrifice in his mind while other Vedic priests performed the ritual. If a mistake was made, the meditating Brahmin would interrupt and correct the other priests. The Upanishads develop the process of meditating on the ritual, and they interiorize the meaning of sacrifice. The key to liberation is to understand the proper meaning of the sacrifice, not to perform it outwardly. The sacrifice teaches our identity with *brahman*. The Upanishads began to question the value of animal sacrifices, and the movements of Jainism and Buddhism sought to eliminate sacrifice altogether and replace it with *ahimsa*,[†] nonviolence. Because violence was believed to create bad karma and bring evil consequences, the motive for nonviolence was generally enlightened self-interest.[56]

The Upanishads offer their readers a salvific knowledge that frees humans from suffering and the cycle of rebirth. Ordinarily, humans act out of desire in ignorance of their true nature. Such actions bind the self to particular impressions, memories, and consequences. These actions also imprison humans in the cycle of suffering. To know the unchanging *brahman* is to find release. Knowledge that the true self is one with ultimate reality cuts through the bonds of ignorance and desire. The result is a unified consciousness, fearlessness, bliss, and tranquillity.

This has often been understood as a monistic philosophy which denies the reality of all distinctions. The refrain of many Upanishads, "That art thou [*tat tvam asi*]," has often been interpreted as denying any ultimate distinctions between humans and the ultimate. This was the basis for the later philosophical interpretation of nondualism called Advaita Vedanta[†] (nondual Vedanta) proposed by Shankara, which came to be the most broadly accepted philosophical system in India.[57] Advaita Vedanta denies that distinctions are ultimately real.[58]

The Upanishads themselves, however, insist on the logic of "not this, not that"; and they have been interpreted by Indian thinkers in a wide variety of ways, not all of them monistic. Some have seen in the Upanishads an affirmation of unity in diversity.[59] The *Shvetashvatara* Upanishad proposes a theistic perspective, maintaining that there is one God who creates and saves: "Some wise men say it is inherent nature, while others say it is time—all totally deluded. It is rather the greatness of God present in the world by means of which this wheel of *brahman* goes around." (*Shvetashvatara* Upanishad 6.1; p. 263). God is "the creator of all; the knower of all; . . . and the cause of liberation from remaining within, and bondage to the rebirth cycle" (*Shvetashvatara* Upanishad 6:16; p. 264).

THE *BHAGAVAD GITA*

Closely related to the *Shvetashvatara* Upanishad is the *Bhagavad Gita*. The full title of this work is *Bhagavad-gitopanishad*, "The Upanishad Sung by the Lord."[60] The *Bhagavad Gita* is one small section of the *Mahabharata* ("The Song of the Great Bharata Dynasty"), the enormously long warrior epic that recounts a great struggle over the succession to the throne of a kingdom in northern India. The family of the Pandavas are pitted against their rivals, the Kuravas. War becomes inevitable, and both parties raise armies and make alliances. Just before the climactic battle, the Pandava warrior Arjuna hesitates, not wishing to kill his kinsmen on the other side. The god Vishnu, who is incarnate as an avatar in Krishna, the charioteer, has a lengthy discussion with Arjuna right before the battle in the middle of the battlefield.

Vishnu was a minor god in the Vedas and the Upanishads, but in the *Mahabharata* he is the one supreme God, ultimate reality. He is variously a personal God and the impersonal Absolute. He enters the world in times of crisis to restore *dharma* (order). Vishnu becomes incarnate in a series of avatars, taking the form of the charioteer Krishna to advise Arjuna on his duty as a member of the warrior caste. Krishna describes himself as the maker of the Vedanta, which means the Upanishads (*Bhagavad Gita* 15:15). Thus the *Bhagavad Gita* presents itself as the summing up of the meaning of the Vedic revelation.

On the battlefield, just before combat is about to begin, Arjuna has doubts about the fighting. He worries about the moral dilemma of killing his opponents, who include relatives he has known all his life. Among the enemy army are wise statesmen and noble, virtuous men. Arjuna worries that no possible gain is worth killing them. He is not afraid to die, and he does not want to kill others. Killing will bring karmic effects that will create future suffering for him. In reply, Krishna delivers a series of discourses on the proper duty of the warrior, though many other topics are brought into the discussion. On one level, the advice of Krishna to Arjuna is to perform the actions proper to his caste. The warrior's responsibility is to fight and kill. Doing this duty well is better than doing the duty of someone else. Arjuna should do the *dharma* of a warrior (*kshatriya*), not that of a world-renouncer.

When Arjuna still refuses to fight, preferring to be a beggar than to feast on the blood of his kinsmen and teachers, Krishna offers a longer exhortation to do battle. Krishna distinguishes between the apparent transience of human existence and the eternal within us that never dies: "Because we all have been for all time: I and thou, and those kings of men. And we all shall be for all time, we all for ever and ever" (2:12; p. 49). Death itself is an illusion: "If any man thinks he slays, and if another thinks he is slain, neither knows the ways of truth. The Eternal in man cannot kill: the Eternal in man cannot die" (2:19: p. 50). The discipline of knowledge (*jnana-yoga*†) teaches the indestructibility of the true self.

In another argument Krishna stresses the glory of doing one's duty as a warrior: "There is no greater good for a warrior than to fight in a righteous war. There is a war that opens the doors of heaven, Arjuna! Happy the warriors whose fate is to fight such war. But to forgo this fight for righteousness is to forgo thy duty and honour" (2:31-32; p. 51).

In addition to the discussion of the warrior's duty, there are also extended passages regarding *brahman* in the style of the Upanishads. In these passages Vishnu is the source of *brahman* and all the gods. All other gods are simply aspects of Vishnu's being.

Krishna instructs Arjuna on the necessity of action without attachment to the consequences. *Karma-yoga*† teaches the way to act according to the duty of a warrior without building up negative karma for the future. If we worry about the results of our work, we are caught in the bonds of desire and selfhood and will not achieve integration of the self and spiritual growth. In response to this danger, *karma-yoga* appears as a practical system of mental and spiritual discipline to help us gain complete detachment. A fully developed yogi views all persons equally without discriminating between friends and enemies, good and evil (6:9). "Day after day, let the Yogi practise the harmony of the soul: in a secret place, in deep solitude, master of his mind, hoping for nothing, desiring nothing" (6:10; p. 70). Freedom from attachment brings freedom from karma. Like the teachers of the Upanishads, Krishna teaches that when we abandon all desire we find *brahman*.

There is still another dimension to the *Bhagavad Gita* which presents Vishnu as the supreme God and absolute reality and calls for devotion (*bhakti*) to him. Vishnu is the God of love, seeking love from humans and intervening in human history to help humans. *Bhakti-yoga*,† the discipline of devotion, offers another path to spiritual development which is open to all. People in the world who do not practice yoga for hours at a time can perform actions of devotion, offering a leaf, a flower, a piece of fruit, a libation of water. These offerings need not be expensive, but they must be given with the proper spirit of loving devotion. Whatever the devotee does should be done for the love and glory of God, without thinking of one's own personal advantage. Through *bhakti*, devotees are freed from the shackles of past karma and receive the grace of Krishna. Especially crucial is the attitude of the person at the moment of death. Krishna promises that someone who at the hour of death bears him in mind with devotion will go straight to him (8:5). Thus humans should bear Krishna in mind at all times, especially when going into battle. The path of devotion, unlike the earlier Vedic rituals and knowledge, is open to all humans, to women as well as men, to members of every caste, the evil and the virtuous. Devoting the fruits of one's actions to God makes possible full devotion to God in every walk of life.

Krishna is one of a series of avatars, or incarnations, of Vishnu. Krishna variously appears as an ordinary human being and also as the unborn Lord of all beings, who through his supernatural power has come to be in human form. The *Bhagavad Gita* does not try to explain this process; it simply asserts it. Later on, Hindus would develop various lists of avatars, including a series of animal forms, Rama, and sometimes also the Buddha. Early in the twentieth century some Hindus would interpret Jesus as one of the avatars of Vishnu, thus making a place for devotion to Jesus as an incarnation of God within the Hindu *bhakti* tradition.

The climactic revelatory scene in the *Bhagavad Gita* comes when Arjuna asks Krishna to reveal his divine glory. Arjuna, having heard Krishna explain the divine glory, wishes to experience it for himself. In reply Krishna invites him: "See now the whole universe with all things that move and move not, and whatever thy soul may yearn to see. See it all as One in me" (11:7; p. 89). Krishna then endows Arjuna with divine sight and appears to him in his divine form. Arjuna sees infinite power and majesty, infinite beauty, and all the gods and other beings in unity within God. The glory is both beautiful and terrible, and so Arjuna asks for a further revelation, seeking to know God more fully (11:31). Krishna replies: "I am all-powerful Time which destroys all things, and I have come here to slay these men. Even if thou dost not fight, all warriors facing thee shall die" (11:32; p. 92). At this, Arjuna proclaims that all people should love and adore God and sing God's praises. Exalted and terrified, Arjuna presents his homage, laments his earlier forgetfulness and easy-going manner with his charioteer, and asks Krishna to show again his human form (11:45). Krishna declares that this vision has been a unique revelation, which cannot be obtained through the Vedas or sacrifices or studies or rituals. Only to Arjuna has it been granted to see the divine form. "Only by love can men see me, and know me, and come unto me" (11:54; p. 95).

There is a stark contrast between the image of Vishnu as the God of love and the stern commands to kill one's kinsmen in war. Many Indians, uncomfortable with the violence demanded by Krishna in the text, have taken the *Bhagavad Gita* out of its original context in the *Mahabharata* and interpreted it as a spiritual struggle within the human soul. On this understanding, the war is not a concrete historical struggle but a symbolic one. As Origen interpreted the bloody conquest narratives of the Hebrew Bible not as outward military battles but as allegories of the human soul, so many interpreters of the *Bhagavad Gita* have stressed that this battle is an internal struggle. Juan Mascaró finds a basis in the text itself for this reading: Krishna tells Arjuna: "Be a warrior and kill desire, the powerful enemy of the soul" (4:43; pp. 23, 60). Later on, Krishna reinforces the symbolic sense of battle: "Kill therefore with the sword of wisdom the doubt born of ignorance that lies in thy heart" (4:42; p. 65). Mascaró comments: "Arjuna becomes the soul of man and Krishna becomes the charioteer of the soul."[61]

Early in the twentieth century the *Bhagavad Gita* came to be regarded as the most significant of the Hindu scriptures, a position it did not have before. Mohandas Gandhi took the ideals of the *Bhagavad Gita* in an allegorical sense as referring to the battle within the soul, and he combined these with the teaching of Jesus in the Sermon on the Mount as a basis for practical nonviolent strategies of political protest. Gandhi popularized the *Bhagavad Gita*'s call to be actively involved in one's duty in the world without clinging to results and consequences. He commented: "Krishna is the Dweller within, ever whispering to a pure heart. . . . Under the guise of physical warfare [the *Gita*] described the duel that perpetually went on in the hearts of mankind. . . . Physical warfare was brought in merely to make the description of the internal duel more alluring."[62] For Gandhi, self-rule meant primarily mastery of one's self. It is one of the great ironies of the history of religious thought that Gandhi could take a text that explicitly urges violence in obedience to duty, interpret it as a text of nonviolence, relate this text to the teaching of Jesus on nonviolence in the Sermon on the Mount, and demonstrate the practical effectiveness of nonviolent tactics on an unprecedented scale.

Hinduism and Christianity

Many of the assumptions of Hindu revelation are radically different from those of Judaism and Christianity. While Hindus often note the lack of a single dogma in their tradition, the belief in rebirth and karma was an unquestioned assumption of all classical Hindu schools from the time of the Upanishads on. The Hindu belief in rebirth sets up a perspective on human existence that is very different from that of the Bible.

Hindus generally hold that there is no eternal hell, no possibility of humans falling into endless suffering. One passage in the *Bhagavad Gita*, however, has been understood to imply a final separation from Vishnu, with no hope of salvation. Zaehner maintains that Krishna's words about those who choose evil repeatedly "seem to be final": "Birth after birth in this revolving round, these vilest among men, strangers to [all] good, obsessed with hate and cruel, I ever hurl into devilish wombs. Caught up in devilish wombs, birth after birth defiled, they never attain to Me: and so they tread the lowest way."[63] For most of the Hindu tradition, however, evil deeds bring their own punishment; but even the worst karmic consequences can be worked through in time.

The teaching of the Upanishads has often been understood as a monism that contradicts the Jewish and Christian sense of a transcendent God who creates the world. The Upanishads themselves, however, offer a variety of perspectives, which are reflected in the later Hindu tradition. Many Hindus affirm the immanence of God in the world, but they do not simply identify God with the universe. In the eleventh century, Ramanuja taught belief in a personal *brahman* who transcends the world but is intimately involved in the world. Ramanuja denied that the Upanishads' basic principle implied an undifferentiated monism: "In texts, again, such as 'Thou art that,' the co-ordination of the constituent parts is not meant to convey the idea of the absolute unity of a non-differenced substance; on the contrary, the words 'that' and 'thou' denote a *Brahman* distinguished by difference."[64] All beings are one in *brahman* without losing their individual identity. Ramanuja stressed the need for devotion (*bhakti*) to God, and for divine grace to free persons from ignorance.[65] Ramanuja's affirmation of unity in distinction can be compared to Nicholas of Cusa's understanding of God as not other than the universe. Both thinkers see ultimate reality as in all things and all things as in ultimate reality, but both also affirm distinction and individual identity.

Of all the world's religions, Hinduism in some ways comes closest to Christianity in proclaiming revelation as the incarnation of a God of love.[66] While Jews and Muslims vigorously deny the possibility of God becoming incarnate and while Buddhists do not believe in a creating and redeeming God, the *Bhagavad Gita* presents Vishnu, the creator of all things, as entering into this world in human form to establish order, oppose evil, and offer salvation to humans. The central purpose of an avatar is to restore *dharma* in the world. An avatar reveals the gracious love of a personal God and invites humans to love God in return and to act in accordance with *dharma*. Avatars also offer examples of proper conduct for humans to follow. As Geoffrey Parrinder notes, this special revelation of God's love presupposes and builds on a more general knowledge of God available in scripture, conscience, and the natural world.[67]

While there is certainly a similarity between Christianity and Hinduism in the general notion of the God of love who creates the universe and comes into the world in human form to offer salvation to humans, nonetheless, it is impossible to identify the Christian understanding of incarnation with the Hindu notion of the avatars. For most Christians, the historical character of the incarnation of God in Jesus Christ is of central importance for Christian faith. For many Hindus, such as Sri Aurobindo and Mohandas Gandhi, the historical character of an avatar is not important at all. Rama and Krishna may have been historical figures, but nothing is known of them for certain. For many Hindus, it would not make a difference if they existed or not. Christian faith, by contrast, has placed great importance on the historical existence of Jesus.

Moreover, the incarnation of God in Jesus Christ is proclaimed as unique, while becoming an avatar is a repeated process in Hinduism. Vishnu takes on a series of lives, including animals. More recently, Ramakrishna (1834-1886) and Gandhi (1869-1948) have been regarded as avatars. Hindus often regard the Christian claim of the uniqueness of the incarnation of God in Jesus Christ as a rather provincial narrowness. Ramakrishna himself viewed avatars as human messengers of God, "human beings with extraordinary original powers and entrusted with a divine commission" (*The Gospel of Ramakrishna* 300).[68] This is, however, rather different from the view of the *Bhagavad Gita* itself, where Krishna is not simply a human messenger but a divine theophany.

Another difference from the Christian tradition is that there is no idea of a suffering God in Hinduism, and no narrative of an avatar falling victim to evil powers in this world. In the *Bhagavad Gita* Krishna does not take part in the battle directly. At the end of his life, he is killed by being shot in the heel by a hunter who mistakes him for a deer. This is simply the end of his earthly life at a time when he is ready to leave the earth. There is no sense of the suffering being central. To many Hindus, the centrality of the cross in Christianity is puzzling.

BUDDHISM

Buddhism is the only major world religion that does not claim to be based upon a revelation coming from God. Siddhartha Gautama, who became Shakyamuni Buddha through his enlightenment, presented himself not as a prophet who had received a divine message but as a pathfinder who had discovered the way to freedom from suffering. The liberating insight of the Buddha is at the center of Buddhist life. The heart of the Buddhist path lies in the inseparable virtues of wisdom and compassion. While there are many different varieties of Buddhist practice in different cultures and epochs, the distinctive shape of wisdom and compassion comes originally from the awakening and example of Shakyamuni Buddha himself. The great variety of Buddhist perspectives and practices precludes any brief summary from being comprehensive. What follows is a cursory attempt to name widespread Buddhist teachings and values. Because of the great flexibility and adaptability of Buddhism over the centuries, there will be exceptions to most generalizations somewhere in the Buddhist world.

Buddhism arose from the awakening of Prince Siddhartha Gautama, a prince born into a royal family in Nepal who became dissatisfied with his pampered life at court and decided to seek a radical liberation from suffering. According to the *Buddhacarita*, one of the most influential narratives of the life of the Buddha, the prince's father had been told that his newborn son would become either a great political ruler or a great religious leader.[69] Desiring a son who would reign in power and glory, King Suddodhana decided to shield his son from all awareness of suffering so that he would never become dissatisfied with his life as a prince.

As a young man, however, Siddhartha had a series of encounters outside the palace walls that changed his life. On successive journeys, he met an old man, an extremely ill man, a corpse, and a wandering ascetic dressed as a beggar. His eyes were opened to the pervasiveness of suffering in the world, and he resolved to leave his wife and son and palace in order to find a cure. His search took him through various meditation teachers and included rigorous ascetic practices. No external guide or ascetic practice could teach him the ultimate truth, however. In the end, he rejected all extreme forms of asceticism, preferring the Middle Way between extremes. After prolonged searching, solitary meditation led him to a solution.

The Buddha expressed the wisdom that he discovered in the Four Noble Truths, the traditional summary of his first preaching after his enlightenment.[70] The First Noble Truth proclaims that life is *dukkha*,[†] a word often translated as "suffering," but more broadly meaning "unsatisfactory." No matter how joyful any given moment may be, it is transitory and impermanent and thus fails to satisfy. All life, all union, all relationships lead to separation. The Second Noble Truth teaches that the origin of the unsatisfactoriness of life is *tanha*, a word often translated as "desire," but perhaps better translated as "thirsting" or "craving" or "grasping." Our craving for people and things and existence itself traps us in patterns of grasping at realities that cannot satisfy us. *Tanha* is desire out of control that imprisons us in unnecessary suffering. Craving in turn arises from a fundamental misconception about human identity, the belief in a perduring, substantial self.

The Third Noble Truth promises that there is an end to suffering and the unsatisfactoriness of life. Nirvana[†] is the extinguishing of the flame of craving and desire. It is not annihilation or escape from this world; it is the stillness that brings tranquillity and the ability to encounter other beings free from the distorting lens of our own addictions. Liberation involves seeing through the delusions of the illusory self so that we can see reality as it is. Nirvana serves as a name for the unconditioned, the timeless, the absolute. Mahayana Buddhists in particular insist that nirvana is not other than the world of impermanence and suffering and change. Thus the experience of nirvana is not only something that happens after death; it is a possibility for us in the present moment. The Fourth Noble Truth points to a concrete way to be free from unsatisfactoriness: the Eightfold Path.

The Four Noble Truths can be compared to the identification and diagnosis of an illness, the promise of a cure, and the specific remedy to be followed. Shakyamuni Buddha's insight is a concrete path of liberation. What may appear strange to Christians is that there is no reliance upon a creating and redeeming God. The Buddha is neither a God incarnate nor a prophet from God; according to the earliest Buddhist texts, he is a pathfinder who points the way to freedom. Refusing to become embroiled in intellectual debates over theory, he pointed to the Eightfold Path and invited others to experience it for themselves.

The Eightfold Path is often divided into the three trainings: morality, meditation, and wisdom. While later Mahayana Buddhists have frequently talked about transcending the opposition between good and evil, the Buddhist Path always presupposes a foundation in morality (*shila*): right speech, right action, and right livelihood. The core of Buddhist morality is contained in the Five Precepts: do not kill, do not take what is not one's own, do not engage in sexual misconduct, do not speak falsely, and do not use intoxicants. Apart from basic moral conduct, Buddhists warn, no spiritual practice can help us.

The Eightfold Path develops depth and strength through training in meditation (*samadhi*): right effort, right mindfulness, and right concentration. Here steady and patient mental discipline tames the mind and calms the emotions. Training in meditation is the hinge of Buddhist spirituality, providing the means of moving beyond the basic moral practice enjoined on all Buddhists to the deeper wisdom of the enlightened. The Eightfold Path culminates in wisdom or salvific insight (*prajna*), which consists of right insight and right thought. The order of the three trainings can vary, with right insight and right thought sometimes being placed at the beginning, as the cognitive reorientation that is necessary for practice. The sequence is not simply a chronological progression because on the Path each of the steps is interdependent with all the others. Progress in one area leads to progress in the others. Buddhism is the practice of realizing the Four Noble Truths in one's own life by following the Eightfold Path. It is not a speculative theory about the universe to be debated but a path to be explored in practice.

At the center of the Buddha's view of human existence is the teaching that there is no substantial, self-existent self (*anatta/anatman*). The scriptures of Mahayana Buddhism proclaim paradoxically that a bodhisattva[†] (a future Buddha) is to liberate countless beings, but there is no bodhisattva to accomplish liberation and there are no beings to be liberated.[71] For Christians accustomed to affirming the reality and value of the self, this is one of the most paradoxical teachings of Buddhism and may well sound nonsensical; but it is important to note that it is grounded in a deep sense of the interdependence of all realities. Even though it appears in negative form, the teaching of no-self is actually a positive affirmation of the interrelatedness of human life.[72] The denial of the self does not reject the beauty and value and importance of human life; instead, it relates humanity to the entire cosmos. Our identity is not found in being an independent, isolated, self-contained unit; it is rather an ongoing process of constantly interacting with all the other beings around us. Even our body itself, though it appears to be solid, is not an impermeable barrier but rather a process of taking in and giving forth. Each breath relates us to the cosmos and the cosmos to us. Our consciousness, our thoughts, our emotions are in constant flux. For Buddhists, to say that we have no self means that there is no independently existing, substantial self. We are an interconnected network of relationships.

Buddhists view humanity as an integral part of the entire cosmos, and thus the context for understanding humanity is the interdependent nature of the entire universe. There is a mutual causality between us and every other being, but there is no ultimate ground or creating God in the Christian sense. Mahayana Buddhists often insist that nirvana, ultimate reality, is *samsara*,[†] the passing world of suffering and change. This sets up a view of human existence and the cosmos that is very different from that of Christianity. Nonetheless, in the Christian tradition, Nicholas of Cusa taught a vision of the universe that often comes surprisingly close to Buddhist language. Nicholas insisted that even though God is radically transcendent and infinite, God is not other (*non aliud*) than the world; for if God were other, God would be another finite thing. The infinite Oneness is never experienced apart from the manifold things of the universe, but it is their deepest point of unity. Nicholas of Cusa, rooted in the age-old Christian Neoplatonic tradition, also insisted that all things in the universe are in all other things: "For in each created thing the universe is this created thing; and each thing receives all things in such a way that in a given thing all things are, contractedly, this thing."[73] This sets up a deep sense of the interconnectedness of all things in the universe that can be compared to, but not identified with, Buddhist perspectives.

For Buddhists, the cosmic vision of the interconnectedness of all things forms the context for human life. Humans have a special place in the cosmos because we alone can escape from the cycle of rebirth and suffering. While humans have a privileged opportunity and responsibility, humans are not of intrinsically higher value than other beings in the cosmos. All beings are to be valued just as they are, not in relation to some allegedly higher form of existence. The world is not given to us to be exploited or dominated, and the First Precept commands that we respect the life of every living being in whatever state of existence. While Buddhists acknowledge that in its strict form this precept is an ideal that is impossible to realize perfectly, it demands respect for the value of life in all its forms. At a time when ecological awareness is increasing, the Buddhist sense of interdependence can be illuminating for all traditions.

In the original context of northern India, Shakyamuni Buddha's teaching of no-self challenged the underlying assumptions of the caste system. In traditional Hindu society, the reality of a permanent self determined one's responsibilities according to caste from the moment of one's birth until death. As we have seen, the *Purusha-Sukhta* in the *Rig Veda* grounded the caste system in the sacrifice of the primordial man. In the *Bhagavad Gita*, Krishna insisted that Arjuna should perform the *dharma* of a warrior rather than renounce fighting. For the Buddha to deny the reality of the self meant that there was no permanent reality whose fate was fixed at birth in one caste or another. In light of this principle, the Buddha modeled a new way of shaping human life. Thus the early Buddhist monastic community was very different from anything in earlier Indian history. In traditional Indian society, it would have been unthinkable for an upper-caste monk to beg from a lower-caste lay person. Buddhist monks, however, begged food from persons of all castes, and thus the begging bowl concretely expressed the interdependence of all people in society. The Buddhist *sangha,*† the monastic community, offered an example for a new way of organizing social relations.

SUFFERING

According to the Buddha, suffering arises from a fundamental mistake in our thinking, the belief in an independent, substantial self. Suffering then spreads through the inevitable law of cause and effect which is called karma. Shakyamuni Buddha taught that the source of unnecessary suffering is craving and grasping. Craving and grasping in turn come from the vain effort to deny the basic truths of impermanence and no-self. Even though all things pass, we refuse to admit this and thus grasp at other beings in a vain effort to wring security and safety from them. We bid them guarantee our identity, but they cannot do this. To make matters worse, we make a sharp distinction between "me" and "you" and between "mine" and "yours," and in so doing we cut ourselves off from other people and the world of nature. We usher ourselves into a world of envy, rivalry, and competition. Trapped in the illusion of an independent, separate self, we ceaselessly create suffering for ourselves and others.

The law of karma ensures that suffering has further effects. Thoughts inevitably shape actions, and actions inevitably produce results. The thoughts and actions may be good, bad, or neutral; their effects will inevitably reflect their own character. This is not an extrinsic system of reward and punishment. It is the automatic functioning of the universe. Westerners have often thought that belief in karma leads to pessimism and fatalism. If everything is determined by karma, it seems that action is useless. For Buddhists, however, the conclusion is just the opposite. The doctrine of karma teaches us that we can shape our own lives. While we inevitably must suffer the effects of our past misdeeds, we can radically reorient our thoughts and actions and thereby produce good results in the future. The beginning of the *Dhammapada*, a traditional collection of sayings of the Buddha, proclaims: "What we are today comes from our thoughts of yesterday, and our present thoughts build our life of tomorrow: our life is the creation of our mind."[74] The doctrine of karma can be compared to the belief in the act–consequence relation in the wisdom tradition of the Bible. The sages of Israel saw actions as carrying intrinsic consequences that followed inevitably according to the moral order of the universe. The central difference is that Buddhist thought on karma has usually assumed the teaching on rebirth.

Buddhists often warn that because we do not like to suffer, for the most part we block out awareness of suffering by deadening our consciousness and our feelings. Thus we are not even aware of the seriousness of our true condition. The denial of suffering can occur explicitly through deadening our consciousness by the abuse of alcohol and drugs, or it can come through refusing to focus on problematic areas of our lives, or simply through a hectic schedule that allows no time for reflection on ourselves. We can pretend that everything is satisfactory when in fact it is not. The story of Prince Siddhartha's early life is a parable of the denial of suffering.[75] The prince's father scrupulously prevented the young prince from seeing any sign of sickness, poverty, or death. Siddhartha grew up in an unreal world where people do not grow old or die or suffer from want. In this world separation does not threaten relationships. The extreme conditions of his upbringing represent in dramatic form the wide variety of ways in which we can block out suffering from our awareness. While most people are not given the luxury of denying suffering to the same degree as the young Prince Siddhartha, the temptation is universal.

The first step in Buddhist awakening is to become aware of suffering with an eye to liberation. This means to be aware of the suffering in our own lives and also to open our eyes and ears and minds to the tremendous suffering around us throughout the world. The beginning of Buddhist meditation practice opens our awareness to the countless forms of suffering that we have kept from surfacing. Simply sitting in quiet meditation is a powerful tool to open oneself to the awareness of suffering. The physical discomfort of the beginning practitioner often combines with memories of past misdeeds and awareness of emotional turbulence. The initial stages of meditation practice may well be extremely challenging, physically, mentally, and emotionally.

Buddhists sometimes compare suffering to a nightmare. It is terrifying as long as it lasts; but when we awake, we realize that it is based on an illusion and we do not have to be afraid. Buddhist hope comes from the possibility of awakening. At the center of the Buddha's awakening was the realization that suffering is not necessary. The identification of the cause of suffering leads to the hope for a cure.

THE END OF SUFFERING

The Third Noble Truth expresses the fundamental Buddhist confidence: There is an end to suffering. The negative, grasping patterns in which we trap ourselves are not necessary, are not our true identity, are not even ultimately real themselves. For Buddhist meditation traditions, the heart of Buddhist confidence is that the truth will manifest itself if there is adequate time and a proper structure of morality and meditation. It is not a question of finding what is absent but of opening ourselves to the truth that has been present all along. At the beginning of Buddhist practice, students must trust in the wisdom of the teacher. After time, however, the students come to experience insight for themselves, learning in their own minds the truth of their original confidence. The unbroken chain of teachers from Shakyamuni Buddha to the present offers testimony to the power of the Buddhist Eightfold Path. This witness offers Buddhists the concrete grounds for hope in this world.

Other traditions of Buddhism do not place the same importance upon meditation practice. The Pure Land Buddhist tradition is skeptical about the efficacy of human efforts to find enlightenment and instead trusts in the power of Amida Buddha. Pure Land Buddhists traditionally deny that self-power can bring suffering to an end. The source of hope is the vow of Amida Buddha to make available salvation to all who trust in his vow.

The significance of Buddhist hope has been repeatedly misunderstood. Western Christians have often seen Buddhist spirituality as fundamentally pessimistic and world-negating. Buddhism has been seen as encouraging the individual to withdraw from the world and seek a solitary salvation. Then the hope of Buddhism would be an abandonment of the world to itself. The Buddha's teaching on no-self, however, tells us that the problem is that we believe in a separate existence. To seek an individualistic salvation would only make the disease worse. For the Buddha, the goal named *nirodha* (cessation) or nirvana could not be a purely individual matter. Nirvana is liberation from the delusions caused by a self that does not exist, and this has consequences for our relationships with other humans and all the world.

There is a paradoxical character to Buddhist confidence, for it is grounded not simply in a vision of the future but in a deep conviction about the present. Despite the suffering caused by our illusions, many Buddhists affirm that we have never been alienated from our true identity. Oneness with absolute reality is primordially ours; it has never been absent from us; it has never been withheld from us. The Vietnamese Zen Buddhist leader Thich Nhat Hanh teaches: "True Mind is not born at the moment of Awakening, because it is neither created nor destroyed. Awakening only reveals it. This is true of nirvana and Buddhata [the Buddha-nature, ultimate reality]."[76] True Mind is like the bright blue sky, which is always there, even when clouds and storms prevent our seeing it. "The only way to realize this Mind of Unity and Thusness, which is also called True Mind is to return to oneself and to see into one's true nature."[77]

The Buddhist practitioner does not obtain something essentially new but awakens to what already is. Thich Nhat Hanh draws out the implication for practice: "Consequently, the practitioner must not await an Awakening that might come from outside, a transmission or a gift of Wisdom. Wisdom cannot be obtained, the Mind cannot transmit itself. The Heart Sutra . . . assures: 'There is no obtaining because there is no object to obtain.'"[78] Nothing has ever been withheld from us. The truth is manifest right before us at every moment, waiting for us to open our eyes. Thus there is no need for a supernatural revelation from a transcendent God.

MEDITATION

Shakyamuni Buddha originally presented himself as a pathfinder, not as a divine savior or a prophet of God. Buddhists do not believe in a divine revelation, and they do not pray to a creating, redeeming God. Thus, for Buddhists, listening to the Word of God and prayer in the Christian sense are not a part of religious devotion; but for many Buddhist traditions the practice of meditation is of central importance. Instead of accepting a revelatory message from God, Buddhist meditation practice involves opening ourselves to liberating insight and overcoming the false belief in an independent self. This is, however, a paradoxical project. As long as we are willfully and deliberately seeking to accomplish it, we cannot do so because our efforts only reinforce our own ego. The Buddha is free from cravings and desires, and so we cannot become a Buddha through cravings and desires. Buddhist morality traditionally focuses primarily on becoming the type of person who will behave selflessly, morally. But we cannot will to become selfless without increasing the strength of the ego.

One classical Buddhist strategy to overcome the problem is to apply the will not to the personality directly but to training in meditation. The Theravada practice of insight meditation (*vipassana*) instructs the student to focus attention on one's breathing and one's experiences without any reasoning, interpreting, or evaluating. According to the *Sutra on the Full Awareness of Breathing* (*Anapanasati Sutta*), Shakyamuni Buddha taught his followers constant awareness of each thought, feeling, and bodily sensation as it arises.[79] In our normal state of illusion, we grasp at pleasant experiences, we flee from unpleasant experiences, and we are bored with neutral experiences. Grasping and avoiding give rise to much of our suffering. In meditation Buddhists acknowledge all experiences without judging.

While there are a wide variety of Buddhist meditation traditions with important differences, a common Buddhist practice is to attend to the present moment, not clinging to or following after thoughts and feelings. As the mind becomes still in relation to outer stimuli, there will often be a tremendous emotional upheaval within. We become aware of the suffering we have been carrying about within ourselves unawares. A frequent Buddhist strategy is to acknowledge every emotion, no matter how powerful, without clinging or rejecting. As anger, jealousy, greed, lust, and hatred appear, they are neither grasped at nor repulsed but simply acknowledged and observed. Negative emotions often appear as ferocious beings that seek to upset the practitioner. The Buddha himself went through such temptations on the night of his enlightenment; and the later Tibetan Buddhist Milarepa told the story of fierce, ugly demons and monsters who came to his meditation hut to interrupt his practice. When he opened the door, they shook their fangs at him and threatened him. He welcomed them graciously and invited them in. They asked: "But aren't you afraid of us?" Milarepa replied: "No. I have been expecting you. Please come in and have some tea."

Buddhist meditation moves patiently and steadily through the emotional turmoil, building concentration and leading to an experience of clarity and equanimity. As concentration develops, the self deconstructs in the flow of awareness. The illusion of a permanent, stable, independent self is cast off. Peacefulness cannot be directly willed, however. Grasping at peace only increases anxiety.

While there is no reliance upon divine revelation, Buddhist meditators trust that the truth will manifest itself if there is adequate time and a proper structure of meditation and moral practice. Insight into reality cannot be forced, however. It can only be experienced. By focusing on the arising, duration, and cessation of desires and thoughts, we acknowledge and free ourselves from our conditionings; and reality becomes luminously clear. This is the experience of wisdom, enlightenment, insight into what is. It is intensely personal, but it cannot be individualistic, for the illusory individual ego dissolves.

While Buddhist meditation may seem foreign to Western Christians, there are deep roots in the Christian tradition itself for engaging in a similar form of practice in a Christian context. From early times, Christians have been familiar with nonverbal meditation as a form of prayer that could open them to the manifestation of God's presence within. In the fourth century, Evagrius Ponticus advised Christians: "Strive to render your mind deaf and dumb at the time of prayer and then you will be able to pray."[80] Evagrius advised Christians at prayer to clear their mind of all thoughts, paying no heed to thoughts and concerns that arise, and to come by meditation to the state of *apatheia*, stillness. Evagrius knew that this would involve a fierce inner struggle as the unconverted ego resists. Nonetheless, he trusted that the image of God is present all the time in the depths of the self, and the presence of God would be revealed so that Christians could experience quiet, the peacefulness of the Sabbath rest. Evagrius proposed a sequence of development that is similar to the Buddhist Path of morality, meditation, and wisdom/compassion. For Evagrius, *ascesis*, the practice of the commandments, leads to *apatheia*, stillness, which in turn brings forth *agapē*, self-giving love.

NONVIOLENCE AND SOCIETY: BUDDHISM AND GIRARD

As we have seen, René Girard insists on a sharp contrast between the revelation of God in the biblical tradition and all other religions. For Girard, all nonbiblical religions turn to epiphanies of sacred violence to resolve social crises. The primitive sacred demands violence and justifies it, and this dynamic gives birth to rituals of sacrifice.[81] Girard asserts that there is no common ground between the violence-ridden mythologies that dominate all other religions and the revelation of God in Christianity.[82]

Girard's critique misses its mark in Buddhism, however. The Buddha's response to the suffering caused by rivalry and violence was rigorously practical and nonviolent. The Buddha claimed no divine revelation and neither sought nor proclaimed an epiphany of the sacred. His prescription for liberation was not dependent on ritual sacrifice or the expulsion of victims.

Indeed, the Buddhist tradition shares many of the concerns of Girard: It denies the reality of an autonomous, independent self and calls attention to the interdependence of all realities. It challenges its followers to become conscious of the sources of their own feelings and thoughts, to accept responsibility for them, and to be liberated from violence. Like Girard, Buddhists reject the notion that there can be "good violence" as well as bad. The Buddhist tradition and Girard agree in rejecting violence, including sacrificial violence which claims to be necessary for the preservation of social or cosmic order. According to Girard, "The illusion that there is a difference within the heart of violence is the key to the sacrificial way of thinking."[83] While the Buddhist tradition does not name the scapegoating mechanism with the same level of precision as Girard, the Buddha did firmly reject the Vedic system of sacrifices, replacing it with the precept of nonviolence and the practice of generosity (*Kutadanta Sutta* 16-27).

Girard has criticized Buddhism for completely withdrawing from society and offering no constructive solution to the social problems of rivalry and violence, only an individual strategy of escape.[84] However, Buddhist wisdom and compassion are inseparable, not by a conscious act of the will but because wisdom means seeing our interrelationship with all other beings. For Buddhists, as we see the truth, we overcome the false boundaries that separate us from others. We embrace all sentient beings and the entire cosmos with compassion. We see through the conditionings that imprisoned us in our own skin-bag and are freed to live in the network of relations that is the universe. The implications for social and ecological awareness, beginning with our own body, can be profound.

The earliest accounts of the message of Shakyamuni Buddha in the Pali scriptures call for a new way of organizing society freed from the illusions of separate, individual existence and from the resulting struggles for power and domination. The ideal of mutual service and sharing is at the center of this vision. The Buddha established basic principles for social ethics, right livelihood, and the responsibilities of a king. The ideal of the Buddhist king found its most complete actualization in the conversion of the emperor Ashoka in the third century B.C.E. from his earlier path of violent conquest to Buddhist ideals. Ashoka's principles included nonviolence to humans and animals alike, support for education, openness to a variety of religions, and encouragement of meditation as the most important way to advance in *dharma*. While the specific recommendations of Shakyamuni Buddha are inevitably tied to his own cultural context, contemporary Buddhists seek out the underlying wisdom that remains true and interpret it in light of present circumstances. Movements that apply ancient Buddhist wisdom to contemporary social, economic, and political struggles have been called Socially Engaged Buddhism.[85] These efforts share many of the values of Girard's dramatic call for a renunciation of violence.

Girard has explored how mimetic rivalry, envy, and scapegoating rule human relationships. In Buddhist practice, practitioners are taught to become aware of the distrusted, disowned sides of ourselves that we project onto others. Buddhist wisdom is insight into our interrelationship with all other beings; and this means that exclusion, violence, and scapegoating are impossible. Compassion draws the Buddhist into a new form of engagement with the world, freed from the cycle of rivalry and craving.

While the concrete social principles of the Buddha have long been familiar to Theravada Buddhists in Southeast Asia, they have often been neglected in the West, even by scholars of Buddhism. When Joanna Macy, an American Buddhist, asked Western scholars of Buddhism about a contemporary Sri Lankan interpretation of the Four Noble Truths to apply to issues like irrigation, literacy, and marketing cooperatives, they dismissed it as a trivialization of the Buddha's message. However, when she inquired of very learned Buddhist monks in Sri Lanka itself, they were surprised that a Buddhist could even ask the question. They told her: "But it is the same teaching, don't you see? Whether you put it on the psycho-spiritual plane or on the socio-economic plane, there is suffering and there is cessation of suffering." To them it was self-evident that both levels of suffering should be relieved.[86]

Socially Engaged Buddhists generally deny that there is any one Buddhist position on political and economic questions. Their specific programs vary from one culture to another. They seek to increase awareness of unnecessary suffering, to change the consciousness of rich and poor alike, to develop practical projects fostering self-reliance and local empowerment, and to apply religious practice as a force for social transformation. In accordance with the ancient Buddhist precepts, their methods are nonviolent. Engaged Buddhists distrust actions inspired by anger, and they stress the crucial importance of compassion for oppressors. They are attentive to the karmic social and personal conditionings that encourage ignorance and suffering, but they insist that karma only shapes us; it does not determine us. Awareness of our conditionings allows us the freedom to change them, and so mindfulness is a central virtue. The practice of meditation combined with concrete acts of compassion points the way to a better world.

There are, to be sure, many fundamental differences between Buddhist and Christian worldviews. Buddhists themselves sometimes admit that the Christian vision of a God who transcends the world, who enters the world to redeem it, makes little sense to them. While the fundamental assumptions of Buddhist awakening and Christian revelation differ radically, there is much that Christians can affirm in the Buddhist analysis of suffering and in the values of morality, meditation, and wisdom. On the practical level, the centuries-long tradition of Buddhist meditation can be a very powerful tool to increase awareness of the dangers that Girard names and to let go of them. Buddhist practitioners of meditation often insist that the experience of transformation through meditation is the heart of Buddhist life and practice and is more important for Christians than accepting or debating Buddhist ideas and concepts.

THE AXIAL RELIGIONS

This brief survey has noted some of the important aspects of major axial religious traditions that bear on revelation or the manifestation of truth. In each tradition a life-transforming insight shapes a practice that promises to renew human existence, bringing humans into harmony with the order of the universe and opening up new possibilities for human flourishing. Each of the axial traditions asserts a universal claim about human existence in the cosmos from a distinctive perspective. The visions of the cosmos differ significantly, but in each case there are similarities to aspects of Christian experience of revelation.

Confucianism, Taoism, Hinduism, and Buddhism have a long and complex history of relating to each other in various settings, and the additional presence of Judaism, Christianity, Islam, and other religions in both the past and the present compounds the complexity of the relationships in Asia as well as in North America and Europe. On many sides there have been both amicable and hostile exchanges, as each tradition has adjusted to the presence of the others. Hindus and Buddhists both borrowed from each other and debated each other for centuries in India and throughout Southeast Asia. Interpenetration continues to the present day as Thai Buddhists honor Hindu deities and Indonesian Muslims recount the stories of the *Ramayana*. Relations are often problematic. Bitter conflict between Hindus and Buddhists still troubles Sri Lanka; Muslims, Hindus, and Sikhs are frequently in opposition in India. Confucianism and Taoism have been both allies and rivals in shaping Chinese culture together with the Mahayana Buddhist traditions. The development of Chinese Buddhism was heavily indebted to the Confucian and Taoist heritage.

While there are many values that are shared by various traditions, there is no one, overarching conceptual scheme that can do equal justice to each of these traditions. Any attempt to state that each perspective is equally true would risk depriving each tradition of its distinctive claim to truth. Each of the major traditions has its own ways of accounting for the others. Christian revelation can find points of contact with each tradition, but important differences of belief and doctrine remain.

7

Encounters in a World of Dialogue

In the testimonies to revelation in the world's religions, wisdom, overflowing love, and violence intertwine. We have seen that in biblical revelation itself there is a tension between the call to faith and hope in a God of all-encompassing love, on the one hand, and the violent demands of the Israelite holy war and the fierce rhetoric of New Testament authors against opponents of Jesus, on the other. The central narrative of revelation by which the Catholic Church lived for centuries was based on the supersession and displacement of the Jewish people by the church. The Christian reception of revelation was thought to have demonstrated the blindness of the Jewish people to their own scriptures. Today this narrative is exhausted, discredited by the religious animosity and violence to which it has historically been an accomplice. No new overarching narrative has yet taken its place.

Both the diversity and the ambiguity of the world's religions pose challenges for Christian theology. Every major religious tradition has an ambiguous heritage. Each of the major religious traditions has inspired lives of dedication and service which have enriched the human community. Each has shaped human lives in the direction of greater honesty, authenticity, and love. Yet religions have also repeatedly called forth and fostered animosity and violence.

The traditions that see themselves as children of Abraham—Judaism, Christianity, and Islam—share central beliefs and values; but they also disagree pointedly in some of their most important convictions about revelation; and they have a long and tragic history of violence and hatred. The traditions of South and East Asia—Hinduism, Buddhism, Confucianism, and Taoism—present worldviews that are often extremely different from Christian revelation; but again and again there are points of convergence in values that draw the traditions together.

DIVERGENCE AND CONVERGENCE

As we have seen in the brief sampling above, the world's religions differ in their visions of the cosmos, human existence, and the goal of human life in important ways. The religions of the world propose paths of transformation that lead, at least in this world, to extremely diverse forms of fulfillment. A Zen master who challenges aspiring students to awaken holds forth a very different ideal from a Hasidic rabbi teaching the Torah in a *yeshiva*. The religious attainment of a Muslim *fakir* is not that of a Catholic saint. The revelation of God on Mt. Sinai is radically different from the manifestation of the Tao to Lao-tzu. The giving of the *Qur'an* to Muhammad is profoundly different from early Christianity's reception of Jesus as the Son of God. All religions are not simply saying the same message with different emphases. There is no way to synthesize the variety of perspectives on revelation or on the manifestation of truth while also respecting the integrity and identity of each tradition. Nonetheless, Christians hope and trust that the God revealed in Jesus Christ is actively involved in all human experience. If God's offer of salvation is present to all people, then so too is the offer of God's revelation in some form also present throughout all human history. The faith that God's love is in some way manifested to all humans provides a basis for seeking out analogous beliefs and values in dialogue. Yet the stark violence of religious history, including the history of Christianity, forbids any easy, uncritical acceptance of unlimited plurality. Christians are called to a critical appropriation of our own tradition and also to an openness to the truth and grace in other traditions.

For Christians who acknowledge Jesus Christ as the incarnation of God in this world, the center of revelation is the person of Jesus Christ; and thus every other testimony of revelation must be related to the Christ-event. In dialogue, Christians expect that members of other traditions will interpret the Christian claim in light of their own commitments. There is a wide variety of relationships between the Christian revelation and other traditions, ranging from agreement in many shared beliefs and values to differences in doctrines and worldviews and, at times, to stark contradictions regarding both values and doctrines. Often Christians can welcome other religious voices as affirming and sharing values that are also held by Jesus and the Christian tradition. When there are differences in perspectives and yet similar values, Christians can explore the meaning of the differences in an atmosphere of trust. When there are stark conflicts in religious beliefs and values, Christians simply have to disagree. Religions, including Christianity, have justified and even sacralized horrendous violence and cruelty in the name of God or the gods. Dialogue cannot mean the acceptance of every perspective.

Just as Christians assess other religions in light of Jesus Christ, so other traditions have their own central foci, which serve as their respective bases for assessing Christianity. The center of Christian revelation is often the point at which differences are most acute and discussions are most difficult. Judaism and Islam, the traditions that share with Christians a belief in the God of Abraham, pointedly reject the claim that Jesus Christ is the incarnate Son of God. Contemporary Jews sometimes acknowledge Jesus as a leader in the prophetic tradition of Israel; but to the present day, for a Jew to accept Jesus as the Messiah and the Son of God is usually reason to be dismissed from the synagogue. Martin Buber could accept Jesus as a brother in faith and as part of Israel's history of faith, but not as the incarnate Son of God.[1] More recently, Pinchas Lapide accepts belief in the resurrection of Jesus as being in accordance with Jewish tradition; but he denies that Jesus is the Messiah or the incarnation of God.[2] Islam, the only major religion other than Christianity with a revealed teaching about Jesus, accepts him as prophet and Messiah but firmly rejects all claims of divinity. For Muslims, instructed by the Qur'an, traditional Christian claims about Jesus Christ are simply wrong.

The Hindu traditions, while sometimes accepting Jesus as an incarnation of God, do so in a framework that is very different from traditional Christian faith and which transforms this belief radically. Hindus often assume that Christian revelation is simply part of the eternal religion (sanatanadharma), of which the Upanishads are the final summation. Thus they can accept Jesus as an avatar within a Hindu framework without a need for further dialogue. In 1983 Bede Griffiths remarked that in twenty-five years of experience in India, "I have hardly ever found an educated Hindu who is really open to dialogue, who really wanted to understand Christian faith as something 'other.'"[3] Other Christians in India, however, do report more productive experiences in dialogue.[4]

Buddhism, which relies on neither a creating and redeeming God nor an incarnation of God, has its own strategies for interpreting the plurality of religions and poses an even stronger challenge to traditional Christian assumptions about revelation, human existence, and the cosmos itself. Because Buddhism is such a strong counterpoint to Christian perspectives, the next chapter will explore particular Buddhist and Christian views of awakening and revelation in more detail. For many Buddhists, Christian faith in a transcendent God who enters the world and dies on the cross seems implausible or even difficult to conceive of at all. For many Buddhists, religious beliefs are not central, however. Zen Buddhists often stress that direct experience of reality is what is important, not discussions of concepts and ideas about God or ultimate reality. The Dalai Lama accepts the plurality of religions as different forms of medicine to heal different types of people. He cautions against combining Buddhism and Christianity because this would not respect their distinct identities, but he praises all the religions of the world to the degree that they teach values that are coherent with his own Tibetan Buddhist principles.[5]

For Korean Zen Master Seung Sahn, the Zen Buddhist principles of interpretation set the framework for understanding every other religious path and assessing it in light of Zen awareness of "the primary point" and "Zen mind." Seung Sahn explained the contrast between Christian belief in creation and his own Buddhist perspective on the importance of letting go of all ideas in one's practice:

> But in Buddhism, there is no original cause or creator; there is no coming, no going, no existence, no non-existence; all of these are opposites thinking. Sun and moon, light and dark, day and night— all these are names, the world of names is opposites thinking. "God" is also a name; it's also opposites thinking. True God has no name, nor form. In no name/no form, there is no coming, no going—no opposites thinking. That which is beyond all names and forms is always bright. That is true God. . . . Zen mind means put down any idea, any form. If your direction is clear and you completely put down everything, then you will attain something. When you attain something, you connect with everything else. All religions are like different paths to the mountaintop. The top of the mountain is very clear; it's the primary point. But there are many paths leading to this point. . . . [W]hen people begin climbing the mountain, they cannot see the top, so they are very strongly attached to "my way." Having clear direction and try mind means just going up, going up, one step after another. So you don't spend energy in fighting other people or their ideas; you just practice. Then you can reach the mountaintop.[6]

The similarities in the values cherished by the world's religions offer a basis for the image of mountain climbers on different paths to the same peak. In some respects, the transformations of human life at which the world's religions aim share important values. The image of climbing the same mountain, however, is problematic. At times, the differences in worldviews appear to be so profound that one may wonder whether members of different traditions are heading to the same peak or even are climbing the same mountain. By suggesting that all religions really seek the same goal, the metaphor of a common mountain may hinder more than it helps. The differences among the world's religions seem in some ways to be a chasm that cannot be crossed. There is no agreement on the question of what humans are to be liberated from or for, and so the goals of religious practice often differ profoundly. The Buddhist and Hindu traditions have not sought salvation from sin through the grace of God but rather release from suffering in the unending cycles of rebirth. R. C. Zaehner observed: "The only common factor between them [the world's religions] is the observed fact of human unhappiness. . . . And it is precisely on the subject of 'it'—namely that from which release is sought—that the world religions so profoundly disagree."[7] To reduce religions to a lowest common denominator or to a core that would be common to all the world's religious traditions would mean a loss of the distinctive identity of the religions themselves.

Given the amount of data from the world's religions that confronts interpreters of religion and theologians, and given the relatively recent beginning of serious dialogue among most of the major traditions, it may well be premature to seek any final, theoretical, conceptual resolution to the question of the relationship among religions at the present stage of discussion. The impulse to hurry may itself betray the process. More focused conversations between particular viewpoints may be more useful and necessary as a prelude to broader generalizations. Acknowledging the differences among the traditions does not preclude recognizing an important resonance of values and perspectives across traditions. Even though the major religious traditions often differ radically in their assumptions about ultimate reality, human existence, and the universe, they nonetheless agree to a significant, even surprising, degree on many of the values that are most central for human existence. For example, without accepting Buddhist cosmology, a Christian can acknowledge the value of the Buddhist practice of the Brahma-viharas, "the dwelling place of the Buddha," which consists of the virtues of loving-kindness (*metta*), sympathetic joy (*muditha*), compassion (*karuna*), and equanimity (*upekkha*). The *Qur'an* itself advises Muslims to compete with Jews and Christians in virtue until the last day, when God will make known to believers that about which they differ (5:48).

On the ethical level, there can be profound influence across traditions even when there are few or no conversions to the other tradition. Hindus were profoundly influenced by British criticisms of traditional practices, like *suttee*, the burning of widows, and the caste system. Where Muslims rulers had governed regions of India for centuries without seriously affecting Hindu religious self-understanding, the values proclaimed by British Christians posed a radical challenge to which Hindus responded with great energy and creativity.[8] In response to Muslim political and military rule, Hindus became more rigid and orthodox; in response to British critiques of Hindu customs, the Indian renaissance transformed Hinduism itself. Gandhi, himself heavily influenced by Leo Tolstoy, in turn had a profound impact on how Christians around the world came to understand the nonviolent teaching of Jesus himself. For centuries, Christians had thought that the teaching of the Sermon on the Mount was idealistic and impracticable for action in the world; Gandhi, interpreting it in light of the Upanishads and the *Bhagavad Gita*, revealed a practical wisdom that most Christians had not suspected in the principles of Jesus.[9]

There are many dimensions to interreligious exchanges, including profound intellectual and moral differences that sometimes call for considered argument;[10] but the many shared values shape an increasingly common horizon of concern in a threatened world. The Declaration Toward a Global Ethic, signed by the Council of Spiritual and Religious Leaders at the Parliament of the World's Religions in Chicago in 1893, expresses the hopes of many that religious traditions with very different perspectives can agree on fundamental values.[11] Genuine conversations have an unpredictable character, as the to-and-fro of dialogue sometimes elicits insights and discoveries that no single partner could have anticipated in isolation.

Yet openness to religious traditions, whether one's own or others', cannot be unconditional. Each tradition's history is ambiguous. The history of Christianity reveals how different interpretations of revelation have variously supported traditions of peace or have led to violence time and time again. As Origen argued to Celsus, it is impossible to accept everything in the history of religion simply because it has been the tradition of some people at some time (*Against Celsus* 5.36).

In recent years, most discussions of the theology of religions have centered on the typology of attitudes toward other religions that Alan Race proposed in 1982: exclusivism,† inclusivism,† and pluralism.[12] While Christian exclusivists insist that salvation is offered only to Christians, Christian inclusivists allow that faithful members of other traditions can receive salvation because they are included in the redemptive work of Jesus Christ. Pluralists, on the other hand, acknowledge that people can be saved through a wide variety of religious traditions without being included in the work of any single religion or savior. In large measure, the debates have raged between inclusivists and pluralists, but increasingly participants have become dissatisfied with the terms themselves and the restricted range of options they present.[13]

JOHN HICK

John Hick proposes a pluralistic theology of religions that is based on the perception that the major religious traditions have transformed human lives in ways that a wide range of humans can acknowledge as positive and also on the suspicion that absolute claims have led to violence.[14] In response to the plurality of religions and the violence of religious history, Hick challenges Christians to abandon the doctrine that Jesus Christ is the incarnation of God in order to allow other religions to be accepted as equally valid responses to the divine mystery, which he calls "the Real." The Trinity, according to Hick, is not true of God's inner life *in se*, as traditional Christianity had affirmed; it is only the way God has appeared to Christians and is, in principle, no more or less true than Jewish, Muslim, Hindu, or Buddhist notions of ultimate reality. In effect, the traditional self-understanding of each religious tradition is subordinated to Hick's analysis of "the Real."

Hick claims that a pluralistic theology of religions can best interpret and respond to the experience of human religiosity, honoring the manifold goodness of many different traditions and avoiding the violence produced by privileging a single religion as uniquely valid. Hick aims at a global and irenic comprehensiveness. In effect, however, Hick proposes a different form of inclusivism. He includes some forms of religion as good and life-transforming manifestations of "the Real," based on the perceived effects in people's lives, as judged from a particular modern Western perspective. He rejects other forms of religion as false because of the perceived negative ethical effects produced. The criterion of moral transformation serves to judge all religious claims. For Hick, a modern Western notion of morality, grounded in a selective appropriation of major world religions, becomes the arbiter of what counts as genuine religion and what is to be rejected as spurious. The price Hick demands for his pluralistic theology of religions, viz., relinquishing the central beliefs of historical Christianity, will appear to be too high to many Christians. Hick makes a similar demand on every other religious tradition, for all are called to reinterpret themselves in light of his notion of "the Real." In Hick's proposal, interreligious dialogue is entered at the cost of surrendering the classical cornerstones of each religious tradition's identity.

S. MARK HEIM

In contrast to Hick, S. Mark Heim insists on placing the diversity of the salvations offered by religious traditions at the center of reflection on the theology of religions.[15] Members of one tradition can recognize legitimate and genuine values in the very different ideals of another path while continuing to regard their own tradition as normative and definitive. Metaphysically, Heim argues, there is no reason to assume that the diverse fulfillments offered by various religions could not continue eschatologically in the next world as well.[16] We can imagine an afterlife in which a Buddhist would experience nirvana and a Christian would experience communion with the triune God. Each would regard the other's salvation as penultimate, but nonetheless as real and good and genuinely distinct from one's own fulfillment.

The insistence on taking seriously the different goals of religions is the centerpiece of Heim's effort to advance the current debate in the theology of religions. Heim charges that most parties to this discussion have assumed erroneously that one religious fulfillment awaits devout practitioners of all different paths. Heim offers a cogent and searching critique of the major representatives of pluralistic positions, especially John Hick, Wilfred Cantwell Smith, and Paul Knitter. The center of Heim's indictment is that "the most insistent voices calling for the affirmation of religious pluralism seem equally insistent in denying that, in properly religious terms, there is or should be any fundamental diversity at all."[17] If all religious paths lead to the same salvation, there is no reason for accepting one religion rather than another, and the concrete specifications of different traditions lose their importance and interest. The central problem is that most pluralistic theologies of religion "relegate specific individual elements in a tradition and its concrete historical texture to secondary status."[18] Moreover, Heim charges, pluralistic theologies of religion have no specific contribution of their own to make to existing dialogues that search for religious knowledge, spirituality, and social justice. Pluralists seek to abstract from particularity in shaping a meta-theory of religions; but the premises of the modern Western critique of religion inevitably shape the principles of the pluralists, leaving them closer to inclusivist and even exclusivist positions than they acknowledge.

At times Heim may exaggerate the one-sidedness of the pluralists he criticizes and thereby also overstate the differences between their positions and his own. His criticism is most successful in the case of Hick. Knitter, though the object of a vigorous critique by Heim, has expressed his "essential agreement" with Heim's proposal.[19]

Heim proposes an alternative option that affirms both the finality of Jesus Christ and also the validity of other religious paths. This position, which he calls variously pluralistic inclusivism or inclusivistic pluralism or orientational pluralism, claims to hold together the apparently competing values of dialogue and witness. To demonstrate the coherence of acknowledging a legitimate plurality of conflicting perspectives, Heim draws upon the orientational pluralism of philosopher Nicholas Rescher, who has sought to chart a path among the continuing debates of philosophers.[20]

Heim is persuasive in seeking to balance fidelity to his own Christian tradition with openness to the legitimacy of other perspectives. Nonetheless, questions remain about the coherence of the result, especially concerning the suggestion of eschatological pluralism. Left to the sideline, for example, is the question of rebirth. Would those who have followed paths based on the assumption of rebirth return? Would a Tibetan Buddhist go through the processes described in *The Book of the Dead*, while a Catholic encounters the world of Dante's *Divine Comedy*? For those who practice a religious tradition while remaining skeptical and suspending judgment concerning the afterlife, would their judgment continue to be suspended?

Heim's title itself, *Salvations*, indicates a Christian starting point for framing the discussion. For many Jews, Muslims, Hindus, and Buddhists, "salvation" would not be a central religious category. To place salvation at the center of a theology of religions privileges a Christian perspective. This is not itself a liability, for there is no perfectly neutral, uninvolved observing point. The search for a single, all-encompassing theoretical resolution that can accord equal respect to the truth claims of each religion may be itself misguided. Any framework within which we interpret the religions is dependent on the assumptions and categories of a particular culture, and often those of a particular philosophy or religion. A comparative study of religion can simply note similarities and contrasts, but the requirements of interreligious dialogue differ from those of a comparative phenomenological study of religion. A more fruitful approach to dialogue brings the perspectives and commitments of one's religious tradition into the discussion, expecting that others will do the same. Christians need not surrender their central beliefs prior to dialogue. They may engage in dialogue, trusting that greater awareness of the truth will emerge from the to-and-fro of conversation.

CHAOS THEORY AND
THE PLURALITY OF RELIGIONS

The assumptions interpreters bring to interpreting revelation are always shaped by their views about the universe, though they are not completely determined by these. Ancient Near Eastern and medieval European assumptions about cosmology set the stage for understanding the drama of revelation in earlier ages. In recent years science has gone through a revolution in perspectives on the significance of patterns and chaos in natural processes, and the paradoxical study of chaos theory opens up new metaphors not only for the physical world but for viewing human culture as a whole, including the testimonies to revelation in the world's religions.[21] There is, of course, no question of any hard argument from scientific discoveries and metaphors to theological conclusions. Nonetheless, insights and reflections coming from the study of chaos in nature and culture may offer helpful perspectives for viewing patterns in the relations among religions. No scientific theory can determine a theology of revelation; but recent knowledge about the natural world offers a new way of valuing positively the contingency, uncertainty, and chaos of human life and thereby can enrich theological reflection. The complex, unpredictable interactions among the world's religions and even the course of any single religious tradition include chaotic elements that cannot be neatly fit into a coherent system. Thus recent scientific attention to the place of chaos in human life may be illumining for the understanding of revelation itself.

In scientific usage, chaos is not sheer disorder. Rather, "[t]he scientific term 'chaos' refers to an underlying interconnectedness that exists in apparently random events."[22] In the scientific sense, a system is in chaos if scientists cannot predict the future states of the system. The study of chaos has discovered striking mathematical patterns that repeat in an astonishingly wide variety of phenomena, from the formation of galaxies to rugged coastlines, from unpredictable weather currents to the flow of blood in the human body, from population growth to the flow of traffic on expressways and to the rise and fall of the stock market. Wherever there is turbulence and disorder, scientists are discovering complex forms of remarkable detail and mathematical proportions that repeat on greatly different scales from the very large to the microscopic. A new branch of geometry has been developed to explore these patterns, which are called "fractals."[†23] John Briggs and F. David Peat explain:

> "Fractal" is the name given by scientists to the patterns of chaos that we see in the heavens, feel on earth, and find in the very veins and nerves of our bodies. The word was coined by the mathematician Benoit Mandelbrot and now has wide use in chaos theory, where fractals refer to the traces, tracks, marks, and forms made by the action of chaotic dynamical systems.[24]

Earlier modern science had often proposed a closed vision of a world of determined causality, and on this basis some thinkers rejected any understanding of religious revelation. The world seemed to be a closed system of predictable causes and effects. In contrast to the confidence of much early modern science, the contemporary study of chaos teaches humans to be humble, and thus finds points of contact with the ancient wisdom traditions. Briggs and Peat comment:

> Chaos, it turns out, is as much about what we *can't* know as it is about certainty and fact. It's about letting go, accepting limits, and celebrating magic and mystery. . . . Paradoxically, the insights of the newest science share the vision of the world presented in many of the world's oldest indigenous and spiritual traditions.[25]

Chaos theory resonates deeply with the ancient wisdom traditions of China, India, and Israel; it also takes up in a new context themes that were important to Nicholas of Cusa, such as the coincidence of opposites,[†] the paradoxical knowing of what is unknowable, and the intimate relation between each being and the entire universe. Briggs and Peat suggest three themes that emerge from the recent science: (1) the acceptance of uncertainty and contingency instead of the quest for prediction and control; (2) the emergence of creativity from participation in chaos; and

(3) attention to subtle patterns of complexities in nature and in human life.[26] These lessons may well prove helpful for pondering religious diversity as well.

In ancient mythology, chaos was often personified as a frightening, monstrous enemy. In contemporary science, chaos, far from being a threat to creativity, is itself the form that nature's creativity takes. Nature is not composed of static, closed entities, but of dynamic and chaotic open-ended, self-organizing systems that constantly interact with an ever-changing environment. Chaos science insists that one can only understand a part by relating it to the whole, for every part is radically interdependent with the whole, and even a very small part can be extremely influential on the whole.

In the most famous exemplification of this principle, a butterfly flaps its wings in Hong Kong, and a month later there is a storm on the other side of the Pacific Ocean. This principle was discovered in the winter of 1961 by meteorologist Edward Lorenz while he was working on computer projections of weather forecasts. He learned, to his surprise, that a minuscule difference in the figure given to a computer for a weather projection (.506 instead of .506127) led to profoundly different predictions of weather over time.[27] Conventional modern science had assumed that parts could be understood in isolation from the whole and that small changes in input would lead to small differences later on. Thus Lorenz had anticipated that a tiny difference in input would result in a tiny difference in later results. The disconfirmation of this expectation was an important step in the birth of the science of chaos. Chaos theory finds that in chaotic systems, everything is related to everything else and that a small difference early in the process can lead to a radically different outcome. The concrete result of any change of input in such a system, however, cannot be predicted and controlled.

Chaos theorists focus on two forms of feedback that allow self-organizing systems to maintain a balance between order and openness. Negative feedback prevents activity from moving beyond certain limits, as in the case of a thermostat, which controls temperature, turning a furnace or air conditioner on or off when certain limits of heat or cold are reached. Negative feedback provides for continuity amid change. Positive feedback incorporates and amplifies input, putting it into the system in ways that powerfully increase its effect, as in the case of a microphone placed too close to a speaker system. The microphone feeds back the original sounds from the room as well as their amplifications from the speaker system, creating a shrill shriek.[28] Too much negative feedback leads to complete stasis and death; too much positive feedback leads to turbulence and disorder. A balance between the two provides stability and continuity amid openness, growth, and change.

The polemic against idols in ancient Israel or in the early church may be viewed as a form of negative feedback which preserved the identity and continuity of faith in God by rejecting certain options as false and dangerous. The repeated appropriations of imagery, thought patterns, and practices from other nations was a form of positive feedback, often powerfully amplifying the influence of the input from other religious traditions and incorporating it into a new context in Israel's faith and into the life of the early church. As we saw earlier, the religion of ancient Israel and of early Christianity was in a continuous process of both resisting and borrowing from the religions of its neighbors.

Negative and positive feedback loops relate the "inside" of a system to its "outside," but even the meaning of the terms "inside" and "outside" are relative in chaos theory because everything is radically interconnected. According to chaos theory individuals and institutions are not static entities but ongoing self-organizing systems constituted by the flow of materials through them, regulated by positive and negative feedback. Even hierarchical institutions that seek clear, linear patterns of authority have unpredictable, nonlinear moments and depend on the feedback of their members for their own continuing existence. There are feedback loops in every system, and the input of even small, subtle influences can over time make a massive difference later on.

Chaos theory would suggest that even a strongly linear, hierarchical religious institution is open to unpredictable, nonlinear changes because of ongoing feedback. As we have seen, Pope Boniface VIII in the early thirteenth century and the Council of Florence, an ecumenical council of the Catholic Church in the fourteenth century, both solemnly defined that those outside the Catholic Church could not be saved. Pope Gregory XVI centuries later reaffirmed this teaching, declaring that the most sacred dogma of the Catholic Church was that no one could be saved outside of it.[29] In terms of formal authority, the matter seemed closed; but another factor was present: the seemingly insignificant intuition of some Catholics in fifteenth-century Spain who actually knew Jews and Muslims and believed that they too could be saved through the practice of their own religions. Over the long run of history, this intuition would not disappear but would be repeated by others and eventually amplified and shared. Eventually even the solemn, official hierarchical definition would be revised.

In a universe of interdependence and interrelationships, boundaries are of special interest, and chaos theorists have learned much from studying the length and character of coastlines. Mathematician Benoit Mandelbrot asked how long the coastline of Great Britain is. The line on a photograph from a satellite can be measured easily enough, but Mandelbrot realized that as one approaches more closely, every increase in scale leads to a greater level of curvature and complexity and thus to ever longer distances of the coastline. To measure every curve of the coastline on ever more precise scales would lead to the molecular and even the atomic and subatomic levels. On every level,

Mandelbrot discovered that similar jagged, fractal shapes repeated themselves. The angles of a bay or a peninsula continued to appear on ever smaller levels. Mandelbrot concluded that the coastline of Britain, if examined at the microscopic and even subatomic levels, is infinite; and he developed a new form of geometry to study the self-similarity of patterns on vastly different scales.[30] Chaos theory's discovery of self-similarity in nature echoes Nicholas of Cusa's intuition that every part of the universe is intimately related to the whole while remaining itself.

According to chaos theory, there are complex interactions between what is "inside" and what is "outside" any individual, institution, or tradition. Chaos theory suggests that it is misguided either to separate the individual from the whole or to merge the individual in the whole. Boundaries are important but relative.

The constantly changing relationships among the world's religions involve both the incorporation of insights and images from other traditions and also the maintenance of identity through defining and defending boundaries. From a satellite, the coastline of England is clear; from close up it becomes ever more complex. From a broad perspective, one can easily make generalizations about the differences and the boundary lines among religions. As one studies religious traditions on ever more detailed levels, matters become more complex, and one can also discover countless ways in which groups and individual members are influenced by practices of other religious traditions. Thomas Bamat and Jean-Paul Wiest have collected reports from all over the world of the complex interaction between popular Catholic beliefs and practices and those of indigenous religious traditions.[31] The primal traditions do not simply disappear after Christian evangelization has taken place but continue to exert influence, often in unpredictable ways.

Another example of a complex boundary involves Christians who engage in a practice of meditation derived from another religious tradition, such as Buddhism. In terms of general views of ultimate reality and the universe, there appears to be a very clear distinction between Catholic Christianity and Zen Buddhism. Nonetheless, viewed more closely in the lives of individual practitioners, the boundary frequently becomes ever more complex. In the twentieth century some Christian missioners to Japan entered into formal Zen training, following the lead of the German Jesuit Hugo Enomiya-Lassalle, often under the guidance of Yamada Koun Roshi. Some of these students then invited other Christians around the world into Zen meditation.[32] Christian students of Yamada Roshi such as Ruben L. F. Habito, Thomas Hand, and Robert Kennedy came to the United States and began to teach formal Zen practice. Some Christians experimented with "Christian Zen"[33] or "Zen Catholicism";[34] some explored what it would mean to be both Zen and Christian, journeying between the two worlds, while respecting their differences.[35] Enomiya-Lassalle noted the difference in interpretations between Zen

Buddhist enlightenment and Christian union with God, but he tended to see them as the same experience, in itself beyond conceptual expression, though interpreted differently.[36] Joseph Cardinal Ratzinger, prefect of the Congregation for the Doctrine of the Faith, expressed reservations about the Christian practice of meditation techniques coming from other religious traditions in his letter to the Catholic bishops of the world, "Concerning Certain Aspects of Meditation."[37] While the tone of the letter was largely cautious and admonitory and at times very negative in its characterization of other traditions, Ratzinger repeated the principle of Vatican II that the Catholic Church "rejects nothing of what is true and holy in these traditions"; and he clearly affirmed the legitimacy of Christian use of meditation practices from other traditions as long as these are integrated into an orthodox Christian spirituality.[38]

Robert Aitken, one of the most respected American senior teachers in Zen Buddhism, reflects on his own participation in two different traditions:

Speaking personally, as a teacher of Zen Buddhism in the Diamond Sangha tradition, I am a Buddhist, yet nonetheless I am also a Protestant Christian who never converted, in the decisive sense of that term, to Buddhism. I find the metaphorical language of Jesus and Old Testament figures rising to my mind when I speak to my students.[39]

In such cases religious identity is nourished by two radically different traditions that flow together in the lives of practitioners; and the boundary between Zen Buddhism and Christianity becomes difficult, if not impossible, to determine.

Briggs and Peat propose one implication of the scientific discoveries in chaos theory: "Truth and chaos are linked. To live with creative doubt means to enter into chaos so as to discover there the truth that 'cannot be measured by words.'"[40] In language that resonates deeply with many wisdom traditions, they recommend the cultivation of a tolerance for ambiguity and for thinking in opposites and note that creative individuals in a wide variety of fields

come to understand that in order to be creative, they need to give themselves to sensations of "knowing but not knowing," inadequacy, uncertainty, awkwardness, awe, joy, horror, being out of control, and appreciating the nonlinear, metamorphosing features of reality and their own thought processes—the many faces of creative chaos.[41]

They also note the implications for dialogue as a process of discernment that can accept diversity and even chaos as contributing to the richness of experience: "The diverse opinions of a group create chaos and nuances in the polarities and allow for the appearance of creativity and self-organization."[42]

Christian theology has often sought to be systematic and to discover order in the cosmos and in human life. Theologians have sought the essence of Christianity which underlies its ever-changing historical manifestations. The search for coherent order is crucial to human existence and to religious practice, but theology also faces the challenge of adequacy to a tradition and a world where order is never complete and final. Alongside the search for order there is also an ancient recognition of the perduring chaos in the universe that can never be overcome or reduced to order. The unstable conclusion of the Book of Job (in which God reproves Job and then praises him to his friends, while also rebuking Job's friends but nonetheless acting in accord with their theology) and the skeptical wisdom of Qoheleth are two dramatic examples of this recognition that were included in the Bible itself. The diversity of the biblical tradition itself defies attempts to impose a neat conceptual order upon it and resembles the ongoing chaotic, dynamic self-organizing systems studied by chaos theory.

In earlier chapters we have seen something of the complexity of the biblical and later Christian traditions' relations to other religions. There was a constant process of negative feedback, rejecting certain beliefs and values, but also a continual process of positive feedback in the appropriation of insights, images, and practices from other traditions. The age-old practice of borrowing perspectives from other religious traditions finds a resonance in the cosmology of chaos theory. If religions, like all institutions, are ongoing self-organizing systems open to the flow of materials through them, then it is natural for them to borrow and appropriate expressions of truth, goodness, and beauty from their environment, while also rejecting elements that appear to threaten their identity.

Perhaps most importantly, chaos theory suggests an attitude of openness, humility, and patience before the chaotic diversity of the world's religions. Instead of imposing a ready-made systematic order on the religions, we may do well to acknowledge the limits of our own understanding and ability to predict and control, to attend to the fecundity of forms of religious practice, and to look for the subtle nuances that can be significant in shaping future events.

A SAPIENTIAL APPROACH

Relating what is most particular in a religious faith to what is most universal is one of the most pressing and vexing problems facing believers. While the challenges facing the world call for concerted action by members of different religious traditions, the religious basis for such action is not always clear. To water down each faith to a least common denominator threatens to rob every tradition of its distinctive identity and power. Influential forces push toward either an exclusivism that regards its own truth as solely valid or an indifferentism that entertains all claims because none is taken seriously. The radical diversity of religious traditions at times seems to threaten the very possibility of communication across confessional boundaries. In this situation, the trajectory of biblical wisdom, with its openness to other traditions and its interweaving of the particular and the universal, calls attention to another option.

The sages of Israel found God revealed in the activities and patterns of everyday life, and yet they also acknowledged that God was beyond any understanding and that the patterns of life were mysterious. This was not simply a "natural" knowledge of God that prepared for a later "supernatural" revelation. Lady Wisdom offered the fullness of life in God's presence. The sages assumed that this offer was open to the wise of all cultures and nations, and they participated in the broader discussions of wisdom in the ancient Near East. The boundaries between wisdom in Israel and in the ancient Near East were porous and permeable. The wisdom tradition's trust in the offer of wisdom in all human experience was combined with a sharp sense that humans never fully grasp the meaning of wisdom. The sages undercut any claim to have understood adequately the significance of wisdom. The teacher of wisdom warns the students not to think of themselves as wise (Prov 3:7), for those who think they are wise have less hope than fools (Prov 26:12). The wise recognize that God is incomprehensible mystery and that no human wisdom can measure God's ways. The sages of Israel knew that any perspective is limited and that individuals themselves must discern the proper time for applying various proverbs and principles of wisdom. Contemporary chaos theory has rediscovered the ancient sages' awareness of contingency and uncertainty, as well as the lesson of humility that flows from this awareness.

The Bible offers not a closed system of revelation but a rather chaotic and turbulent ongoing tradition of voices with differing perspectives and values. At times the biblical tradition appropriates insights from neighboring cultures; at times it fiercely resists the perspectives of other religious traditions. The process, like the self-organizing systems of chaos theory, was unpredictable. A small influence from outside could have a major impact over time. The inclusion of conflicting voices within the biblical canon itself is an important principle for interreligious dialogue. If the biblical tradition can embrace perspectives that directly challenge one another, then Christians need not impose a rigid standard of consistency in the search for religious truth. The inclusion of the books of Job and Qoheleth in the biblical canon directly calls into question the earlier

assertions of the books of Proverbs and of Deuteronomy. Job and
Qoheleth raise painful questions regarding the intelligibility of experience and the meaning and value of wisdom. They insist that their skeptical challenges have as much right to be called wisdom as the confidence
of earlier sages. By accepting the voices of Job and Qoheleth, the Jewish
and Christian communities were acknowledging a plurality of conflicting perspectives that cannot be easily harmonized in a neat, theoretical
scheme. This chaotic plurality of biblical voices offers a relatively more
adequate witness to God's revelation than any single vantage point.

Similarly, it would have been much simpler and in many respects
more coherent for the early church to have followed either Marcion or
Tatian in accepting a single Gospel narrative as authoritative, but the
church decided to embrace the chaotic tradition of four Gospels which
differ on many points. In accepting four canonical Gospels, the church
was acknowledging that no single narrative could completely capture
the fullness of the Christ-event.

Chaos and order interpenetrate human existence and the cosmos. The
wisdom tradition of Israel and its continuing trajectory in the Christian
church reach for descriptions of the universal presence of wisdom in
human experience, but they also undercut any particular claim to have
understood the ways of God adequately and exhaustively. The juxtaposition of wisdom sayings that contradict each other (e.g., Prov 26:4-5)
forces the hearer to recognize the limited applicability of either perspective. While proverbs promise us wisdom and insight, no proverb can
predict for us the proper time to apply it. The sages challenged their students to recognize the complexity and ambiguity of human experience
and to discern for themselves the proper time for the proper speech or
action. They cultivated a sense of mystery, of paradox, and an openness
to being surprised by the playfulness of Lady Wisdom. Virtually every
culture has a wisdom tradition, and the values of the sages of Israel are
often similar to those of wisdom teachers in other cultures, such as Confucianism and Taoism.

The interpretation of Jesus as the incarnation of Sophia or the Logos
in the New Testament asserts a strong universal claim for the significance of his life, death, and resurrection: Wisdom, or the Logos, through
whom all things were made, has entered the world in Jesus Christ, incar-
nating, demonstrating the love of God for humankind. Wisdom is the
principle of intelligibility, the teacher of the secrets of nature (cf. Wis
7:7-21), but the New Testament also stresses the mysterious character of
this revelation. Many of Jesus' own sayings are unsettling paradoxes,
shocking the hearer into a new vision of the gracious possibilities of life
before God. Paul proclaims that the wisdom of God, Jesus Christ crucified, does not simply conform to the wisdom of the world but appears
as folly to the Greeks and scandal to the Jews (1 Cor 1:23). Moreover,
the rather chaotic plurality of interpretations of Jesus in the New Testa-

ment itself cautions against interpreting any single perspective as fully adequate. The Gospels' portrayal of Jesus' own fierce criticisms of the religious leaders of his day is an example of the need for continual critical assessment of one's religious tradition.

Christian theology has long faced the dilemma of how to move from the turbulent chaotic stream of the Bible to a coherent, systematic vision of the universe. To take any one biblical perspective as the center means relegating other biblical voices to the periphery. Girard's proposal runs into this danger by focusing so strongly and exclusively on one aspect of biblical revelation, the vindication of the victim. Classical Christian theology created a forced harmony from the Bible through a supersessionist narrative which displaced the Jewish people, rejected their understanding of their scriptures, and proclaimed a new Christian triumphalism. The result was repeated violence toward Jews, a catastrophic betrayal of the message of Jesus himself. Chaos theory suggests another image of how a system can operate: an open-ended self-organizing system that constantly interacts with the flow of ideas and energies around it and that includes patterns of interaction and interconnectedness within even the most chaotic turbulence. Such an image corresponds more accurately to the concrete facts of history and avoids the recourse to violence to enforce religious conformity.

NICHOLAS OF CUSA

The sapiential tradition of Israel and the Wisdom Christology of the New Testament have continued to affect Christian thought century after century. Nicholas of Cusa drew heavily from these perspectives, interpreted through the lens of the Christian Neoplatonic mystical tradition, in formulating his own synthesis. While his own efforts at establishing unity among the world's religions were limited by the horizons of his own time and were doomed to failure, many of the principles of his theology continue to offer wisdom today and resonate deeply with the perspectives of contemporary chaos theory.[43] Rejecting any triumphalistic claim to have comprehended God fully, he insisted that all theology is a *docta ignorantia*, a learned ignorance, a knowing that is aware of its own limits and that recognizes that the reality of God is beyond anything that we can think, imagine, or conceive. Nicholas insisted that even the biblical descriptions and images of God are not perfectly adequate to the divine reality and are misleading if taken univocally. All language about God must pass through a purgation, a negation of its literal meaning.

Moreover, Nicholas acknowledged that all peoples know God and speak of God in their respective traditions; and he assumed that God had sent prophets to different nations, suggesting that the plurality of the world's religions is related to the divine economy of revelation and salvation. Nicholas taught that God is both radically transcendent and also radically immanent in the universe. While God is beyond our understanding, God is "not other" than the world, an important principle for dialogue with South and East Asian traditions that teach nonduality.

Nicholas also held forth the ideal of the coincidence of opposites. Things that appear contrary or contradictory in this world may coincide in the divine reality in a way that ordinary understanding cannot grasp. The measure of our reason is not the measure of the divine reality. Each attempt to articulate the coincidence of opposites inevitably uses the language of a particular way of thinking to articulate what is beyond language. Negative theology reminds us that this language falls short of capturing God, but Nicholas trusts that a skillful use of language can evoke an awareness of the unknowable God. These principles do not resolve all the problems posed by the encounter with other traditions, but they offer wisdom and guidance in dialogue.

Rather than constructing new inclusivist or pluralist theologies of religion, what may be more helpful in the present situation is close attention to the dynamics of conversation when perspectives from different traditions are brought together. To this project the next chapter will turn.

8

Buddhist Awakening and
Christian Revelation

A BUDDHIST–CHRISTIAN CONVERSATION

Of all the world's major religious traditions, Buddhism appears in many ways to be the tradition at the furthest remove from fundamental Christian assumptions about revelation. Buddhists do not look to a transcendent creator God or rely on any divine revelation. Precisely because of these important differences, Buddhism has a claim to be among the most provocative of dialogue partners for Christians.

Chaos theory suggests that we cannot predict or control the outcome of many natural processes and cultural encounters. The same is true of any genuine conversation: If the search for the truth becomes more important than each side's desire to be in the right, then conversation can lead all parties to insights they might not have had in isolation. Rather than trying to achieve a final conceptual resolution of the question of religious plurality regarding revelation or the manifestation of truth, we may do better by attending carefully to the often chaotic process of dialogue itself, with its negative and positive feedback loops and its seemingly minor factors which can become amplified into powerful shaping forces over time. As we have seen, John Briggs and F. David Peat suggest that one lesson of chaos theory is patiently to wait in times of confusion in openness and humility. The Christian theologian Karl Rahner and the Buddhist thinker Masao Abe, like many earlier wisdom teachers, also recommend a patient waiting before the mystery of existence, trusting that insight will emerge even in the midst of confusion and chaos. As an example of the type of conversation that can occur between traditions with very different assumptions about transformative insights, this chapter will place in conversation the views of Rahner on Christian revelation and of Abe on Mahayana Buddhist awakening.

Masao Abe (1915-) is a Japanese Zen Buddhist philosopher who is the leading contemporary representative of the Kyoto School of philosophy. The Kyoto School, founded by Japanese philosopher Kitaro Nishida (1870-1945) and continued by Hajime Tanabe (1885-1962) and Keiji Nishitani (1900-1990), is a group of Japanese thinkers who have immersed themselves in both Eastern and Western thought and have reflected deeply on contemporary philosophical issues in light of both traditions. Himself a student of Nishitani, Abe has studied not only Buddhist thought but also Western philosophy and Christian theology, spending two years as a student at Columbia University (1955-57) and studying under Paul Tillich at Union Theological Seminary. Abe later served as visiting professor at a number of American universities, and his work has been the focus of much recent interreligious discussion.[1]

Karl Rahner (1904-1984) was a German Jesuit theologian who greatly influenced Catholic and Protestant theology during the middle of the twentieth century. Early in his career Rahner reinterpreted the metaphysics of knowledge of Thomas Aquinas in light of the more recent modes of thinking of Immanuel Kant and of his own teacher, Martin Heidegger. Later, as a systematic theologian, Rahner began his theological reflections from the experience of the human person in a world shaped by revelation and grace, and he sought to relate all Christian doctrines to contemporary experience of the world. He saw divine revelation as a strictly universal offer of God's love to every human being, whether the person is explicitly aware of Jesus Christ or not; and he interpreted the person and event of Jesus Christ as the concrete and definitive expression of the universal salvific love of God that embraces every person. Rahner described the implicit offer of God's love in all experience as "transcendental revelation,†" and the explicit, historical revelation of God in the history of Israel and the person of Jesus Christ as "categorical revelation.†" The specific events in the history of Israel and the life, death, and resurrection of Jesus are concrete outward expressions of the universal transcendental revelation that embraces every person. While Rahner himself never studied Asian religious traditions in depth, he was very interested in the question of how Christians can welcome other religious traditions as concrete mediations of grace. He assumed that all religious traditions are willed by God as part of the economy of revelation and salvation.

One example of a convergence of opposite perspectives that remain distinct occurred in a conversation between Rahner and a teacher of Masao Abe, the noted Japanese Zen Buddhist philosopher Keiji Nishitani, who was well known as the leader of the Kyoto School of philosophy. Nishitani was aware that Rahner had used the term "anonymous Christian" to describe members of other religious traditions who were embraced by the grace of God given in Jesus Christ, and he asked Rahner what he would say about being called an anonymous Zen Buddhist.

Rahner, with his usual complexity of thought, made several points in reply:

> certainly you may and should do so from your point of view; I feel myself honoured by such an interpretation, even if I am obliged to regard you as being in error or if I assume that, correctly understood, to be a genuine Zen Buddhist is identical with being a genuine Christian, in the sense directly and properly intended by such statements. Of course in terms of objective social awareness it is indeed clear that the Buddhist is not a Christian and the Christian is not a Buddhist.

To this Nishitani responded: "Then on this point we are entirely at one."[2]

In other conversations with Christian theologians in Marburg and in Basel, Nishitani posed a question based on the statement of the apostle Paul: "It is no longer I who live but it is Christ who lives in me" (Gal 2:20). Nishitani told the Christians that he understood this statement immediately from his own Zen experience, but he asked them: "Who is speaking here?"[3] On both occasions the Christian theologians found no satisfactory answer and remained silent in frustration.

In questioning Rahner and his other Christian interlocutors, Nishitani was speaking out of the centuries-old Zen tradition of presenting koans of the true self. Zen masters frequently pose puzzling questions of identity and challenge their hearers to respond immediately from their own direct awareness of reality. Any merely conceptual answer or any imitation of another's response will be sternly rebuffed. The key to answering properly is a transformed consciousness that can be displayed but not defined.

While the worldviews of Buddhists and Christians are profoundly different, the values of the two traditions resonate deeply with each other, suggesting overtones of a unity beyond all differences, a coincidence of opposites that respects differences but unites them. Buddhist and Christian articulations of the opposites and of the unity will, of course, differ dramatically. The encounter of Buddhists and Christians may be taken as a koan in the original sense of the Chinese word *kung-an*, a "public notice" or a "public announcement." A koan invites the hearer to take to heart what has been announced, but the announcement is a baffling, perplexing paradox that cannot be resolved by the intellect. A koan frustrates our ordinary process of thinking and challenges us to move to a new level of consciousness. Rahner's and Nishitani's agreement on the paradoxical identity and difference of the Zen Buddhist and the Christian is one public announcement, or koan; and Nishitani's unanswered question on Paul's Christian identity is another.

One limitation of many recent Western Christian discussions of the theology of religions is that they often use Western philosophical and theological assumptions and concepts to frame the issues. While this can be helpful as an initial stage for internal Western Christian reflection, we cannot assume that the assumptions and concepts of any one religious tradition can automatically provide an adequate framework for understanding and judging another tradition. Interreligious dialogue challenges us to enter into the images and categories of other religious traditions to see questions in a different framework. John Cobb's proposal for the mutual transformation of traditions and David Tracy's call for the praxis of interreligious dialogue challenge us to perform experiments of entering into other traditions' perspectives.[4] The Mahayana Buddhist tradition has a long history of dealing with questions of identity; and its nondual logic of affirming "not one, not two," may be of help in pondering the encounters of the world's religions. As an example of how two traditions can both converge and diverge, respecting other positions while remaining deeply rooted in their own commitments, this chapter will explore the perspectives of Masao Abe and Karl Rahner on awakening and revelation. Both thinkers recommend an attitude of openness and humility before the questions of human existence.

Masao Abe's and Karl Rahner's understandings of religious identity arise from their respective interpretations of the experiences of Buddhist awakening and Christian revelation. At the center of Rahner's theology is a description of the experience of revelation and grace in the language of the Christian tradition, though Rahner also claims that this experience is available to all humans. Abe expresses the implications of Zen Buddhist awakening in relation to contemporary nihilism and to other religious traditions.[5] Abe assumes that the Zen tradition describes experiences that are available to all human beings. Each offers a phenomenology of religious experience to address the challenge of modern secular thought, which dismisses religion in any form.

Abe has also offered his own interpretations of the Christian themes of the Trinity, creation, incarnation, and the crucifixion of Jesus.[6] While these interpretations are very evocative and thought-provoking, his interpretations are more properly part of Buddhist thought than Christian theology because Abe's fundamental assumptions remain Mahayana Buddhist; and the Christian themes are radically reinterpreted in light of the Mahayana principles of nonduality and dependent co-arising.[†] In particular, from Rahner's perspective, Abe's use of the term "God" is misleading and confusing, because Abe treats the God of Christianity as a being within the field of dependent co-arising. Abe asks about the ground of God, and he proposes *jinen* (naturalness or "just-as-it-isness") as the source of every will, human or divine. In this discussion I will focus primarily on Abe's interpretation of his own tradition rather than on his provocative reinterpretation of Christian theology.

PRE-REFLECTIVE EXPERIENCE AND LANGUAGE

For both Abe and Rahner, religious identity arises primordially from awareness of nameless, boundless openness in which all beings are what they are. Religious practice and discourse need to return continually to this unthematic, pre-reflective source experience to be nourished. In boundless openness, the full experience of reality itself awaits us in a dynamic unity at every moment, and conscious appropriation of this experience has the power to transform our lives. For both Abe and Rahner, this primal awareness cannot be captured in conceptual affirmations, and it calls forth paradoxical and seemingly contradictory uses of language to express the nameless. This sets up a major difficulty in comparing the two figures; for no univocal, conceptual understanding of either Buddhist awakening or Christian revelation can be adequate to the full pre-reflective awareness.

For Rahner, the encounter with God takes place primordially on the transcendental level of our original orientation toward absolute mystery, which Rahner describes as the transcendental horizon.[†] Human transcendence is the infinite openness of the finite for the infinite, "a basic mode of being which is prior to and permeates every objective experience."[7] The transcendental horizon can never be objectified because it is the condition of possibility of encountering objects. The horizon is not one experience alongside others, for it "opens us to unlimited possibilities of encountering this or that particular thing."[8]

In Rahner's view, this fundamental, primitive experience of God as gracious transcendental horizon is the condition of possibility and the source for all explicit, thematic knowledge of God in religion and philosophy. The primordial revelation of God is this implicit awareness of the infinite, which approaches us graciously. This revelation finds expression in the symbols of the world's religions. For Abe, the language of Zen Buddhism expresses the direct, nondiscursive awakening to *shunyata,* or the true self. This pre-reflective realization of nondiscursive insight is the creative source of all the images, actions, and stories of the Zen masters. While the awareness itself can never be objectified, it can be displayed in rock gardens and koans and Zen actions and especially in the practice of zazen itself. This awareness is demonstrated in performance, not in concepts. True *shunyata* is not thought but lived.[9]

Since neither *shunyata* nor the transcendental horizon can ever be defined conceptually or distinguished from other things, we do not have two "things" that we can compare and contrast. Nonetheless, in seeking to name the unnameable, Abe and Rahner often choose terms that are quite similar. Both thinkers use the image of boundless openness outside of which there is nothing whatsoever. *Shunyata* and the transcendental horizon can be experienced as no-thing and thus as nihilistic. In both cases, we may seem to lose ourselves in this awareness, and we risk falling into despair. Both *shunyata* and the transcendental horizon, however, are also the creative source of human action and religious insight. Abe's *shunyata* is the universal process of emptying, the process in which beings are just what they are and are equal in their suchness. Rahner describes the transcendental horizon as the self-emptying (*Selbstentäusserung*) of God which allows creatures to be what they are.

Claims of a pre-reflective, nonthematic awareness are notoriously difficult to discuss, and critics have rightly noted that even if a direct, pre-reflective experience of reality were possible, we could not describe it apart from some linguistic interpretation. Abe and Rahner are both aware of the paradoxical demands that their claims make on language, and they both insist than any statements about *shunyata* or the transcendental horizon must be negated. When either *shunyata* or the transcendental horizon is treated as an object, it is falsified; yet every attempt to speak of these experiences inevitably treats *shunyata* or the transcendental horizon at least grammatically as an object. To address this dilemma, Abe uses the traditional logic of the Prajnaparamita Sutras: *shunyata* is not *shunyata*. Rahner for his part insists that all statements about the transcendental horizon are dialectical and dipolar because they use objects within the horizon to symbolize the horizon itself.

For both Abe and Rahner, in communicating the experience of awakening or grace, the choice is not between a pure, unmediated experience of reality and language but between skillful and unskillful uses of language. In Mahayana Buddhist terms, we never experience ultimate truth apart from conventional truth, or *nirvana* apart from *samsara*, or *shunyata* apart from dependent co-arising. In Rahner's language, the experience of God is always a mediated immediacy because God's presence is both manifested in and through finite reality and also hidden in this manifestation. For both Abe and Rahner, language about ultimate reality must be both negated and affirmed if it is to be used properly. In interreligious dialogue, what we can compare are not unthematic experiences themselves, if such exist, but the linguistic forms of expression that seek to convey an experience of transformation that eludes direct conceptual discourse.

AWAKENING AND REVELATION

Both Abe and Rahner see the path to realizing one's true religious identity as a process of surrender and letting go. Our ordinary self must release its grasp on itself and surrender to boundless openness. Abe identifies the central problem of human existence as the split that is created by discriminating, grasping self-consciousness. Because of self-consciousness we

compare ourselves with others, and we regard ourselves from a standpoint outside ourselves. Self-consciousness leads us to make value judgments about things we like or dislike. We become especially attached to
the idea of our own self and thereby establish ourselves as the center of
the world. "Distinction turns into opposition, conflict and struggle as
soon as the distinction becomes an object of attachment."[10] According
to Abe, the view of ourselves from the outside "constitutes the fundamental ignorance inherent in human existence."[11] Self-consciousness
divides us from ourselves and creates our basic restlessness or fundamental anxiety. The raison d'être of religion is to cure this fundamental
restlessness.

For Rahner, the central problem of human existence is the frightening
responsibility of our transcendental freedom. In creating free creatures,
God allows humans the possibility of a fundamental acceptance or rejection of our own absolute origin and future. The ability to make distinctions and to view ourselves from outside flows from our condition as
free, finite creatures, which is good. The restlessness we experience is,
for Rahner, the reaching out of the human spirit through the finite for
the infinite. While this is subject to corruption, the restlessness is not
itself evil. Our relationship to ourselves is grounded in the gift of transcendental freedom, the power to decide about the totality of our lives
and dispose ourselves either toward or against our horizon.

Ultimately, for Rahner, we do not decide about outward things alone;
we decide about our own selves. The problem of human existence is that
in deciding we face the radical threat of guilt. For Rahner, "all sin is only
the refusal to entrust oneself to this measurelessness" which we name
God; sin is "the lesser love which, because it refuses to become greater,
is no longer love."[12] The possibility of finally rejecting the gracious horizon of our lives is a frightening paradox, for human freedom thereby
rejects its own ground of possibility. Even an outwardly minor act or a
complacent state of quiet despair can express a deep-seated rejection of
the gracious horizon.

This radical threat does not exist in Abe's religious universe. To be
sure, ignorance is beginningless and endless and causes untold suffering;
but for Abe, the problem of good and evil is not a problem of the moral
will deciding itself before God but rather of the discriminating mind
which creates duality and distinctions. For Abe, like the Mahayana Buddhist tradition in general, there is no possibility of an ultimate, definitive
separation from *shunyata* or the Buddha-nature. Abe cites an old Zen
principle: "You are already inseparable from Self-Awakening."[13] Abe
does use the Buddhist symbol of hell, but in Buddhist cosmology hell
does not last forever. Abe tells the story of the Zen master who promises
his students that when he dies, he is going straight to hell. When they
respond with amazement, the master asks, "If I do not go to hell, who
will be there waiting to save you when you arrive?"

For both Rahner and Abe, the restless search for human identity gives rise to misguided and futile efforts to find peace. Abe compares the desperate search of self-consciousness to a snake biting its own tail: "Trying to grasp one's self by one's self from the outside may be likened metaphorically to a snake trying to swallow its own tail. When the snake bites its tail, it makes a circle. And the more it tries to swallow its tail, the smaller that circle becomes."[14] If the snake succeeded completely, it would disappear into emptiness. In pursuing itself, the self-conscious ego falls into an ever deeper dilemma until it finally collapses into emptiness. This may happen at different times in different ways, sometimes only on one's deathbed; but sooner or later for Abe, "the realization of no-self is a 'must' for the human ego. We must realize that there is no unchanging, eternal ego-self."[15]

Rahner is also aware of the power of anxiety in human life. Like Abe, Rahner notes that we can grasp at one thing or experience after another in the attempt to secure our identity and quiet the restless spirit; but as long as we cling to something we can grasp or control, we cut ourselves off from the transcendental horizon and from our true selves. But Rahner also repeatedly stresses a temptation that does not fit Abe's usual model of the frantic self, but which Abe could well acknowledge as a danger. For Rahner, modern Westerners face the danger of a safe, mediocre life that settles down in comfort and finds a thousand substitutes for action.[16] This is not the anxious ego swallowing its tail but the quiet despair of one who has given up and settled into an inauthentic peace. "The danger of a spectacular breakdown does exist. But at least equally serious is the danger that our whole life will slowly but surely fade into oblivion: the danger of mediocrity, of no longer really believing in a personal achievement, of giving up everything."[17]

Rahner agrees with Abe that our self-consciousness never successfully and finally grasps who we are, and he draws the further conclusion that our own interpretation of ourselves is no certain measure of our transcendental decision for or against God. "We can in fact refuse to see that our trivial faults and imperfections are a cover for a final basic attitude which is truly mortal sin."[18] Rahner expresses the fundamental choice of human existence in a favorite image that resonates deeply with Abe's perspective. We really have only one choice in life. We can cling to the small, brightly lit island of our own knowledge and mastery and control, and this clinging is what we call hell; or we can surrender to the infinite ocean of mystery, which appears as the blinding darkness that surrounds the island, and this surrender is what we call heaven.[19]

Like Abe, Rahner insists that the ego's quest for the true self must in the end surrender any attempt to establish itself securely against the threats that menace it. For both Rahner and Abe, genuine reflection on our identity plunges us into a dilemma, and both reject any merely conceptual resolution. For Rahner, human beings not only have questions but are questions. To accept divine revelation, for Rahner, allows us to accept and entrust the question that we are to the divine mystery that encompasses without trying to secure our own existence or salvation. Abe notes: "It is not that I *have* a dilemma, but I *am* a dilemma."[20] For both, the objectified self is not the true self. For Abe, it is only when we realize that we are a dilemma which we cannot resolve and let go of the effort to resolve it that we experience *shunyata*: "Once you thoroughly realize that you *are* the dilemma of good and evil you can break through the dilemma and come to a standpoint which is neither good nor evil."[21]

For Abe, the death of the ego discloses emptiness, and through this experience one realizes suchness: "In this realization you are no longer separated from yourself, but are just yourself. No more, no less. There is no gap between you and yourself: you become you."[22] The distinction within the self is overcome. This realization is not only a goal; it is also the point of departure, the basis for a life liberated from anxiety.

Abe, in keeping with the Zen tradition, usually describes this new way of being in the world as total liberation. For the awakened one, every anxiety and fear are broken through. Abe does, however, also acknowledge the legitimacy of the alternative perspective of Shinran, the thirteenth-century founder of the Jodo Shinshu tradition in Japan. According to Shinran, we never completely break through anxiety and fear in this world. For Shinran, we are saved by trusting in the vow of Amida Buddha, but we nonetheless remain foolish and ignorant.[23]

In describing the acceptance of revelation and grace in conversion, Rahner uses images reminiscent of the Zen description of the Great Doubt or the Great Death. While revelation and grace are universally offered and can be received in a wide variety of outward circumstances, Rahner examines the limit-situations where we live on the border between God and the world as paradigmatic of the experience of revelation and grace. These are strange experiences of knowing by not-knowing. He describes these experiences as deeply unsettling, having "the taste of death and destruction." They are, in Heidegger's word, *unheimlich* (uncanny), because they plunge us into an abyss we cannot master or control. According to Rahner, "Then is the hour of grace. Then the seemingly uncanny, bottomless depth of our existence as experienced by us is the bottomless depth of God communicating himself to us, the dawning of his approaching infinity which no longer has any set paths, which is tasted like a nothing because it is infinity."[24] He cites as examples the experiences of absolute loneliness, forgiving or sacrificing without personal benefit, and trying to love God even when it seems pointless: "when we seemed to be calling out into emptiness and our cry seemed to fall on deaf ears, when it looked as if we were taking a terrifying jump into the bottomless abyss, when everything seemed to become incomprehensible and apparently senseless."[25]

For Rahner, the proper human response is to relinquish the effort to control and accept the uncontrollable in faith. We accept our orientation to absolute mystery "in unconditional obedience to conscience, and in the open and trusting acceptance of the uncontrollable in one's own existence in moments of prayer and quiet silence."[26] This acceptance is what is at stake in understanding the meaning of the word "God": "The concept 'God' is not a grasp of God by which a person masters the mystery, but it is letting oneself be grasped by the mystery which is present and yet ever distant."[27] We can jump into the abyss while dreading the leap precisely because our impotence, weakness, and cowardice are encompassed and surpassed by God's power and mercy.[28] Revelation and grace free us for action.

Awareness of boundless openness is elusive, and both Abe and Rahner make concrete suggestions for how to become more conscious of the prediscursive experience of *shunyata* or the transcendental horizon. Abe follows the model of his mentor, Dogen, and recommends zazen, sitting meditation. In sitting meditation, the practitioner refrains from conscious thinking, attends to the breathing, and acknowledges all experiences that arise without conceptualizing, judging, or clinging. Dogen gives instructions on how to meditate: "Do not think good or bad. Do not administer pros and cons. Cease all movements of the conscious mind, the gauging of all thoughts and views. Have no designs on becoming a Buddha."[29] In time, the clinging ego-self will face a crisis and deconstruct, and the practitioner will experience the casting off of body and mind. The immediate presence of things as they are becomes luminous.

Rahner's own spiritual practice was shaped by the *Spiritual Exercises* of Ignatius Loyola, which use images in guided meditation; but Rahner did not recommend this as a universal practice for modern Christians. He noted that modern Catholic theologians have not done much to encourage the more primitive experience of God as the horizon of our lives. Rahner's own advice is not as specific and detailed as Abe's and Dogen's, but the basic principle and movement of the practice are very similar. Dogen, Abe, and Rahner all recommend returning to the source of all experience and thought by disengaging the mind from the usual flow of contents. Rahner advises:

Be still for once. Don't try to think of so many complex and varied things. Give these deeper realities of the spirit a chance now to rise to the surface: silence, fear, the ineffable longing for truth, for love, for fellowship, for God. Face loneliness, fear, imminent death! Allow such ultimate, basic human experiences to come first. Don't go talking about them, making up theories about them, but simply endure these basic experiences. Then in fact something like a primitive awareness of God can emerge. Then perhaps we cannot say much about it; then what we "grasp" first of all about God appears to be nothing, to be absent, the nameless, absorbing and suppressing all that can be expressed and conceived.[30]

Rahner warns that neglect of this primitive experience of God leads to the impoverishment of all language about God: "[I]f we do not develop such experiences, then our religious life is and remains really of a secondary character and its conceptual-thematic expression is false."[31] The similarities to Dogen's and Abe's practice of zazen are clear. By sitting quietly, we allow anxieties to surface and we face them. We relinquish the ego-self's desire for security and see through the deceptive patterns of the ego-self. Ultimate reality manifests itself on a new level, in ways that can be described both as nothingness and as wondrous Being.

Dogen and Abe promise that attending to the pre-reflective aspect of experience through zazen can free us from selfishness, awaken us to the true self, and open us to wisdom, compassion, and equanimity. In quiet Christian attention to the primitive experience of God as horizon, Rahner finds a similar transformation from the insecure self-centeredness of our ego to the infinite openness of knowledge becoming love. The Christian life is "ultimately a transcendentality, dying, [being] crucified, becoming torn apart with Christ, not as a theory but as what happens in us in our concrete existence when we confront this life with its ultimate dependence on the incomprehensible mystery of God."[32] Accepting our transcendental orientation to God allows us to love our neighbor, accept our own death, and hope in the future beyond any this-worldly calculation.

WHO IS SPEAKING HERE?
BECOMING WHAT WE ARE

For both Abe and Rahner, the most important aspect of religious life is the experience of transformation in which we cast off our ordinary self and awaken to our true identity. Nishitani's question, "Who is speaking here?" challenges both traditions. Both Abe and Rahner agree that the answer must be paradoxical, including both an affirmation and a negation. Any univocal, conceptual response will miss the point. Both agree that we become ourselves by losing ourselves in the realization of oneness with reality itself, but their respective perspectives on dependent co-arising and creation shape very different interpretations of these claims.

For Rahner, the meaning of dispossessing ourselves and becoming one with God is structured by the fundamental relationship of creation. Normally we think of relationships in this world as being between two independently existing realities. Creation does not fit this pattern, however, for there is no other independent reality to which God can be related.

All creatures are in a relationship of absolute dependence on God, but God includes this relationship within Godself, and so, as Nicholas of Cusa had also insisted, God is not simply opposed to the world as another finite being. Thus there is no self in the sense of an independent, permanent ego that can be a secure refuge unto itself. Abe's doctrine of no-self rejects any notion of an unchanging, eternal ego-self. For Rahner, we are not a permanent substance but rather the action of becoming who we are, the contingent, dependent "performance" of ourselves as the dynamic process reaching out for God.

In accepting revelation and grace, the self that depends radically on God for its very existence surrenders itself and becomes one with God in a nondual unity. Revelation is God's self-communication and our transformation in it. Rahner models his interpretation of this nondual oneness on the union of the human and divine natures in Jesus Christ, which is expressed in the terms of the Council of Chalcedon (451 C.E.): The two natures are joined inseparably but remain unconfused. Like Jesus Christ, though never to the same degree, we become the real-symbolic expression of the reality of God, so that our very being is the self-utterance of God. When Paul says, "It is no longer I who live but Christ who lives in me" (Gal 2:20), Rahner understands the "I" who speaks as the human person dispossessed of its curved-in-on-itself sub-jectivity, taken up into the divine life, and empowered by God. The self has become dispossessed of itself and has become transparent to the divine without losing itself. There is no opposition between the human and the divine in the voice speaking, however, because they are not two opposed entities. In the union of grace, God and humans become one and thus are inseparable but unconfused.

Abe, like the Buddhist tradition in general, does not rely on a creat-ing and redeeming God, but speaks of dependent co-arising, the inter-dependence of all things in the universe. For Abe, no reality radically transcends the universe; and thus there is no incomprehensible, tran-scendent God. Abe asserts: "There is absolutely nothing behind the world or the universe, the fact of which is to be realized by one's self."[33] Nonetheless, because nonduality escapes all conceptual determination, it would be misleading to label Abe a monist. For Abe, Rahner's descrip-tion of our union with God as inseparable and unconfused remains dual-istic; these terms must themselves be negated in a movement to a more radical nonduality. Abe's vision of dependent co-arising implies that every relationship without exception must be symmetrical. The true self of Abe realizes itself in awakening, and the true self is not other than *shunyata*, the boundless openness that is the universe. Thus any concep-tual answer to Nishitani's question of who is speaking in Paul's state-ment (Gal 2:20) would be wrong. As an old Zen master said: "Anything I could possibly say would miss the point." For Rahner, the "I" who is speaking has surrendered itself in an act that is and is not its own because it is constituted in both the order of nature and of grace by itself and by God. We come most truly to be ourselves when we are not ourselves, for freedom and dependence on God increase in direct and not inverse proportionality. We become who we are when we have abandoned any effort at calculation or control of the mystery that envelops us. The grasping ego-self has died. And yet, for Rahner, not unlike the Japanese Pure Land Buddhist Shinran, we never completely actualize this state in this world. We remain in a certain sense *simul justus et peccator*, at once justified and sinner, dependent on the grace of God.

Nishitani's question "Who is speaking here?" includes another question as well: Is the new identity the same as or different from the old? What remains and what is changed? Here again no direct answer is adequate. For both Abe and Rahner, the experience of awakening or revelation allows us to be what we already are, and thus the new identity received in Buddhist awakening or Christian revelation is both new and not new. A real transformation has taken place, but this transformation is an appropriation of who we have always been.

For Rahner, God is universally present as revelation and grace; thus, if we are seeking God, we have in some sense always already found God and been found by God. God is always already known prior to being consciously experienced or reflected upon. Since the transcendental horizon is always gracious, there is nothing absolutely new to find in religious experience. Even the proclamation of the Christian gospel to those who have never heard it does not bring "new News." What happens in prayer and religious practice and metaphysical reflection is that "we are only making explicit for ourselves what we already know implicitly about ourselves in the depths of our personal self-realization."[34]

Rahner also negates the linear temporal sequence suggested by the terms of human guilt, the need for redemption, and salvation. "We cannot interpret this world in a Christian way by saying that formerly there was a very evil world burdened with guilt, and that by the redemption of Jesus Christ it then became essentially different in an empirical and tangible way."[35] Even in individual experience, where there is a real process of transformation, the awareness of guilt comes after the experience of forgiveness and grace. We may think that formerly we were guilty and now we are forgiven, but it is only by accepting God's forgiveness and grace that we can understand what the guilt is that is being forgiven.[36] Thus Rahner uses the image of a circle of guilt and forgiveness, a circle in which the elements mutually condition one another. A cry for forgiveness is itself the expression of grace and not the search for it. In the conscious acceptance of grace, we realize that we are always sinners and that the horizon of God's grace is always present. We allow grace to manifest itself in our lives.

Abe also insists that awakening is a realization of who we already are, and thus the experience both does and does not bring a new identity.

Mahayana Buddhism traditionally discussed this issue under the rubric of original enlightenment and acquired enlightenment. As Abe notes, "Zen always emphasizes that you are originally in enlightenment."[37] Thus there is nothing to seek and nothing to find, no realization and no attainment. Original enlightenment is the pre-reflective, universally present realization of *shunyata*. Acquired enlightenment is the conscious awakening through the discipline of Buddhist practice.

Abe's main guide to interpreting the relation between the two is Dogen, for whom this issue constituted the central existential crisis of his own life and practice. The young Dogen could not see why rigorous Buddhist meditation practice was necessary if original enlightenment was already present. Dogen went to China in search of an answer, and he resolved the crisis by coming to see practice and attainment not as two distinct experiences but rather, in Abe's words, as "indispensable and inseparable components of a dynamic relationship."[38] Rahner views a prayer for forgiveness as itself the expression of grace even though it seems to be a search for grace. Abe, following Dogen, describes the practice of zazen as being the expression of enlightenment even though it may seem to be the search for enlightenment. "[W]e realize that we are not simply on the way towards enlightenment but have *originally* been *in* enlightenment. There is a dynamic unity of being on the way and having reached the goal. Zazen has no purpose. True zazen in itself is true enlightenment."[39] Rahner also asserts a dynamic unity of being on the way and of having reached the goal: The experience of Christian prayer means that we are not simply on the way toward revelation and grace but have originally been in revelation and grace.

The final question of Rahner's discussion with Nishitani remains: Are these realizations of Buddhist awakening and Christian grace the same or different? On one level, as Rahner and Nishitani agreed, it is clear that the objectifications of religious awareness of Abe and Rahner are quite different. In addition to the differences already noted, Rahner, with the Christian tradition in general, always relates his thought to the concrete historical events of the life, death, and resurrection of Jesus in a way that finds no exact parallel in Abe. For Rahner, in Jesus Christ God expresses Godself outside Godself in a unique and definitive way. For Abe, by contrast, the Buddha is not a historical savior and bears no supernatural gift. The historical figure Shakyamuni Buddha points out our own identity, and in awakening we ourselves are the Buddha, the *dharma*, suchness.[40] For Abe, there is no one event in history that plays the role of the Christ-event.

Nonetheless, there are dynamics in both Abe's and Rahner's perspectives that open a space for the further agreement between Nishitani and Rahner that, in the direct and proper sense, to be a Zen Buddhist is not other than to be a Christian. While the expressions of Zen and Christian experiences are very different, both Abe and Rahner nonetheless assume the strict universality of the pre-reflective horizon of experience and thus allow for the possibility of analogous experiences and expressions in other traditions: Abe's *shunyata* is the universal process of emptying which is the dynamic movement of all beings just as they are, whether people use Buddhist categories or not; Rahner's God is the horizon of all finite reality, universally present whether people use Christian categories or not.

This is not to say that Buddhist and Christian experiences are the same, for the experience of the ultimate always comes through a particular tradition and is shaped by it. Both Abe and Rahner recognize that every experience of *shunyata* or of the transcendental horizon takes place in a concrete historical and cultural setting that is inseparable from the awareness of ultimate reality.

Both Abe and Rahner also acknowledge the relative legitimacy of other religious traditions to mediate the experience of awakening or revelation, but each uses the assumptions and criteria of his own tradition to judge others. Rahner assumes that the Christ-event is the definitive real symbol of the universal salvific will of God, normative for every religious tradition. But Rahner also asserts that other religious traditions are in fact also positively willed by God as the path of divine salvation for their members.[41] Abe assumes that the Mahayana principles of nonduality, dependent co-arising, and universally reciprocal relationships offer norms to evaluate every other form of religion and philosophy. But Abe also acknowledges that *shunyata* is manifested and realized in other religious awakenings as well. Both Abe and Rahner interpret the other's tradition as relatively adequate, but as being en route toward a more fully adequate self-understanding.

While each clearly affirms his own religious tradition, the final movement for both thinkers is beyond the one-sided certainties of all conceptual claims, including those of their own respective religious traditions. For Abe, wisdom inevitably becomes compassion; in light of nondiscriminating consciousness, the awakened one can use conceptual knowledge to return to the world of particularity without clinging to concepts or objects. Even Buddhist perspectives and concepts must be negated in order to serve as tools of compassion. For Rahner, the experience of God transforms knowledge into love. In the movement into God, knowledge must choose either to cling to itself in despair or to negate itself and become love. If we use our knowledge as an instrument of power and conquest, then we are not really knowing.

Abe calls the result of his path a positionless position, a position that negates itself and thus allows a space for every other position, including a framework for a theology of religions.[42] Rahner claims that the Christian realizes that no individual truth is true except in the process of becoming a question that remains unanswered because it is asking about the incomprehensible God. Thus he can boldly argue: "The Christian is the true and the most radical skeptic" because the Christian has to deal with "that otherwise maddening experience in which . . . one can hold no opinion to be completely true and no opinion to be completely false."[43]

From the perspective of the Zen tradition, this entire discussion has been far too conceptual and thus has long since missed the point. A well-known Zen story expresses the paradoxical transformation of reality in Zen practice. The Chinese Ch'an master Ching yüan Wei-hsin of the Tang dynasty recalled his experience of Zen practice:

> Thirty years ago, before I began the study of Zen, I said, "Mountains are mountains, waters are waters."
>
> After I got an insight into the truth of Zen through the instruction of a good master, I said, "Mountains are not mountains, waters are not waters."
>
> But now, having attained the abode of final rest [that is, awakening], I say, "Mountains are really mountains, waters are really waters."

Abe notes that after recounting his experience, Wei-hsin then asks the crucial question, "Do you think these three understandings are the same or different?"[44] Abe himself answers the question of Wei-hsin: "They are different and yet not different; they are the same and yet different at once."[45] By including both of the earlier stages in a dynamic whole, the third stage both affirms them and overcomes them. *Shunyata* is realized in awakening, but Abe tells us: "this dynamic identity of self and *shunyata* is equally true of everyone and everything throughout the universe."[46]

To return to the spirit of Nishitani's questions, perhaps we can substitute "Buddhism" and "Christianity" for the mountains and waters that Wei-hsin described above. At the beginning of dialogue, Buddhism is Buddhism and Christianity is Christianity. During the course of dialogue, both traditions will be negated only to become more truly themselves. Or one could turn to another old Zen story from the Blue Cliff Records, a brief dialogue that for Nishitani expressed the core of Zen identity:

> Kyozan Ejaku asked Sansho Enen, "What is your name?"
> Sansho said, "Ejaku!"
> "Ekaju!" replied Kyozan, "that's my name."
> "Well then," said Sansho, "my name is Enen."
> Kyozan roared with laughter.[47]

Epilogue

Christians bring to the dialogue with other religions and to the challenge of violence a sense of the presence of God entering into human life in Jesus Christ and extending healing and reconciliation to all the world. From biblical times to the present, Christians have experienced the presence of God moving in their lives in mysterious, uncanny ways.

For Christians, the heart of revelation is that God is infinite, overflowing love, love without measure, love beyond reason, love like a fountain that flows and flows and flows until the water floods everything all around. This unceasing flood of love is the most attractive and frightening, elusive and mysterious reality in a Christian's life. Attractive, because this love is what we yearn for most deeply; frightening, because this love will not leave us alone but wants to purify us and transform us. If we truly surrender to this love, our lives will never again be the same. For Christians, the ultimate power in this universe is the relentless love of God. Beyond our fears, beyond our addictions, beyond our doubts, beyond our cruelty and hatred, beyond our envy and rivalry, the infinite love of God is pursuing us.

There is something frightening about this love, and we draw back because we are afraid we do not deserve it. We fear we do not belong in the presence of God. We feel ashamed and want to hide. For Christians, the deepest problem of our existence is not our finitude, it is not that we become sick, grow old, and die. The greatest danger of our lives is that we can separate ourselves from the love of God, and on some level we have already done so. We choose something finite in place of God and make it the center of our lives. God knocks at the door of our lives, but we have to open the door to allow God in.

Christians experience in Jesus a revelation of God, who is present throughout all of human existence. In proclaiming Jesus Christ as the incarnation of Lady Wisdom, of the Logos, the early church was asserting that the love of God revealed in him extends to the entire cosmos. Indeed, it is difficult to imagine a God who is infinite, overflowing love being absent from some portion of human existence. The patterns of Jesus' ministry, life, death, and resurrection reveal to Christians the meaning of our own lives. The revelation of God in Jesus does not promise an easy peace. Often the first awareness of God is

201

disheartening, disorienting, disrupting. Christians may become aware of God through some type of loss or threat to our being that reminds us of our absolute dependence upon God. To encounter God can be like falling into an abyss. We lose all security. We are in a free fall, and there is nothing we can grasp onto for support. All we can do is trust that God is there waiting to catch us.

But Christians also experience God as the source of the most important values in our lives, as source of all that is true, good, and beautiful. What lures us in the quest for justice is ultimately the presence of God. What fascinates us in the experience of beauty, whether natural or artistic, is the presence of God. What draws the scientist or the explorer onward, through search after search, is the desire for the truth. In each case there is a loss of concern for the self. If we are focused on justice, on beauty, on truth, there is a healthy self-forgetfulness. Christians can trust that as members of other religious traditions experience the true, the good, and the beautiful, they too experience the God who is love, whether they believe in God or not.

The light of revelation illumines and transforms, offering insight and healing, calling forth community; but, as we have seen, understandings of revelation, from biblical times to the present, have fostered hatred and violence. The biblical witness to God's revelation calls for an openness, even a surrender of our self-understanding. We do not measure the revelation of God; it measures us. Yet the concrete, violent content of some scriptural demands and the later history of violence of the Christian tradition itself demand that we scrutinize carefully what is claimed to be revelatory of God's will. Biblical commands and traditional Christian perspectives have caused too much unnecessary, unjust suffering to allow for an uncritical acceptance. To be effective witnesses demands a conversion of mind and heart, both personally and as representatives of an ambiguous tradition stretching back for centuries. It also demands an openness to the revelatory presence of God in other religious traditions, indeed throughout all human life and the entire cosmos. Christians bring the message of the revelation of God in Jesus Christ to the world, a message that challenges all humans, especially those who claim to be his followers, to live lives of forgiveness and love.

Notes

PREFACE

1. See Donald W. Mitchell and James A. Wiseman, eds., *The Gethsemani Encounter: A Dialogue on the Spiritual Life by Buddhist and Christian Monastics* (New York: Continuum, 1997).

1
REVELATION, THE RELIGIONS, AND VIOLENCE

1. John Paul II, *Tertio Millennio Adveniente*, nos. 33-53, *Origins* 24/24 (Nov. 24, 1994): 410-15.

2. Quoted by Daniel Goldhagen, *Hitler's Willing Executioners: Ordinary Germans and the Holocaust* (New York: Alfred A. Knopf, 1996), 53.

3. Wyndham Lewis, *The Jews: Are They Human?* (London: George Allen & Unwin, 1939).

4. Georges Passelecq and Bernard Suchecky, *The Hidden Encyclical of Pius XI* (New York: Harcourt Brace & Co., 1997), 249.

5. Karl Barth, *Church Dogmatics*, vol. 2, part 2, *The Doctrine of God* (Edinburgh: T. & T. Clark, 1957), 206-9; idem, *Dogmatics in Outline* (New York: Harper Torchbooks, 1959), 74-81.

6. Jules Isaac, *The Teaching of Contempt: Christian Roots of Anti-Semitism*, ed. Claire Huchet-Bishop (New York: Holt, Rinehart and Winston, 1964).

7. Council of Florence, Bull of Union with the Copts, Session 11, 4 February 1442, in *Decrees of the Ecumenical Councils*, ed. Norman P. Tanner (2 vols.; London: Sheed & Ward; Washington, D.C.: Georgetown University Press, 1990), 1:578. Unless otherwise noted, all quotations from Catholic ecumenical councils will be taken from Tanner.

8. Raymond E. Brown, *The Death of the Messiah: From Gethsemane to the Grave: A Commentary on the Passion Narratives in the Four Gospels*, Anchor Bible Reference Library (2 vols.; New York: Doubleday, 1994), 1:385.

9. See Miika Ruokanen, *The Catholic Doctrine of Non-Christian Religions According to the Second Vatican Council* (Leiden: E. J. Brill, 1992); and Avery Dulles, *The Assurance of Things Hoped For: A Theology of Christian Faith* (New York and Oxford: Oxford University Press, 1994), 269.

10. Vatican I, Dogmatic Constitution on the Catholic Faith (*Dei Filius*), no. 2; p. 806.

11. Gerald O'Collins, *Retrieving Fundamental Theology* (New York: Paulist, 1993), 79-86.

12. Pontifical Council for Interreligious Dialogue and the Congregation for the Evangelization of Peoples, *Dialogue and Proclamation*, in *Origins* 21/8 (July 4, 1991): 130.

13. Ibid., 129.

14. Francis Cardinal Arinze, "Message for End of Ramadan," *Origins* 27/29 (Jan. 8, 1998): 485.

15. See, e.g., Donald W. Mitchell and James A. Wiseman, eds., *The Gethsemani Encounter: A Dialogue on the Spiritual Life by Buddhist and Christian Monastics* (New York: Continuum, 1997).

16. Pope John Paul II, "The Challenge and the Possibility of Peace," *Origins* 16/21 (Nov. 6, 1986): 370.

17. Ibid.

18. Jorge Mejía, "World Religions: Together to Pray," *Origins* 16/21 (Nov. 6, 1986): 369.

19. Vivekananda, "Hinduism," in *The Dawn of Religions Pluralism: Voices from the World's Parliament of Religions, 1893*, ed. Richard Hughes Seager (LaSalle, Ill.: Open Court, 1993), 430.

20. Joseph Mitsuo Kitagawa, *The Quest for Human Unity: A Religious History* (Minneapolis: Fortress, 1990), 208.

21. Two works that were widely influential in broadening Christian attitudes are Mircea Eliade, *The Sacred and the Profane: The Nature of Religion* (New York: Harcourt, Brace, & World, 1959); and idem, *Patterns in Comparative Religion* (New York: New American Library, 1963).

22. *The Dhammapada: The Path of Perfection*, trans. Juan Mascaró (Harmondsworth, England: Penguin Books, 1973), 85.

23. Leo D. Lefebure, *Life Transformed: Meditations on the Christian Scriptures in Light of Buddhist Perspectives* (Chicago: ACTA Publications, 1989); idem, *The Buddha and the Christ: Explorations in Buddhist-Christian Dialogue* (Maryknoll, N.Y.: Orbis, 1993).

24. *No Religion Is an Island: Abraham Joshua Heschel and Interreligious Dialogue*, ed. Harold Kasimow and Byron L. Sherwin (Maryknoll, N.Y.: Orbis, 1991).

25. His Holiness the Dalai Lama, "Harmony, Dialogue and Meditation," in *The Gethsemani Encounter*, 46-48.

26. D. T. Suzuki, *Outlines of Mahayana Buddhism* (New York: Schocken Books, 1963 [1907]), 259-76.

27. John Hick, *God Has Many Names: Britain's New Religious Pluralism* (London: Macmillan, 1980); idem, *An Interpretation of Religion: Human Responses to the Transcendent* (New Haven and London: Yale University Press, 1989).

28. Walter Burkert, *Homo Necans: The Anthropology of Ancient Greek Sacrificial Ritual and Myth* (Berkeley: University of California Press, 1983).

29. See R. C. Zaehner, *The City within the Heart* (New York: Crossroad, 1981), 27-56; and Walter Brueggemann, *Revelation and Violence: A Study in Contextualization* (Milwaukee, Wis.: Marquette University Press, 1986).

30. Craig L. Nessan, "Sex, Aggression, and Pain: Sociobiological Implications for Theological Anthropology," *Zygon* 33 (1998): 451.

31. James Gilligan, *Violence: Reflections on a National Epidemic* (New York: Vintage Books, 1997), 65.

32. Ibid., xi.

33. See Norman F. Cantor, *The Civilization of the Middle Ages* (rev. ed.; New York: HarperCollins, 1993), 1-13.

34. Abbé Pierre and Bernard Kouchner, *Dieu et les Hommes: Dialogue et propos recueillis par Michel-Antoine Burnier* (Paris: Robert Laffont, 1993), 40-42.

35. Richard L. Rubenstein, *After Auschwitz: Radical Theology and Contemporary Judaism* (Indianapolis: Bobbs-Merrill Educational Publishing, 1966), 204; for a survey of Jewish reflections, see Stephen T. Katz, *Post-Holocaust Dialogues: Critical Studies in Modern Jewish Thought* (New York: New York University Press, 1983).

36. Richard L. Rubenstein, "Emptiness, Holy Nothingness, and the Holocaust," in *Masao Abe: A Zen Life of Dialogue*, ed. Donald W. Mitchell (Boston: Charles E. Tuttle, 1998), 184-95.

37. Edward Schillebeeckx, *Christ: The Experience of Jesus as Lord* (New York: Crossroad, 1981), 724-30.

38. Emil Fackenheim, *To Mend the World: Foundations of Post-Holocaust Jewish Thought* (New York: Schocken Books, 1982), 135.

39. On the theology of revelation, see Avery Dulles, *Models of Revelation* (Garden City, N.Y.: Doubleday, 1983); John F. Haught, *Mystery and Promise: A Theology of Revelation* (Collegeville, Minn.: Liturgical Press, 1993); Gerald O'Collins, *Fundamental Theology* (New York and Ramsey, N.J.: Paulist, 1981); Gabriel Fackre, *The Doctrine of Revelation: A Narrative Interpretation* (Grand Rapids: Eerdmans, 1997); René Latourelle and Gerald O'Collins, eds., *Problems and Perspectives of Fundamental Theology* (New York and Ramsey, N.J.: Paulist, 1982); Theron D. Price, *Revelation and Faith: Theological Reflections on the Knowing and Doing of Truth* (Macon, Ga.: Mercer University Press, 1987).

40. René Girard, *Violence and the Sacred* (Baltimore and London: Johns Hopkins University Press, 1977); and René Girard, with Jean-Michel Oughourlian and Guy Lefort, *Things Hidden since the Foundation of the World* (Stanford, Calif.: Stanford University Press, 1987).

41. René Girard, *Deceit, Desire, and the Novel: Self and Other in Literary Structure* (Baltimore and London: Johns Hopkins University Press, 1965); idem, *Resurrection from the Underground: Feodor Dostoevsky*, ed. and trans. James G. Williams (New York: Crossroad, 1997).

42. See René Girard, *A Theater of Envy: William Shakespeare* (New York and Oxford: Oxford University Press, 1991), 29-79.

43. René Girard, *"To Double Business Bound": Essays on Literature, Mimesis, and Anthropology* (Baltimore: Johns Hopkins University Press, 1978).

44. Susan Niditch, *War in the Hebrew Bible: A Study in the Ethics of Violence* (New York and Oxford: Oxford University Press, 1993), 60-61, 74.

45. René Girard, *Job: The Victim of His People* (Stanford, Calif.: Stanford University Press, 1987).

46. Girard, *Violence and the Sacred*, 55, 221, 235, 237.

47. Joseph Henninger, "Sacrifice," in *The Encyclopedia of Religion*, ed. Mircea Eliade (12 vols.; New York: Macmillan; London: Collier Macmillan, 1987), 12:553-54.

48. Valerio Valeri, *Kingship and Sacrifice: Ritual and Society in Ancient Hawaii* (Chicago and London: University of Chicago Press, 1985), 68.

49. Ibid., 69.

2
BIBLICAL REVELATION AND OTHER RELIGIONS

1. Gabriel Moran, *Uniqueness: Problem or Paradox in Jewish and Christian Traditions* (Maryknoll, N.Y.: Orbis, 1992), 18-24.

2. Ibid., 46.

3. Gerhard von Rad, *Old Testament Theology* (2 vols.; New York: Harper & Row, 1962, 1965).

4. Karl Barth, "The Christian Understanding of Revelation," in Karl Barth, *Against the Stream: Shorter Post-War Writings 1946-52* (New York: Philosophical Library, 1954), 208, 226.

5. G. Ernest Wright, *God Who Acts: Biblical Theology as Recital* (London: SCM, 1952), 19.

6. Wright, *God Who Acts*; idem, *The Old Testament against Its Environment* (London: SCM, 1950).

7. H. D. Preuss, "Erwägungen zum theologischen Ort alttestamentlischer Weisheitsliteratur," *Evangelische Theologie* 30 (August 1970): 393-417; idem, "Das Gottesbild der älteren Weisheit Israels," in *Studies in the Religion of Ancient Israel* (Leiden: E. J. Brill, 1972), 117-45.

8. Walter Brueggemann, "Scripture and an Ecumenical Life-Style," *Interpretation* 24 (1970): 3-19.

9. James L. Crenshaw, "Method in Determining Wisdom Influence Upon 'Historical' Literature," *Journal of Biblical Literature* 88 (1969): 129-42.

10. Morton Smith, "The Common Theology of the Ancient Near East," *Journal of Biblical Literature* 71 (1952): 135-47.

11. Norman K. Gottwald, *The Tribes of Yahweh: A Sociology of the Religion of Liberated Israel 1250-1050 BCE* (Maryknoll, N.Y.: Orbis, 1979), 670.

12. Smith, "Common Theology," 146.

13. Bertil Albrektson, *History and the Gods: An Essay on the Idea of Historical Events as Divine Manifestations in the Ancient Near East and in Israel,* Coniectanea Biblica, OT (Lund: Gleerup, 1967).

14. Jon D. Levenson, *Sinai and Zion: An Entry into the Jewish Bible* (San Francisco: Harper & Row, 1985), 10; H. W. F. Saggs, *The Encounter with the Divine in Mesopotamia and Israel* (London: University of London/Athlone, 1976).

15. Mark S. Smith, *The Early History of God: Yahweh and the Other Deities in Ancient Israel* (San Francisco: Harper & Row, 1990).

16. Ibid., 164-65.

17. Ibid., 161.

18. Robert Karl Gnuse, *No Other Gods: Emergent Monotheism in Israel,* Journal for the Study of the Old Testament Supplement 241 (Sheffield, England: Sheffield Academic Press, 1997), 180-94.

19. René Girard, with Jean-Michel Oughourlian and Guy Lefort, *Things Hidden since the Foundation of the World* (Stanford, Calif.: Stanford University Press, 1987), 151-52.

20. Ibid., 153.

21. *The Story of Two Brothers,* in *Ancient Near Eastern Texts Relating to the Old Testament,* ed. James D. Pritchard (3rd ed. with supplement; Princeton, N.J.: Princeton University Press, 1969), 23-25.

22. See James Henry Breasted, *Development of Religion and Thought in Ancient Egypt* (Philadelphia: University of Pennsylvania Press, 1959 [1912]), 165-256.

23. See H. and H.A. Frankfort, John A. Wilson, Thorkild Jacobsen, and William A. Irwin, *The Intellectual Adventure of Ancient Man: An Essay on Speculative Thought in the Ancient Near East* (Chicago and London: University of Chicago Press, 1977 [1946]), 108-10.

24. A. Leo Oppenheim, *Ancient Mesopotamia: Portrait of a Dead Civilization*, ed. Erica Reiner (rev. ed.; Chicago: University of Chicago Press, 1977), 102, 107.

25. John Bright, *A History of Israel* (2nd ed.; Philadelphia: Westminster, 1972), 120.

26. Leo G. Perdue, *The Collapse of History: Reconstructing Old Testament Theology* (Minneapolis: Fortress, 1994).

27. Donald B. Redford, *Egypt, Canaan, and Israel in Ancient Times* (Princeton, N.J.: Princeton University Press, 1992), 257-65.

28. For example, John Van Seters commented that the account of the deliverance at the Sea of Reeds in Exodus was created by a writer during the exile or later: the "exilic Yahwist *created* the sea event and then placed it between the exodus and the wilderness, providing the transition between the two." *The Life of Moses: The Yahwist as Historian in Exodus-Numbers* (Louisville, Ky.: Westminster/John Knox Press, 1994), 145; see also idem, *In Search of History: Historiography in the Ancient World and the Origins of Biblical History* (New Haven: Yale University Press, 1983).

29. Gnuse, *No Other Gods*, 32-58.

30. Levenson, *Sinai and Zion*, 16-17.

31. G. Van der Leeuw, *L'homme primitif et la religion* (Paris: Presses universitaires de France, 1940), 101; quoted by Mircea Eliade, *Patterns in Comparative Religion* (New York: New American Library, 1963), 395.

32. Eliade, *Patterns*, 401.

33. Frank Moore Cross, *Canaanite Myth and Hebrew Epic: Essays in the History of the Religion of Israel* (Cambridge, Mass., and London: Harvard University Press, 1973), 77-144.

34. Bernard F. Batto, *Slaying the Dragon: Mythmaking in the Biblical Tradition* (Louisville, Ky.: Westminster/John Knox Press, 1992), 123.

35. *Enuma Elish* 93-140, in *Ancient Near Eastern Texts Relating to the Old Testament*, ed. James H. Pritchard (3rd ed.; Princeton, N.J.: Princeton University Press, 1969), 67.

36. Walter Wink, *Engaging the Powers: Discernment and Resistance in a World of Domination* (Minneapolis: Fortress, 1992), 14. See Paul Ricoeur, *Symbolism of Evil* (Boston: Beacon, 1967), 175-210.

37. Wink, *Engaging the Powers*, 15.

38. Batto, *Slaying the Dragon*, 119.

39. Ibid., 112.

40. Unless otherwise noted, biblical quotations will be from *The New Jerusalem Bible* (New York: Doubleday, 1985).

41. John Briggs and F. David Peat, *Turbulent Mirror: An Illustrated Guide to Chaos Theory and the Science of Wholeness* (New York: Harper & Row, 1990), 19-21.

42. Rudolf Otto, *The Idea of the Holy: An Inquiry into the Non-rational Factor in the Idea of the Divine and Its Relation to the Rational* (2nd ed.; Oxford: Oxford University Press, 1950, 1975), 12-59.

43. Levenson, *Sinai and Zion*, 46-48.

44. Batto, *Slaying the Dragon*, 120.

45. J. Lindblom, *Prophecy in Ancient Israel* (Philadelphia: Fortress, 1962); Thomas Overholt, *Channels of Prophecy: The Social Dynamics of Prophetic Activity* (Minneapolis: Fortress, 1989); Robert R. Wilson, *Prophecy and Society in Ancient Israel* (Philadelphia: Fortress, 1980); and David E. Aune, *Prophecy in Early Christianity and the Ancient Mediterranean World* (Grand Rapids: Eerdmans, 1983).

46. Joseph Blenkinsopp, *A History of Prophecy in Israel* (Philadelphia: Westminster, 1983), 61-66.

47. Overholt, *Channels of Prophecy,* 15-58.

48. Ibid., 21-25.

49. Abraham Joshua Heschel, "No Religion Is an Island," in *No Religion Is an Island: Abraham Joshua Heschel and Interreligious Dialogue,* ed. Harold Kasimow and Byron L. Sherwin (Maryknoll, N.Y.: Orbis, 1991), 14.

50. Hermann Vorländer, *Mein Gott: Die Vorstellungen vom persönliche Gott (*Kevelaer: Butzon and Bercker, 1975*);* idem, "Der Monotheismus Israels als Antwort auf die Krise des Exils," in *Der einzige Gott: Die Geburt des biblischen Monotheismus,* ed. B. Lang (Munich: Kösel, 1981).

51. Gerd Theissen, *Biblical Faith: An Evolutionary Approach*, trans. John Bowden (Philadelphia: Fortress, 1985).

52. Gnuse, *No Other Gods,* 41-46.

53. Karl Jaspers, *The Origin and Goal of History* (New Haven: Yale University Press, 1953).

54. Gnuse, *No Other Gods,* 214.

55. See John G. Gammie and Leo G. Perdue, eds., *The Sage in Israel and the Ancient Near East* (Winona Lake, Ind.: Eisenbrauns, 1990).

56. On the wisdom tradition, see James L. Crenshaw, *Old Testament Wisdom: An Introduction* (Atlanta: John Knox Press, 1981); Leo G. Perdue, *Wisdom and Creation: The Theology of Wisdom Literature* (Nashville: Abingdon, 1994); and Leo G. Perdue, Bernard Brandon Scott, and William Johnston Wiseman, eds., *In Search of Wisdom: Essays in Memory of John G. Gammie* (Louisville: Westminster/John Knox Press, 1993).

57. William P. Brown, *Character in Crisis: A Fresh Approach to the Wisdom Literature of the Old Testament* (Grand Rapids: Eerdmans, 1996).

58. Gerhard von Rad, *Wisdom in Israel*, trans. James D. Martin (Nashville: Abingdon, 1972), 37.

59. Ibid., 144-76.

60. Bernhard Lang, *Wisdom and the Book of Proverbs: An Israelite Goddess Redefined* (New York: Pilgrim Press, 1986), 126-36.

61. Christa Kayatz, *Studien zu Proverbien 1-9,* Wissenschaftliche Monographien zum alten und neuen Testament 22 (Neukirchen-Vluyn: Neukirchener Verlag, 1966), 86-87. See also H. H. Schmid, *Wesen und Geschichte der Weisheit*, Beihefte zur *Zeitschrift für die alttestamentliche Wissenschaft* 101 (Berlin: Alfred Töpelmann Verlag, 1966), 159.

62. Helmer Ringgren, *Word and Wisdom: Studies in the Hypostatization of Divine Qualities and Functions in the Ancient Near East* (Lund: Ohlsson, 1947).

63. John J. Collins, "The Biblical Precedent for Natural Theology," *Journal of the American Academy of Religion* 45 Supplement (1977): 35-67.

64. James Barr, *Biblical Faith and Natural Theology* (Oxford: Clarendon Press, 1993).

65. See Barth's use of the term "natural theology" in the sense defined by the Dogmatic Constitution on the Catholic Faith (*Dei Verbum*) of Vatican I: Karl Barth, *The Doctrine of God*, vol. 2, part 1 of *Church Dogmatics*, ed. G. W. Bromiley and T. F. Torrance (Edinburgh: T. & T. Clark, 1957), 2/1:79-85. Barr cites Barth's usage as one precedent for his own use (p. 3).

66. Roland E. Murphy, "The Interpretation of Old Testament Wisdom Literature," *Interpretation* 23 (1969): 289-301; idem, "Wisdom and Creation," *Journal of Biblical Literature* 104 (1985): 3-11; idem *The Tree of Life: An Exploration of Biblical Wisdom Literature*, Anchor Bible Reference Library (New York: Doubleday, 1990), 124-25.

67. Crenshaw, *Old Testament Wisdom*, 149-73.

68. See Helmut Koester, *Introduction to the New Testamant* (2 vols.; Philadelphia: Fortress, 1982).

69. Aristotle, *Magna Moralia*, 2.11(1208b26-28), in *The Complete Works of Aristotle*, ed. Jonathan Barnes (rev. ed.; Princeton, N.J.: Princeton University Press, 1984), 2:1913.

70. See Raymond E. Brown, *The Gospel according to John (I-XII)*, Anchor Bible (Garden City, N.Y.: Doubleday, 1966).

71. Dale C. Allison, *Jesus of Nazareth: Millenarian Prophet* (Minneapolis: Fortress, 1998).

72. M. Jack Suggs argues that Matthew did identify Jesus with Sophia (*Wisdom, Christology, and Law in Matthew's Gospel* [Cambridge, Mass.: Harvard University Press, 1970]). For a critical rejoinder, see Marshall D. Johnson, "Reflections on a Wisdom Approach to Matthew's Christology," *Catholic Biblical Quarterly* 36 (1974): 44-64.

73. Charles E. Carlston, "Proverbs, Maxims, and the Historical Jesus," *Journal of Biblical Literature* 99 (1980): 91.

74. Hans Dieter Betz, *The Sermon on the Mount: A Commentary on the Sermon on the Mount including the Sermon on the Plain*, ed. Adela Yarbro Collins (Minneapolis: Fortress, 1995).

75. James G. Williams, *Those Who Ponder Proverbs: Aphoristic Thinking and Biblical Literature* (Sheffield, England: Almond, 1981), 47-63.

76. William A. Beardslee, "Parable, Proverb, and Koan," *Semeia* 12 (1978): 159-68.

77. Joseph A. Loya, Wan-Li-Ho, and Chang-Shin Jin, *The Tao of Jesus: An Experiment in Inter-Traditional Understanding* (New York and Mahwah, N.J.: Paulist, 1998).

3
THE DIVINE WARRIOR AND THE CRUCIFIED GOD

1. See Roland H. Bainton, *Christian Attitudes toward War and Peace* (Nashville: Abingdon, 1960).

2. Gustavo Gutiérrez, *A Theology of Liberation: History, Politics and Salvation*, trans. and ed. Caridad Inda and John Eagleson (Maryknoll, N.Y.: Orbis, 1973), 155.

3. Ibid., 157.

4. George V. Pixley, *On Exodus: A Liberation Perspective*, trans. Robert R. Barr (Maryknoll, N.Y.: Orbis, 1987). For a range of essays inspired by this approach, see Norman K. Gottwald and Richard A. Horsley, eds., *The Bible and Liberation: Political and Social Hermeneutics* (rev. ed.; Maryknoll, N.Y.: Orbis; London: SPCK, 1993).

5. Julius Wellhausen, *Prolegomena to the History of Ancient Israel* (Cleveland: Cleveland World, 1957 [1885]), 434.

6. See Gerhard von Rad, *Holy War in Ancient Israel*, trans. Marva J. Dawn (Grand Rapids: William B. Eerdmans, 1991); Susan Niditch, *War in the Hebrew Bible: A Study in the Ethics of Violence* (New York and Oxford: Oxford University Press, 1993).

7. Donald B. Redford, *Egypt, Canaan, and Israel in Ancient Times* (Princeton, N.J.: Princeton University Press, 1992), 276.

8. Ibid., 422.

9. Niditch, *War*, 28-149.

10. Ibid., 123.

11. Babylonian Talmud, *Megillot* 10b; quoted by Niditch, *War*, 150.

12. Walter Brueggemann, *Revelation and Violence: A Study in Contextualization* (Milwaukee, Wis.: Marquette University Press, 1986), 3.

13. Ibid., 17, 18.

14. Ibid., 23.

15. Walter Brueggemann, *Theology of the Old Testament: Testimony, Dispute, Advocacy* (Minneapolis: Fortress, 1997), 250.

16. Martin Buber, "Autobiographical Fragments," in *The Philosophy of Martin Buber*, ed. Paul Arthur Schilp (LaSalle, Ill.: Open Court, 1967), 32.

17. Ibid., 32-33.

18. Jon D. Levenson, "Is There a Counterpart in the Hebrew Bible to New Testament Antisemitism?" *Journal of Ecumenical Studies* 22 (1985): 248-51.

19. National Conference of Catholic Bishops, *The Challenge of Peace: God's Promise and Our Response: A Pastoral Letter on War and Peace* (Washington, D.C.: United States Catholic Conference, 1983); John Paul II, *The Gospel of Life* [*Evangelium Vitae*] (New York: Random House Times Books, 1995).

20. Joseph Cardinal Ratzinger, "Commentary on Profession of Faith's Concluding Paragraphs," *Origins* 28/8 (July 16, 1998): 118.

21. Abraham J. Heschel, *The Prophets* (2 vols.; New York: Harper Colophon Books, 1969 [1962]), 1:112.

22. Ibid., 1:56.

23. Ibid., 1:151.

24. Ibid., 1:166.

25. Ibid., 1:166.

26. See Richard A. Horsley and Neil Asher Silberman, *The Message and the Kingdom: How Jesus and Paul Ignited a Revolution and Transformed the Ancient World* (New York: Grosset/Putnam, 1997).

27. Walter Wink, *The Powers*: vol. 1, *Naming the Powers: The Language of Power in the New Testament*; vol. 2, *Unmasking the Powers: The Invisible Forces that Determine Human Existence*; and vol. 3, *Engaging the Powers: Discernment and Resistance in a World of Domination* (Philadelphia and Minneapolis: Fortress, 1984, 1986, 1992).

28. René Girard, *The Scapegoat* (Baltimore: Johns Hopkins University Press, 1986), 125-29.

29. Ibid., 135.

30. Ibid., 145.

31. Ibid., 146.

32. Hans Dieter Betz, *The Sermon on the Mount: A Commentary on the Sermon on the Mount including the Sermon on the Plain*, ed. Adela Yarbro Collins (Minneapolis: Fortress, 1995), 301-9.

33. See Willard M. Swartley, *The Love of Enemy and Nonretaliation in the New Testament* (Louisville, Ky.: Westminster/John Knox Press, 1992).

34. See Michel Desjardins, *Peace, Violence and the New Testament* (Sheffield, England: Sheffield Academic Press, 1997), 20.

35. Ibid., 78-82.

36. Richard A. Horsley, *Jesus and the Spiral of Violence: Popular Jewish Resistance in Roman Palestine* (Minneapolis: Fortress, 1993), 163.

37. Desjardins, *Peace,* 83-92.

38. Ibid., 84.

39. Adela Yarbro Collins, *Crisis and Catharsis: The Power of the Apocalypse* (Philadelphia: Westminster, 1984), 130.

40. Rosemary Radford Ruether, *Faith and Fratricide: The Theological Roots of Anti-Semitism* (New York: Seabury, 1979). See the responses to Ruether in Alan Davies, ed., *Antisemitism and the Foundations of Christianity* (New York: Paulist, 1979).

41. See Craig A. Evans and Donald A. Hagner, eds., *Anti-Semitism and Early Christianity: Issues of Polemic and Faith* (Minneapolis: Fortress, 1993); and Krister Stendahl, *Paul among Jews and Gentiles and Other Essays* (Philadelphia: Fortress, 1976).

42. Raymond E. Brown, *An Introduction to the New Testament*, Anchor Bible Reference Library (New York: Doubleday, 1997), 166-67.

43. Luke T. Johnson, "The New Testament's Anti-Jewish Slander and the Conventions of Ancient Polemic," *Journal of Biblical Literature* 108 (1989): 419-41.

44. Raymond E. Brown, *The Gospel according to John (I-XII)*, Anchor Bible (Garden City, N.Y.: Doubleday, 1966), 358.

45. René Girard, with Jean-Michel Oughourlian and Guy Lefort, *Things Hidden since the Foundation of the World* (Stanford, Calif.: Stanford University Press, 1987), 161.

46. Ibid., 165.

47. Joseph Cardinal Bernardin, *Antisemitism: The Historical Legacy and the Continuing Challenge for Christians: An Address at Hebrew University of Jerusalem, March 23, 1995* (Fairfield, Conn.: Center for Christian-Jewish Understanding, 1995), 13.

48. See Raymond E. Brown, *The Death of the Messiah: From Gethsemane to the Grave: A Commentary on the Passion Narratives in the Four Gospels,* Anchor Bible Reference Library (2 vols.; New York: Doubleday, 1994), 1:862-77.

49. Cited by Girard, *Things Hidden,* 168.

50. Girard, *Scapegoat.* 106.

51. Girard, *Things Hidden,* 219.

52. See Wink, *Engaging the Powers,* 175-93.

4
REVELATION AND OTHER RELIGIONS
IN THE EARLY AND MEDIEVAL CHURCH

1. See Kurt Rudolph, *Gnosis: The Nature and History of Gnosticism*, trans. and ed. Robert McLachlan Wilson (San Francisco: Harper & Row, 1983); and James M. Robinson, ed., *The Nag Hammadi Library in English* (rev. ed.; San Francisco: Harper & Row, 1988).

2. *Nag Hammadi Library*, 126.

3. See Hans Jonas, *The Gnostic Religion: The Message of the Alien God and the Beginnings of Christianity* (2nd ed., rev.; Boston: Beacon, 1963).

4. *Nag Hammadi Library*, 40.

5. Jonas, *Gnostic Religion*, 81.

6. *Nag Hammadi Library*, 473.

7. Jonas, *Gnostic Religion*, 254.

8. See Robert M. Grant, *Irenaeus of Lyons* (London and New York: Routledge, 1997).

9. See Jean Daniélou, *A History of Early Christian Doctrine before the Council of Nicaea*, vol. 2, *Gospel Message and Hellenistic Culture* (London: Darton, Longman, & Todd; Philadelphia: Westminster, 1973), 445-500.

10. See E. C. Blackman, *Marcion and His Influence* (London: SPCK, 1948).

11. See also Eusebius, *Ecclesiastical History* 5.14-19.

12. Clement of Alexandria, *Exhortation to the Greeks,* trans. G. W. Butterworth, Loeb Classical Library (Cambridge, Mass.: Harvard University Press; London: William Heinemann, 1919) 9.72; p. 195.

13. Cited by Daniélou, *History,* 51.

14. Clement is quoting Ps 96:5.

15. Origen, *Contra Celsum*, trans. Henry Chadwick (Cambridge: Cambridge University Press, 1980 [1953], 293.

16. See Robert L. Wilken, "Religious Pluralism and Early Christian Thought," *Pro Ecclesia* 1 (1992): 33-35.

17. *Agadah Bereshit* 31; quoted by Hans Joachim Schoeps, *The Jewish-Christian Argument: A History of Theologies in Conflict* (New York: Holt, Rinehart and Winston, 1963), 23.

18. Jeffrey S. Siker, *Disinheriting the Jews: Abraham in Early Christian Controversy* (Louisville, Ky.: Westminster/John Knox Press, 1991), 163-84.

19. Henri de Lubac, *The Sources of Revelation* (New York: Herder & Herder, 1968), 113-14. The quotations are from Justin Martyr, *Dialogue with Trypho* 44; Bernard of Clairvaux, *Sermon on the Canticle of Canticles* 73.2 (cf. also Augustine, *On the Psalms* 56:9, and *City of God* 1.4.34); and Justin Martyr, *Dialogue with Trypho* 29.2; 11.5.

20. See Robert L. Wilken, *John Chrysostom and the Jews: Rhetoric and Reality in the Late 4th Century* (Berkeley: University of California Press, 1983).

21. Ambrose of Milan, *Letter* 40 *to Theodosius;* see *The Early Church and the State*, ed. Agnes Cunningham, trans. Michael Di Maio and Agnes Cunningham (Philadelphia: Fortress, 1982), 87-99.

22. See F. Van der Meer, *Augustine the Bishop: Religion and Society at the Dawn of the Middle Ages* (New York: Harper Torchbooks, 1961), 32-75.

23. Ibid., 34.

24. See Marshall G. S. Hodgson, *The Venture of Islam* (3 vols.; Chicago and London: University of Chicago Press, 1974).

25. See Fazlur Rahman, *Islam* (2nd ed.; Chicago and London: University of Chicago Press, 1979); idem, *Major Themes of the Qur'an* (Minneapolis and Chicago: Bibliotheca Islamica, 1980); and John L. Esposito, *Islam: The Straight Path* (3rd ed.; New York and Oxford: Oxford University Press, 1998).

26. See W. Montgomery Watt, *Muhammad: Prophet and Statesman* (London and Oxford: Oxford University Press, 1974).

27. All translations of the Qur'an are from *The Koran*, trans. H. J. Dawood (4th rev. ed.; Harmondsworth, England: Penguin, 1974).

28. See Kenneth Cragg, *Jesus and the Muslim: An Exploration* (London: George Allen & Unwin, 1985).

29. The term "Nestorian" is misleading and is rejected by members of the Church of the East today. The Church of the East did accept the teaching of Nestorius as affirming its own traditional faith, and it refused to refer to Mary as "Mother of God" because it feared the term would be misleading.

30. Contemporary leaders of the Oriental Orthodox Churches reject the term "Monophysite," because they do not hold that there is a singular nature (*monos physis*) in Jesus Christ. Rather, in acclaiming Jesus, they profess "one nature" (*mia physis*), which is composite and complex, including both divinity and humanity. Thus they prefer to be called "miaphysites."

31. Cited by Gustave E. von Grunebaum, *Medieval Islam: A Study in Cultural Orientalism* (2nd ed.; Chicago: University of Chicago Press, 1953), 57.

32. In *Apocalyptic Spirituality*, trans. Bernard McGinn (New York: Paulist, 1979), 89-96.

33. See Andrew Colin Gow, *The Red Jews: Antisemitism in an Apocalyptic Age: 1200-1600* (Leiden: E. J. Brill, 1995).

34. Cited by Alan T. Davies, *Anti-Semitism and the Christian Mind: The Crisis of Conscience after Auschwitz* (New York: Herder & Herder, 1969), 69-70.

35. See Joshua Trachtenburg, *The Devil and the Jews: The Medieval Conception of the Jew and Its Relation to Modern Antisemitism* (Philadelphia: Jewish Publication Society of America, 1943), 88-108.

36. Samuel Hugh Moffett, *A History of Christianity in Asia*, vol. 1, *Beginnings to 1500* (San Francisco: HarperSanFrancisco, 1992), 351.

37. Wilfred Cantwell Smith, *Towards a World Theology: Faith and the Comparative History of Religions* (Philadelphia: Westminster, 1981), 7-9. See also Aloysius Pieris, *Love Meets Wisdom: A Christian Experience of Buddhism* (Maryknoll, N.Y.: Orbis, 1988), 25-26.

38. Abu'l Faraj, *Kitab al Fihrist*; cited by Moffett, *History,* 302-3.

39. *Fontes Iudaeorum regni Castellae*, ed. Carlos Carrete Parrondo, vol. 2, *Ed Tribunal de la Inquisición en el Obispado de Soria (1486-1502)* (Salamanca, 1985), 122; cited by Henry Kamen, *The Spanish Inquisition: An Historical Revision* (London: Weidenfeld & Nicolson, 1997), 6.

40. C. Carrete Parrondo, "Duelos os dé Dios, e avrá Christianidad: nueva página sobre el criptojudaismo castellano," *Sefarad* 2 (1992): 369; cited by Kamen, *Spanish Inquisition,* 6.

41. Kamen, *Spanish Inquisition,* 5.

42. John of Segovia, *Letter to Nicholas of Cusa*; see James E. Biechler, "A New Face Toward Islam: Nicholas of Cusa and John of Segovia," in *Nicholas of*

Cusa in Search of God and Wisdom, ed. Gerald Christianson and Thomas M. Izbicki, Studies in the History of Christian Thought 45 (Leiden: E. J. Brill, 1991), 191.

43. Nicholas of Cusa, *Letter to John of Segovia*, December 29, 1454; cited by Biechler, "New Face," 200.

44. See John Patrick Dolan, ed., *Unity and Reform: Selected Writings of Nicholas de Cusa* (South Bend, Ind.: University of Notre Dame Press, 1962).

45. See Jasper Hopkins, *Nicholas of Cusa On Learned Ignorance: A Translation and Appraisal of De Docta Ignorantia* (2nd ed.; Minneapolis: Arthur J. Banning, 1985), 158.

46. Jasper Hopkins, *Nicholas of Cusa on God as Not-Other: A Translation and Appraisal of De Li Non Aliud* (Minneapolis: University of Minnesota Press, 1979).

47. For an introduction and translation of the text, see Dolan, *Unity and Reform*, 185-237; and also William F. Wertz Jr., *Toward a New Council of Florence: "On the Peace of Faith" and Other Works by Nicholas of Cusa* (Washington, D.C.: Schiller Institute, 1993).

48. Nicholas of Cusa, *On the Peace of Faith*, in Dolan, *Unity and Reform*, 201.

5

REVELATION AND VIOLENCE
IN THE EARLY AND MEDIEVAL CHURCH

1. See W. H. C. Frend, *Martyrdom and Persecution in the Early Church: A Study of a Conflict from the Maccabees to Donatus* (Grand Rapids: Baker Book House, 1965).

2. See Louis J. Swift, *The Early Fathers on War and Military Service* (Wilmington, Del.: Michael Glazier, 1983); and John Helgeland, Robert J. Daly, and J. Patout Burns, *Christians and the Military: The Early Experience*, ed. Robert J. Daly (Philadelphia; Fortress, 1985).

3. C. John Cadoux, *The Early Christian Attitude to War: A Contribution to the History of Christian Ethics* (New York: Seabury, 1982 [1919]), 241.

4. See Donald B. Redford, *Egypt, Canaan, and Israel in Ancient Times* (Princeton, N.J.: Princeton University Press, 1992).

5. See Robert M. Grant, *Early Christianity and Society: Seven Studies* (San Francisco: Harper & Row, 1977), 124-45; Martin Hengel, *Property and Riches in the Early Church: Aspects of a Social History of Early Christianity* (Philadelphia: Fortress, 1974).

6. *Patrologiae cursus completus,* Series graeca, ed. J.-P. Migne (Paris, 1857–), 31:276-77.

7. See Justin Martyr, *First Apology* 67.6; Tertullian, *Apology* 39.5-7; and Pontianus, *Biography of Cyprian*, cited by Rodney Stark, *The Rise of Christianity: A Sociologist Reconsiders History* (Princeton, N.J.: Princeton University Press, 1996), 87.

8. Stark, *Rise of Christianity*, 84; see also Grant, *Early Christianity*, 124-25.

9. Stark, *Rise of Christianity*, 86.

10. Ibid., 103-11.

11. Ibid., 117-28.

12. See Frend, *Martyrdom*; and Robert M. Grant, *Augustus to Constantine: The Rise and Triumph of Christianity in the Roman World* (1970; reprint ed., San Francisco: Harper & Row, 1990).

13. See Frend, *Martyrdom*, 181-505.

14. Herbert Musurillo, ed. and trans., *The Acts of the Christian Martyrs* (Oxford: Clarendon Press, 1972), 67.

15. Origen, *An Exhortation to Martyrdom, Prayer, First Principles Book IV, Prologue to the Commentary on the Song of Songs Homily XXVII on Numbers*, trans. Rowan A. Greer (New York: Paulist, 1979), 73.

16. Stark, *Rise of Christianity*, 163-89.

17. See *The Sayings of the Desert Fathers: The Alphabetical Collection*, trans. Benedicta Ward (Kalamazoo, Mich.: Cistercian Publications, 1975; rev. ed. 1984).

18. On Constantine's attitudes toward the Jews, see Eusebius, *Life of Constantine* 3.18.

19. See W. H. C. Frend, *The Rise of Christianity* (Philadelphia: Fortress, 1984), 639-40.

20. Ambrose, *Exposition of Psalm* 35.25; see Helgeland et al., *Christians and the Military*, 74-75.

21. In *The Early Church and the State*, ed. Agnes Cunningham, trans. Michael Di Maio and Agnes Cunningham, Sources of Early Christian Thought (Philadelphia: Fortress, 1982), 90.

22. Trans. R. S. Pine-Coffin (Harmondsworth, England: Penguin, 1961), 52.

23. See Helgeland et al., *Christians and the Military*, 76-78.

24. James A. Brundage, *Medieval Canon Law and the Crusader* (Madison, Milwaukee, and London: University of Wisconsin Press, 1969), 19-21.

25. See Peter Brown, *Augustine of Hippo: A Biography* (Berkeley: University of California Press, 1967), 234-43.

26. See Frend, *Rise of Christianity*, 721-892; and Peter Brown, *The Rise of Western Christendom: Triumph and Diversity AD 200-1000* (Malden, Mass., and Oxford: Blackwell, 1996).

27. Philippe Ariès and Georges Duby, eds., *A History of Private Life*, vol. 2, *Revelations of the Medieval World* (Cambridge, Mass., and London: Belknap Press of Harvard University Press, 1988), 48, 66.

28. Leonardo Boff, *Saint Francis: A Model for Human Liberation* (New York: Crossroad, 1988), 167 n. 17.

29. See Norman F. Cantor, *The Civilization of the Middles Ages* (rev. ed.; New York: HarperCollins, 1993), 205-23; and Gerd Tellenbach, *Church, State and Christian Society at the Time of the Investiture Contest* (1940; reprint ed., Atlantic Highlands, N.J.: Humanities Press, 1979).

30. See Walter Ullman, *A Short History of the Papacy in the Middle Ages* (London and New York: Methuen, 1972), 142-278.

31. See Cantor, *Civilization*, 243-76, 392-415.

32. Marc Bloch, *Feudal Society*, vol. 2, *Social Classes and Political Organization* (Chicago: University of Chicago Press, 1961), 353-54.

33. Boff, *Saint Francis*, 55.

34. Ibid., 56.

35. See Raul Manselli, *St. Francis of Assisi* (Chicago, Ill.: Franciscan Herald Press, 1988).

36. From Al-Muttaqi, *Kanz* 2:252-86, in Bernard Lewis, ed. and trans., *Islam from the Prophet Muhammad to the Capture of Constantinople* (New York and Oxford: Oxford University Press, 1987), 210-11.

37. Brundage, *Medieval Canon Law,* 22.

38. Ibid., 23.

39. Edward Peters, ed., *The First Crusade: The Chronicle of Fulcher of Chartres and Other Source Materials* (Philadelphia: University of Pennsylvania Press, 1971), 9.

40. Quoted by Edward H. Flannery, *The Anguish of the Jews: Twenty-three Centuries of Anti-Semitism* (New York: Macmillan; London: Collier-Macmillan, 1965), 90-91.

41. Bernard of Clairvaux, *Letter* 363; see Jean Leclercq, *Bernard of Clairvaux and the Cistercian Spirit,* Cistercian Studies 16 (Kalamazoo, Mich.: Cistercian Publications, 1976), 65.

42. Steven Runciman, *A History of the Crusades,* vol. 3, *The Kingdom of Acre and the Later Crusades* (Cambridge: Cambridge University Press, 1954), 480; cited by Sarvepalli Radhakrishnan, *Indian Religions* (New Delhi and Bombay: Orient Paperbacks, 1979), 16-17.

6
ENCOUNTERING THE RELIGIONS
OF CHINA AND INDIA

1. See Emile Bréhier, *The Philosophy of Plotinus* (Chicago: University of Chicago Press, 1971 [1958]), 106-32.

2. Ewert H. Cousins, *Christ of the 21st Century* (Rockport, Mass.: Element, 1992).

3. Karl Jaspers, *The Origin and Goal of History,* trans. Michael Bullock (New Haven: Yale University Press, 1953), 2.

4. Ibid., 4.

5. David L. Hall and Roger T. Ames, *Anticipating China: Thinking through the Narratives of Chinese and Western Culture* (Albany: State University of New York Press, 1995), xiii.

6. Benjamin I. Schwartz, *The World of Thought in Ancient China* (Cambridge, Mass., and London: Belknap Press of Harvard University Press, 1985), 3.

7. Jaspers, *Origin and Goal,* 19-20.

8. Joseph Mitsuo Kitagawa, *The Quest for Human Unity: A Religious History* (Minneapolis: Fortress, 1990), 1-2.

9. Tu Wei-Ming, *Centrality and Commonality: An Essay on Confucian Religiousness* (rev. ed.; Albany: State University of New York Press, 1989), x.

10. John C. H. Wu, *Chinese Humanism and Christian Spirituality,* ed. Paul K. T. Sih (Jamaica, N.Y.: St. John's University Press, 1965), 8-9.

11. Rodney L. Taylor, "Confucianism: Scripture and Sage," in *The Holy*

Book in Comparative Perspective, ed. Frederick M. Denny and Rodney L. Taylor (Columbia: University of South Carolina Press, 1993), 182.

12. Hans Küng and Julia Ching, *Christianity and Chinese Religions* (New York: Doubleday, 1989), 131; see also Julia Ching, *Chinese Religions* (Maryknoll, N.Y.: Orbis, 1993).

13. See Thomas Merton, *The Wisdom of the Desert: Sayings from the Desert Fathers of the Fourth Century* (New York: New Directions, 1960).

14. Confucius, *The Analects*, trans. D. C. Lau (Harmondsworth, England: Penguin, 1979) 7:30; p. 90. All quotations will be from this translation unless otherwise noted.

15. Herbert Fingarette, *Confucius—Secular as Sacred* (New York: Harper Torchbooks, 1972), 1-17.

16. Ibid., 37-56; Schwartz, *World of Thought*, 72-75.

17. Fingarette, *Confucius*, 68.

18. Tu Wei-Ming, "Confucianism," in *Our Religions*, ed. Arvind Sharma (San Francisco: HarperSanFrancisco, 1993), 145.

19. Ibid., 146.

20. Schwartz, *World of Thought*, 94.

21. H. H. Rowley, *Prophecy and Religion in Ancient China and Israel* (New York: Harper and Brothers, 1956), 17-26.

22. R. C. Zaehner, *Concordant Discord: The Interdependence of Faiths* (Oxford: Clarendon Press, 1970), 25.

23. Tu Wei-Ming, "Confucianism," 152.

24. See Liu Xiaogan, "Taoism," in *Our Religions*, ed. Arvind Sharma (San Francisco: HarperSanFrancisco, 1993), 231-89.

25. See Livia Kohn, *The Taoist Experience: An Anthology* (Albany: State University of New York Press, 1993).

26. Liu Xiaogan, "Taoism," 240.

27. On this translation, see J. Shih, "The Tao: Its Essence, Its Dynamism, and Its Fitness as a Vehicle of Christian Revelation," in *L'Eglise et les Religions*, Studia Missionalia 15 (Rome: Gregorian University Press, 1966), 117-33.

28. Unless otherwise noted, all translations are from *Tao Te Ching*, trans. Ch'u Ta-Kao (London: Unwin Paperbacks, 1989).

29. Küng and Ching, *Christianity*, 133.

30. See Liu Xiaogan, "Taoism," 242-43.

31. Küng and Ching, *Christianity*, 134.

32. Burton Watson, ed. and trans., *The Complete Works of Chuang Tzu* (New York and London: Columbia University Press, 1968), 39-40; see Liu Ziaogan, "Taoism," 248-49.

33. Schwartz, *World of Thought*, 191.

34. See Kohn, *Taoist Experience*, 281-82.

35. Watson, *Works of Chuang Tzu*, 57-58; quoted by Küng and Ching, *Christianity*, 135.

36. Wu, *Chinese Humanism*, 68-70.

37. Ibid., 86-91; Schwartz, *World of Thought*, 193-94.

38. See *The Sayings of the Desert Fathers: The Alphabetical Collection*, trans. Benedicta Ward (rev. ed.; Kalamazoo, Mich.: Cistercian Publications, 1984); and *The Philokalia: The Complete Text Compiled by St. Nikodimos of*

the Holy Mountain and St. Makarios of Corinth, trans. G. E. H. Palmer et al. (3 vols.; London: Faber & Faber, 1979).

39. Peter Brown, *Society and the Holy in Late Antiquity* (Berkeley and Los Angeles: University of California Press, 1982), 103-65.

40. Merton, *Wisdom of the Desert, 5.*

41. Thomas Merton, *The Way of Chuang Tzu* (New York: New Directions, 1965), 11.

42. Wu, *Chinese Humanism,* 96-97.

43. See Arvind Sharma, "Hinduism," in *Our Religions,* ed. Arvind Sharma (San Francisco: HarperSanFrancisco, 1993), 5.

44. *Hindu Scriptures,* ed. Dominic Goodall (Berkeley and Los Angeles: University of California Press, 1996); *Textual Sources for the Study of Hinduism,* ed. and trans. Wendy Doniger O'Flaherty with Daniel Gold, David Haberman, and David Shulman (Chicago: University of Chicago Press, 1988); and Harold Coward, *Sacred Word and Sacred Text: Scripture in World Religions* (Maryknoll, N.Y.: Orbis, 1988), 106-29.

45. M. Dhavamony, "Revelation in Hinduism," in *Revelation in Christianity and Other Religions,* Studia Missionalia 20 (Rome: Gregorian University Press, 1971), 173.

46. Sarvepalli Radhakrishnan, *Indian Religions* (New Delhi and Bombay: Orient Paperbacks, 1979), 22.

47. Sri Sarvepalli Radhakrishnan, *The Hindu View of Life* (London: Unwin Paperbacks, 1980 [1927]), 13-15.

48. On Vivekananda, see Anantanand Rambachan, *The Limits of Scripture: Vivekananda's Reinterpretation of the Vedas* (Honolulu: University of Hawaii Press, 1994); for Western interpretations of Hindu revelation, see R. C. Zaehner, *Mysticism Sacred and Profane* (London: Oxford University Press, 1978 [1957]); Geoffrey Parrinder, *Mysticism in the World's Religions* (London: Sheldon, 1976).

49. Anantanand Rambachan, *Accomplishing the Accomplished: The Vedas as a Source of Valid Knowledge in Shankara,* Society for Asian and Comparative Philosophy 10 (Honolulu: University of Hawaii Press, 1991), 118-19.

50. Rambachan, *Accomplishing,* 123.

51. *Brihadaranyaka Upanishad* 4.4.5; quoted by Zaehner, *Concordant Discord,* 37.

52. *The Rig Veda: An Anthology,* ed. and trans. Wendy Doniger O'Flaherty (Harmondsworth, England: Penguin, 1981), 10:90; pp. 29-32.

53. *Upanishads,* trans. Patrick Olivelle (Oxford and New York: Oxford University Press, 1996), lii. Unless otherwise noted, all translations of the Upanishads will be from this edition.

54. Zaehner, *Concordant Discord,* 68.

55. Ibid.

56. A. L. Basham, *The Origins and Development of Classical Hinduism,* ed. Kenneth G. Zysk (Boston: Beacon, 1989), 66-67.

57. See Sarvepalli Radhakrishnan and Charles A. Moore, eds., *A Sourcebook in Indian Philosophy* (Princeton, N.J.: Princeton University Press, 1957), 506-43.

58. See Eliot Deutsch, *Advaita Vedanta: A Philosophical Reconstruction* (Honolulu: University of Hawaii Press, 1969).

59. Zaehner, *Concordant Discord*, 84.

60. Basham, 82; *Bhagavad Gita,* trans. Juan Mascaró (Harmondsworth, England; Penguin, 1962). Unless otherwise noted, all translations from the *Bhagavad Gita* will be from this edition.

61. Mascaró, "Introduction" to *Bhagavad Gita,* 22.

62. Quoted by Louis Fischer, *The Life of Mahatma Gandhi* (New York: Harper & Row, 1950), 32.

63. R. C. Zaehner, *The Bhagavad Gita with a Commentary Based on the Original Sources* (London: Oxford University Press, 1969), 16:19-20; p. 24.

64. *The Vedanta Sutras with the Commentary of Ramanuja,* trans. George Thibaut, Sacred Books of the East 48 (Oxford: Clarendon Press, 1904), in Radhakrishnan and Moore, *A Source Book in Indian Philosophy,* 551.

65. See John B. Carman, *Majesty and Meekness: A Comparative Study of Contrast and Harmony in the Concept of God* (Grand Rapids: Eerdmans, 1994), 79-100.

66. For reflections on the *Bhagavad Gita* as a spiritual guide for Christians, see Bede Griffiths, *River of Compassion* (Warwick, N.Y.: Amity House, 1987).

67. Geoffrey Parrinder, *Avatar and Incarnation* (New York: Oxford University Press, 1982), 124-25.

68. Quoted by Parrinder, 230.

69. See Ashvaghosha, *The Buddhacarita or, The Acts of the Buddha,* Part 1: Sanskrit Text, ed. and trans. E. H. Johnston (Lahore: University of the Punjab, 1936; reprint, New Delhi: India Oriental Books Reprint Corp. 1972), 1.34; p. 8.

70. See Walpola Rahula, *What the Buddha Taught* (New York: Grove Press, 1959).

71. *Ashtasahasrika Sutra (The Perfection of Wisdom in 8,000 Lines),* I, 20-21, in Edward Conze, ed. and trans., *Selected Sayings from the Perfection of Wisdom* (1955; reprint, Boulder, Colo.: Prajna Press, 1978), 99.

72. See Thich Nhat Hanh, *The Heart of Understanding: Commentaries on the Prajnaparamita Heart Sutra,* ed. Peter Levitt (Berkeley, Calif.: Parallax Press, 1988).

73. Jasper Hopkins, *Nicholas of Cusa On Learned Ignorance: A Translation and Appraisal of De Docta Ignorantia* (2nd ed.; Minneapolis: Arthur J. Banning, 1985), 98.

74. *The Dhammapada: The Path of Perfection,* trans. Juan Mascaró (Harmondsworth, England: Penguin Books, 1973), 1:1; p. 35.

75. See *Buddhacarita,* 2:25-56; 3:1-43.

76. Thich Nhat Hanh, *Zen Keys* (Garden City, N.Y.: Anchor Books, 1974), 78.

77. Ibid., 76.

78. Ibid., 78.

79. See Thich Nhat Hanh, *Breathe! You Are Alive: Sutra on the Full Awareness of Breathing* (Berkeley, Calif.: Parallax Press, 1990).

80. Evagrius Ponticus, *The Praktikos; Chapters on Prayer,* trans. John Eudes Bamberger (Kalamazoo, Mich.: Cistercian Publications, 1981), 11; p. 57.

81. René Girard, *Violence and the Sacred* (Baltimore and London: Johns Hopkins University Press, 1977), 1-67.

82. René Girard, *The Scapegoat* (Baltimore: Johns Hopkins University Press, 1986), 166.

83. René Girard, with Jean-Michel Oughourlian and Guy Lefort, *Things Hidden since the Foundation of the World* (Stanford, Calif.: Stanford University Press, 1987), 266.

84. "Seminaire de recherche sur l'oeuvre de René Girard tenu au RIER (Regroupement Interuniversitaire pour l'Etude de la Religion)," *Studies in Religion/Sciences Religieuses* 10, no. 1 (1981): 81, 83.

85. See Thich Nhat Hanh et al., *For a Future to Be Possible: Commentaries on the Five Wonderful Precepts* (Berkeley, Calif.: Parallax Press, 1993); Ken Jones, *Beyond Optimism: A Buddhist Political Ecology* (Oxford: Jon Carpenter, 1993); Joanna Macy, *World as Lover, World as Self* (Berkeley, Calif.: Parallax Press, 1991); Thich Nhat Hanh, *Vietnam: Lotus in a Sea of Fire* (New York: Hill & Wang, 1967).

86. Joanna Macy, "In Indra's Net: Sarvodaya and Our Mutual Efforts for Peace," in *The Path of Compassion: Writings on Socially Engaged Buddhism*, ed. Fred Eppsteiner (rev. 2nd ed.; Berkeley, Calif.: Parallax Press, 1988), 179.

7

ENCOUNTERS IN A WORLD OF DIALOGUE

1. Martin Buber, *Two Types of Faith* (New York: Harper Torchbooks, 1961 [1951]), 12-13.

2. Pinchas Lapide, *The Resurrection of Jesus: A Jewish Perspective* (Minneapolis: Augsburg, 1983), 123-53.

3. Bede Griffiths, *The Cosmic Revelation: The Hindu Way to God* (Springfield, Ill.: Templegate, 1983), 113.

4. See A. Pushparajan, ed., *Pilgrims of Dialogue* (Munnar, India: Sangam Dialogue Centre, 1991).

5. The Dalai Lama, "Harmony, Dialogue and Meditation," in *The Gethsemani Encounter: A Dialogue on the Spiritual Life by Buddhist and Christian Monastics*, ed. Donald W. Mitchell and James A. Wiseman (New York: Continuum, 1997), 46-50.

6. Seung Sahn, "True God, True Buddha," *Primary Point* 9, no. 2 (Sept. 1992): 3.

7. R. C. Zaehner, *Concordant Discord: The Interdependence of Faiths* (Oxford: Clarendon Press, 1970), 436.

8. See Anantanand Rambachan, *The Limits of Scripture: Vivekananda's Reinterpretation of the Vedas* (Honolulu: University of Hawaii Press, 1994), 11-40.

9. See Robert Ellsberg, ed., *Gandhi on Christianity* (Maryknoll, N.Y.: Orbis, 1991); and Mohandas K. Gandhi, *Autobiography: The Story of My Experiments with Truth* (New York: Dover, 1983 [1948]).

10. Paul J. Griffiths, *An Apology for Apologetics: A Study in the Logic of Interreligious Dialogue*, Faith Meets Faith Series (Maryknoll, N.Y.: Orbis, 1991).

11. Hans Küng and Karl-Josef Kuschel, eds., *A Global Ethic: The Declaration of the Parliament of the World's Religions* (New York: Continuum, 1993).

12. Alan Race, *Christians and Religious Pluralism: Patterns in the Christian Theology of Religions* (Maryknoll, N.Y.: Orbis, 1982).

13. See Terrence W. Tilley, "'Christianity and the World Religions,' A Recent Vatican Document," *Theological Studies* 60, no. 2 (1999): 318-37.

14. John Hick, *An Interpretation of Religion: Human Responses to the Transcendent* (New Haven and London: Yale University Press, 1989); and idem, *A Christian Theology of Religions: The Rainbow of Faiths* (Louisville, Ky.: Westminster/John Knox Press, 1995).

15. S. Mark Heim, *Salvations: Truth and Difference in Religion* (Maryknoll, N.Y.: Orbis, 1995).

16. Ibid., 129-44.

17. Ibid., 3.

18. Ibid., 6.

19. Paul Knitter, *One Earth Many Religions: Multifaith Dialogue and Global Responsibility* (Maryknoll, N.Y.: Orbis, 1995), 197 n. 6.

20. Nicholas Rescher, *The Strife of Systems* (Pittsburgh: Pittsburgh University Press, 1985); idem, *Pluralism: Against the Demand for Consensus* (Oxford: Clarendon, 1993).

21. John Briggs and F. David Peat, *Seven Life Lessons of Chaos: Timeless Wisdom from the Science of Change* (New York: HarperCollins, 1999) 1-10; see also James Gleick, *Chaos: Making a New Science* (New York: Penguin, 1987); and John Briggs and F. David Peat, *Turbulent Mirror: An Illustrated Guide to Chaos Theory and the Science of Wholeness* (New York: Harper & Row, 1990).

22. Briggs and Peat, *Seven Lessons*, 2.

23. Briggs and Peat, *Turbulent Mirror*, 83-113; Gleick, *Chaos*, 81-118.

24. Briggs and Peat, *Seven Lessons*, 100.

25. Ibid., 7; see also John F. Haught, *Chaos, Complexity and Theology*, Teilhard Studies 30 (Chambersburg, Pa.: Anima Books,1994).

26. Briggs and Peat, *Seven Lessons*, 7-10.

27. Gleick, *Chaos*, 16.

28. Briggs and Peat, *Seven Lessons*, 4-16.

29. Gregory XVI, 1834, in Mansi 51, 570; cited by Edward Schillebeeckx, *Church: The Human Story of God* (New York: Crossroad, 1990), 247.

30. Briggs and Peat, *Seven Lessons*, 100-102; Gleick, *Chaos*, 94-96.

31. For examples from around the world, see Thomas Bamat and Jean-Paul Wiest, *Popular Catholicism in a World Church* (Maryknoll, N.Y.: Orbis, 1999).

32. H. M. Enomiya-Lassalle, *Zen Meditation for Christians* (LaSalle, Ill.: Open Court, 1974).

33. William Johnston, *Christian Zen* (New York: Harper Colophon Books, 1971); idem, *The Still Point: Reflections on Zen and Christian Mysticism* (New York: Fordham University Press, 1970).

34. Dom Aelred Graham, *Zen Catholicism* (New York: Crossroad; York, England: Ampleforth, 1994 [1963]).

35. John Dykstra Eusden, *Zen and Christian: The Journey Between* (New York: Crossroad, 1981).

36. Hugo Enomiya-Lassalle, *Living in the New Consciousness* (Boston and Shaftesbury: Shambhala, 1988), 121-23.

37. Joseph Cardinal Ratzinger, "Letter to the Bishops of the Catholic Church on Some Aspects of Christian Meditation," *Buddhist-Christian Studies* 11 (1991): 123-38.

38. Ibid., 129.

39. Robert Aitken, "The Intrareligious Realization: Ruminations of an American Zen Buddhist," in *John Paul II and Interreligious Dialogue*, ed. Byron L. Sherwin and Harold Kasimow (Maryknoll, N.Y.: Orbis, 1999), 103.

40. Briggs and Peat, *Seven Lessons*, 22.

41. Ibid., 24.

42. Ibid., 97.

43. Ibid., 80.

8

BUDDHIST AWAKENING AND CHRISTIAN REVELATION

1. See Donald W. Mitchell, ed., *Masao Abe: A Zen Life of Dialogue* (Boston: Charles E. Tuttle, 1998).

2. Karl Rahner, "The One Christ and the Universality of Salvation," in *Theological Investigations,* vol. 16, trans. David Morland (New York: Crossroad, 1983), 219.

3. Quoted by Hans Waldenfels, *Absolute Nothingness: Foundations for a Buddhist-Christian Dialogue*, trans. J. W. Heisig (New York: Paulist, 1980), 157.

4. John B. Cobb Jr., *Beyond Dialogue: Toward a Mutual Transformation of Christianity and Buddhism* (Philadelphia: Fortress, 1982); David Tracy, *Dialogue with the Other: The Inter-Religious Dialogue*, Louvain Theological and Pastoral Monographs (Louvain: Peeters; Grand Rapids: Eerdmans, 1990).

5. Masao Abe, *Zen and Western Thought*, ed. William R. LaFleur (Honolulu: University of Hawaii Press, 1985).

6. Masao Abe, "Kenosis and Emptiness," in *Buddhist Emptiness and Christian Trinity: Essays and Explorations*, ed. Roger Corless and Paul F. Knitter (New York: Paulist, 1990); idem, "Kenotic God and Dynamic Sunyata," in *Divine Emptiness and Historical Fullness: A Buddhist-Jewish-Christian Conversation with Masao Abe*, ed. Christopher Ives (Valley Forge, Pa.: Trinity Press International, 1995); and Masao Abe, *Buddhism and Interfaith Dialogue*, ed. Steven Heine (Honolulu: University of Hawaii Press, 1995).

7. Karl Rahner, *Foundations of Christian Faith: An Introduction to the Idea of Christianity*, trans. William V. Dych (New York: Crossroad, 1982), 34.

8. Ibid., 61.

9. Abe, "Kenotic God and Dynamic Sunyata," 28.

10. Masao Abe, "Emptiness Is Suchness," in *The Buddha Eye: An Anthology of the Kyoto School*, ed. Frederick Franck (New York: Crossroad, 1982), 206.

11. Ibid.

12. Karl Rahner, *The Practice of Faith: A Handbook of Contemporary Spirituality*, ed. Karl Lehman and Albert Raffelt (New York: Crossroad, 1986), 133.

13. Abe, *Zen and Western Thought*, 187.

14. Abe, "Emptiness Is Suchness," 206.

15. Ibid.

16. Rahner, *Practice of Faith*, 108.

17. Ibid., 110.

18. Ibid., 112.

19. Rahner, *Foundations*, 22.

20. Abe, *Zen and Western Thought*, 201.

21. Ibid., 192.

22. Abe, "Emptiness Is Suchness," 207.

23. Shinran, *Tannisho: A Shin Buddhist Classic*, trans. Taitetsu Unno (Honolulu: Buddhist Study Center Press, 1984).

24. Karl Rahner, "Reflections on the Experience of Grace," in *Theological Investigations*, vol. 3, trans. Karl-H. and Boniface Kruger (London: Darton, Longman & Todd; New York: Seabury Press, 1974), 89.

25. Ibid., 87.

26. Rahner, *Foundations*, 54.

27. Ibid., 54.

28. Rahner, *Practice of Faith*, 113.

29. Dogen, "Dogen's Fukanzazengi and Shobogenzo Zazengi," trans. Norman Wadell and Masao Abe; cited by T. P. Kasulis, *Zen Action, Zen Person* (Honolulu: University of Hawaii Press, 1981), 70.

30. Rahner, *Practice of Faith*, 63.

31. Ibid., 63.

32. Ibid., 187.

33. Abe, *Zen and Western Thought*, 167-68.

34. Rahner, *Foundations*, 53.

35. Ibid., 90.

36. Ibid., 93.

37. Abe, *Zen and Western Thought*, 187.

38. Masao Abe, "Dogen's View of Time and Space," *Eastern Buddhist*, New Series 21, no. 2 (1988): 6.

39. Abe, *Zen and Western Thought*, 200.

40. Abe, "Kenotic God and Dynamic Sunyata," 29-30.

41. Karl Rahner, "Christianity and the Non-Christian Religions," in *Theological Investigations*, vol. 5, trans. Karl-H. Kruger (Baltimore: Helicon, 1966), 125-29.

42. Abe, *Buddhism and Interfaith Dialogue*, 40-50.

43. Karl Rahner, "The Incomprehensibility of God in Thomas Aquinas," *Journal of Religion* 58 Supplement (1978): S125.

44. Abe, *Zen and Western Thought*, 4.

45. Ibid.

46. Abe, "Kenotic God and Dynamic Sunyata," 28.

47. Keiji Nishitani, "The I-Thou Relation in Zen Buddhism," in *The Buddha Eye: An Anthology of the Kyoto School*, ed. Frederick Franck (New York: Crossroad, 1982), 48.

Glossary

Advaita Vedanta—a leading school of Hindu thought, influenced by Shankara, which teaches the nonduality of ultimate reality and this world

ahimsa—nonviolence

atman—the individual self

avatar—an incarnation of God in Hinduism

Axial Age—the period from 800 to 200 B.C.E. during which the cultures of China, India, Greece, and Israel went through major religious transformations

bhakti-yoga—the discipline of devotion to a personal God in Hinduism

bodhisattva—a future Buddha; a being who delays entry into nirvana until all sentient beings can enter together

brahman—ultimate reality in Hinduism

caritas—Augustine's term for the self-giving love that is modeled on God

categorical revelation—Karl Rahner's term for the self-communication of God in and through concrete historical events and the literary expressions of these

chaos theory—contemporary scientific study of the patterns in unpredictable systems

coincidence of opposites (*coincidentia oppositorum*)—Nicholas of Cusa's idea that opposites in finite thought may coincide in the infinite

cupiditas—Augustine's term for the distorted, self-destructive love that is centered on something finite

dharma—the cosmic order; the teaching of the Buddha

dharmakaya—ultimate reality

dependent co-arising (*pratitya-samutpada*)—the interdependence of all realities in Mahayana Buddhism

dukkha—unsatisfactoriness, suffering

exclusivism—the claim that only members of a particular religious tradition can be saved

external mediation—a term of René Girard for imitation of a model who greatly exceeds the imitator in power

fractals—patterns in chaos that are traces of dynamic systems

gnosis—knowledge, a term in early Christianity for a special, saving knowledge

inclusivism—the position that all people can be saved by being included in a particular religious tradition's mediation of salvation

internal mediation—a term of René Girard for imitation of a model by an imitator who approaches the model in power and becomes a threat

jnana-yoga—the discipline of knowledge in Hinduism

karma—the law of cause and effect that governs the universe in Indian thought

karma-yoga—the way of action without attachment to consequences

learned ignorance (*docta ignorantia*)—the term of Nicholas of Cusa for a knowing of the infinite that acknowledges its own limits and recognizes the unknowability of the infinite

mimesis—a term of René Girard for the imitation of others' desires, whether conscious or unconscious

mimetic rivalry—a term of René Girard for the competition that arises when an imitator approaches a model in power and becomes a threat

mimetic theory—the theory of desire, imitation, and violence of René Girard

nirvana—the extinction of craving; ultimate reality

pluralism—the position that a variety of religions offer equal opportunities for knowledge of the ultimate and salvation

samsara—the world of suffering and change in Buddhist though

sangha—Buddhist monastic community; more broadly, the entire Buddhist community

scapegoat mechanism—René Girard's term for channeling hostility onto a victim to achieve a relative stability and peace

Shakyamuni Buddha—the title of Siddhartha Gautama after his enlightenment; Shakyamuni literally means "the silent one of the Shakya clan"

surrogate victim mechanism—the scapegoat mechanism

Tao—the Way; the principle of cosmic order in Chinese thought

transcendental horizon—Karl Rahner's term for the implicit experience of God as the limit of all experience, knowing, and action

transcendental revelation—Karl Rahner's term for the implicit self-communication of God in all human experience

Upanishads—ancient Hindu scriptures that guide seekers to liberation through insight

Vedas—the most ancient Hindu scriptures

via negativa—a term in Christian theology for theology that stresses the difference between all human thought and God; God is known more truly by not knowing

List of References

Abe, Masao. *Buddhism and Interfaith Dialogue.* Ed. Steven Heine. Honolulu: University of Hawaii Press, 1995.

———. "Dogen's View of Time and Space." *Eastern Buddhist,* New Series 21, no. 2 (1988): 1-35.

———. *A Study of Dogen: His Philosophy and Religion.* Ed. Steven Heine. Albany: State University of New York Press, 1992.

———. *Zen and Western Thought.* Ed. William R. LaFleur. Honolulu: University of Hawaii Press, 1985.

Aitken, Robert. "The Intrareligious Realization: Ruminations of an American Zen Buddhist." In *John Paul II and Interreligious Dialogue,* ed. Byron L. Sherwin and Harold Kasimow, 96-107. Maryknoll, N.Y.: Orbis, 1999.

Albrektson, Bertil. *History and the Gods: An Essay on the Idea of Historical Events as Divine Manifestations in the Ancient Near East and in Israel.* Coniectanea Biblica, OT. Lund: Gleerup, 1967.

Allison, Dale C. *Jesus of Nazareth: Millenarian Prophet.* Minneapolis: Fortress, 1998.

Ariès, Philippe, and Georges Duby, eds. *A History of Private Life.* Vol. 2, *Revelations of the Medieval World.* Cambridge, Mass., and London: Belknap Press of Harvard University Press, 1988.

Arinze, Francis Cardinal. "Message for End of Ramadan." *Origins* 27/29 (Jan. 8, 1998): 485.

Aristotle. *Magna Moralia.* In *The Complete Works of Aristotle,* ed. Jonathan Barnes. Rev. ed. Princeton, N.J.: Princeton University Press, 1984.

Ashvaghosha. *The Buddhacarita or, The Acts of the Buddha.* Part 1: Sanskrit Text. Ed. and trans. E. H. Johnston. Lahore: University of the Punjab, 1936. Reprint, New Delhi: India Oriental Books Reprint Corp., 1972.

Augustine. *Confessions.* Trans. R. S. Pine-Coffin. Harmondsworth, England: Penguin, 1961.

Aune, David E. *Prophecy in Early Christianity and the Ancient Mediterranean World.* Grand Rapids: Eerdmans, 1983.

Bainton, Roland H. *Christian Attitudes toward War and Peace.* Nashville: Abingdon, 1960.

Bamat, Thomas, and Jean-Paul Wiest. *Popular Catholicism in a World Church* Maryknoll, N.Y.: Orbis, 1999.

Barr, James. *Biblical Faith and Natural Theology.* Oxford: Clarendon Press, 1993.

Barth, Karl. *Against the Stream: Shorter Post-War Writings 1946-52.* New York: Philosophical Library, 1954.

————. *Church Dogmatics*. Vol. 2, pts. 1 and 2, *The Doctrine of God*. Edinburgh: T. & T. Clark, 1957.

————. *Dogmatics in Outline*. New York: Harper Torchbooks, 1959.

Basham, A. L. *The Origins and Development of Classical Hinduism*. Ed. Kenneth G. Zysk. Boston: Beacon, 1989.

Batto, Bernard F. *Slaying the Dragon: Mythmaking in the Biblical Tradition*. Louisville, Ky.: Westminster/John Knox Press, 1992.

Beardslee, William A. "Parable, Proverb, and Koan." *Semeia* 12 (1978): 151-73.

Bernardin, Joseph Cardinal. *Antisemitism: The Historical Legacy and the Continuing Challenge for Christians: An Address at Hebrew University of Jerusalem, March 23, 1995*. Fairfield, Conn.: Center for Christian-Jewish Understanding, 1995.

Betz, Hans Dieter. *The Sermon on the Mount: A Commentary on the Sermon on the Mount including the Sermon on the Plain*. Ed. Adela Yarbro Collins. Minneapolis: Fortress, 1995.

Bhagavad Gita. Trans. Juan Mascaró. Harmondsworth, England: Penguin, 1962.

Biechler, James L. "A New Face Toward Islam: Nicholas of Cusa and John of Segovia." In *Nicholas of Cusa in Search of God and Wisdom*, ed. Gerald Christianson and Thomas M. Izbicki. Studies in the History of Christian Thought 45. Leiden: E. J. Brill, 1991.

Blackman, E. C. *Marcion and His Influence*. London: SPCK, 1948.

Blenkinsopp, Joseph. *A History of Prophecy in Israel*. Philadelphia: Westminster, 1983.

Bloch, Marc. *Feudal Society*. Vol. 2, *Social Classes and Political Organization*. Chicago: University of Chicago Press, 1961.

Boff, Leonardo. *Saint Francis: A Model for Human Liberation*. New York: Crossroad, 1988.

Breasted, James Henry. *Development of Religion and Thought in Ancient Egypt*. Philadelphia: University of Pennsylvania Press, 1959 [1912].

Briggs, John, and F. David Peat. *Seven Life Lessons of Chaos: Timeless Wisdom from the Science of Change*. New York: HarperCollins, 1999.

————. *Turbulent Mirror: An Illustrated Guide to Chaos Theory and the Science of Wholeness*. New York: Harper & Row, 1990.

Bright, John. *A History of Israel*. 2nd ed. Philadelphia: Westminster, 1972.

Brown, Peter. *Augustine of Hippo: A Biography*. Berkeley: University of California Press, 1967.

————. *The Rise of Western Christendom: Triumph and Diversity AD 200-1000*. Malden, Mass., and Oxford: Blackwell, 1996.

————. *Society and the Holy in Late Antiquity*. Berkeley and Los Angeles: University of California Press, 1982.

Brown, Raymond E. *The Death of the Messiah: From Gethsemane to the Grave: A Commentary on the Passion Narratives in the Four Gospels*. Anchor Bible Reference Library. 2 vols. New York: Doubleday, 1994.

————. *The Gospel according to John*. Anchor Bible. 2 vols. Garden City, N.Y.: Doubleday, 1966, 1970.

————. *An Introduction to the New Testament*. Anchor Bible Reference Library. New York: Doubleday, 1997.

Brown, William P. *Character in Crisis: A Fresh Approach to the Wisdom Literature of the Old Testament*. Grand Rapids: Eerdmans, 1996.

Brueggemann, Walter. *Revelation and Violence: A Study in Contextualization.* Milwaukee, Wis.: Marquette University Press, 1986.

———. "Scripture and an Ecumenical Life-Style." *Interpretation* 24 (1970): 3-19.

———. *Theology of the Old Testament: Testimony, Dispute, Advocacy.* Minneapolis: Fortress, 1997.

Brundage, James A. *Medieval Canon Law and the Crusader.* Madison, Milwaukee, and London: University of Wisconsin Press, 1969.

Buber, Martin. "Autobiographical Fragments." In *The Philosophy of Martin Buber,* ed. Paul Arthur Schilpp. LaSalle, Ill.: Open Court, 1967.

Burkert, Walter. *Homo Necans: The Anthropology of Ancient Greek Sacrificial Ritual and Myth.* Berkeley, Calif.: University of California Press, 1983.

Cantor, Norman F. *The Civilization of the Middle Ages.* Rev. ed. New York: HarperCollins, 1993.

Carlston, Charles E. "Proverbs, Maxims, and the Historical Jesus." *Journal of Biblical Literature* 99 (1980): 91.

Carman, John B. *Majesty and Meekness: A Comparative Study of Contrast and Harmony in the Concept of God.* Grand Rapids: Eerdmans, 1994.

Ching, Julia. *Chinese Religions.* Maryknoll, N.Y.: Orbis, 1993.

Clement of Alexandria. *Exhortation to the Greeks.* Trans. G. W. Butterworth. Loeb Classical Library. Cambridge, Mass.: Harvard University Press; London: William Heinemann, 1919.

Cobb, John B., Jr. *Beyond Dialogue: Toward a Mutual Transformation of Christianity and Buddhism.* Philadelphia: Fortress, 1982.

Collins, Adela Yarbro. *Crisis and Catharsis: The Power of the Apocalypse.* Philadelphia: Westminster, 1984.

Collins, John J. "The Biblical Precedent for Natural Theology." *Journal of the American Academy of Religion* 45 Supplement (1977): 35-67.

Confucius. *The Analects.* Trans. D. C. Lau. Harmondsworth, England: Penguin, 1979.

Conze, Edward. *Buddhist Thought in India: Three Phases of Buddhist Philosophy.* Ann Arbor: University of Michigan Press, 1967 [1962].

———, ed. and trans. *Buddhist Wisdom Books, Containing the Diamond Sutra and The Heart Sutra.* 2nd ed. London: George Allen & Unwin, 1975.

———, ed. and trans. *Selected Sayings from the Perfection of Wisdom.* Boulder, Colo.: Prajna Press, 1978 [1955].

Corless, Roger, and Paul F. Knitter, eds. *Buddhist Emptiness and Christian Trinity: Essays and Explorations.* New York: Paulist, 1990.

Cousins, Ewert H. *Bonaventure and the Coincidence of Opposites.* Chicago: Franciscan Herald Press, 1978.

———. *Christ of the 21st Century.* Rockport, Mass.: Element, 1992.

Coward, Harold. *Sacred Word and Sacred Text: Scripture in World Religions.* Maryknoll, N.Y.: Orbis, 1988.

Cragg, Kenneth. *Jesus and the Muslim: An Exploration.* London: George Allen & Unwin, 1985.

Crenshaw, James L. "Method in Determining Wisdom Influence upon 'Historical' Literature." *Journal of Biblical Literature* 88 (1969): 129-42.

———. *Old Testament Wisdom: An Introduction.* Atlanta: John Knox Press, 1981.

Cross, Frank Moore. *Canaanite Myth and Hebrew Epic: Essays in the History of the Religion of Israel*. Cambridge, Mass., and London: Harvard University Press, 1973.

Cunningham, Agnes, ed. *The Early Church and the State*. Trans. Michael Di Maio and Agnes Cunningham. Philadelphia: Fortress, 1982.

Daniélou, Jean. *A History of Early Christian Doctrine before the Council of Nicaea*. Vol. 2, *Gospel Message and Hellenistic Culture*. London: Darton, Longman, & Todd; Philadelphia: Westminster, 1973.

Davies, Alan, ed. *Antisemitism and the Foundations of Christianity*. New York: Paulist, 1979.

Desjardins, Michel. *Peace, Violence and the New Testament*. Sheffield, England: Sheffield Academic Press, 1997.

Deutsch, Eliot. *Advaita Vedanta: A Philosophical Reconstruction*. Honolulu: University of Hawaii Press, 1969.

The Dhammapada: The Path of Perfection. Trans. Juan Mascaró. Harmondsworth, England: Penguin Books, 1973.

Dhavamony, M. "Revelation in Hinduism." In *Revelation in Christianity and Other Religions*, 163-89. Studia Missionalia 20. Rome: Gregorian University Press, 1971.

Dolan, John Patrick, ed. *Unity and Reform: Selected Writings of Nicholas de Cusa*. South Bend, Ind.: University of Notre Dame Press, 1962.

Dulles, Avery. *The Assurance of Things Hoped For: A Theology of Christian Faith*. New York and Oxford: Oxford University Press, 1994.

Eliade, Mircea. *Patterns in Comparative Religion*. New York: New American Library, 1963.

———. *The Sacred and the Profane: The Nature of Religion*. New York: Harcourt, Brace & World, 1959.

Ellsberg, Robert, ed. *Gandhi on Christianity*. Maryknoll, N.Y.: Orbis, 1991.

Enomiya-Lassalle, H. M. *Living in the New Consciousness*. Boston and Shaftesbury: Shambhala, 1988.

———. *Zen Meditation for Christians*. LaSalle, Ill.: Open Court, 1974.

Esposito, John L. *Islam: The Straight Path*. 3rd ed. New York and Oxford: Oxford University Press, 1998.

Eusden, John Dykstra. *Zen and Christian: The Journey Between*. New York: Crossroad, 1981.

Evagrius Ponticus. *The Praktikos; Chapters on Prayer*. Trans. John Eudes Bamberger. Kalamazoo, Mich.: Cistercian Publications, 1981.

Fackenheim, Emil. *To Mend the World: Foundations of Post-Holocaust Jewish Thought*. New York: Schocken Books, 1982.

Fingarette, Herbert. *Confucius—Secular as Sacred*. New York: Harper Torchbooks, 1972.

Fischer, Louis. *The Life of Mahatma Gandhi*. New York: Harper & Row, 1950.

Flannery, Edward H. *The Anguish of the Jews: Twenty-three Centuries of Anti-Semitism*. New York: Macmillan; London: Collier-Macmillan, 1965.

Franck, Frederick, ed. *The Buddha Eye: An Anthology of the Kyoto School*. New York: Crossroad, 1982.

Frankfort, H., and H. A. Frankfort, John A. Wilson, Thorkild Jacobsen, and William A. Irwin. *The Intellectual Adventure of Ancient Man: An Essay on Speculative Thought in the Ancient Near East*. Chicago and London: University of Chicago Press, 1977 [1946].

Frend, W. H. C. *Martyrdom and Persecution in the Early Church: A Study of a Conflict from the Maccabees to Donatus.* Grand Rapids: Baker Book House, 1965.

———. *The Rise of Christianity.* Philadelphia: Fortress, 1984.

Gammie, John G., and Leo G. Perdue, eds. *The Sage in Israel and the Ancient Near East.* Winona Lake, Ind.: Eisenbrauns, 1990.

Gandhi, Mohandas K. *Autobiography: The Story of My Experiments with Truth.* New York: Dover, 1983 [1948].

Gilligan, James. *Violence: Reflections on a National Epidemic.* New York: Vintage Books, 1997.

Girard, René. *Deceit, Desire, and the Novel: Self and Other in Literary Structure.* Baltimore and London: Johns Hopkins University Press, 1965.

———. *Job: The Victim of His People.* Stanford, Calif.: Stanford University Press, 1987.

———. *Resurrection from the Underground: Feodor Dostoevsky.* Ed. and trans. James G. Williams. New York: Crossroad, 1997.

———. *The Scapegoat.* Baltimore: Johns Hopkins University Press, 1986.

———. *A Theater of Envy: William Shakespeare.* New York and Oxford: Oxford University Press, 1991.

———. *"To Double Business Bound": Essays on Literature, Mimesis, and Anthropology.* Baltimore: Johns Hopkins University Press, 1978.

———. *Violence and the Sacred.* Baltimore and London: Johns Hopkins University Press, 1977.

Girard, René, with Jean-Michel Oughourlian and Guy Lefort. *Things Hidden since the Foundation of the World.* Stanford, Calif.: Stanford University Press, 1987.

Gleick, James. *Chaos: Making a New Science.* New York: Penguin, 1987.

Gnuse, Robert Karl. *No Other Gods: Emergent Monotheism in Israel.* Journal for the Study of the Old Testament Supplement 241. Sheffield, England: Sheffield Academic Press, 1997.

Goldhagen, Daniel. *Hitler's Willing Executioners: Ordinary Germans and the Holocaust.* New York: Alfred A. Knopf, 1996.

Goodall, Dominic, ed. *Hindu Scriptures.* Berkeley and Los Angeles: University of California Press, 1996.

Gottwald, Norman K. *The Tribes of Yahweh: A Sociology of the Religion of Liberated Israel 1250-1050 BCE.* Maryknoll, N.Y.: Orbis, 1979.

Gottwald, Norman K., and Richard A. Horsley, eds. *The Bible and Liberation: Political and Social Hermeneutics.* Rev. ed. Maryknoll, N.Y.: Orbis; London: SPCK, 1993.

Gow, Andrew Colin. *The Red Jews: Antisemitism in an Apocalyptic Age: 1200-1600.* Leiden: E. J. Brill, 1995.

Graham, Dom Aelred. *Zen Catholicism.* New York: Crossroad; York, England: Ampleforth, 1994 [1963].

Grant, Robert M. *Augustus to Constantine: The Rise and Triumph of Christianity in the Roman World.* San Francisco: Harper & Row, 1990 [1970].

———. *Early Christianity and Society: Seven Studies.* San Francisco: Harper & Row, 1977.

———. *Irenaeus of Lyons.* London and New York: Routledge, 1997.

Griffiths, Bede. *The Cosmic Revelation: The Hindu Way to God.* Springfield, Ill.: Templegate, 1983.

―――. *River of Compassion.* Warwick, N.Y.: Amity House, 1987.

Griffiths, Paul J. *An Apology for Apologetics: A Study in the Logic of Interreligious Dialogue.* Faith Meets Faith Series. Maryknoll, N.Y.: Orbis, 1991.

Grunebaum, Gustave E. von. *Medieval Islam: A Study in Cultural Orientalism.* 2nd ed. Chicago: University of Chicago Press, 1953.

Gutiérrez, Gustavo. *A Theology of Liberation: History, Politics and Salvation.* Trans. and ed. Caridad Inda and John Eagleson. Maryknoll, N.Y.: Orbis, 1973.

Hall, David L., and Roger T. Ames. *Anticipating China: Thinking through the Narratives of Chinese and Western Culture.* Albany: State University of New York Press, 1995.

Heim, S. Mark. *Salvations: Truth and Difference in Religion.* Maryknoll, N.Y.: Orbis, 1995.

Helgeland, John, Robert J. Daly, and J. Patout Burns. *Christians and the Military: The Early Experience.* Ed. Robert J. Daly. Philadelphia: Fortress, 1985.

Hengel, Martin. *Property and Riches in the Early Church: Aspects of a Social History of Early Christianity.* Philadelphia: Fortress, 1974.

Henninger, Joseph. "Sacrifice." In *The Encyclopedia of Religion,* ed. Mircea Eliade. 12 vols. New York: Macmillan; London: Collier Macmillan, 1987.

Heschel, Abraham J. *The Prophets.* 2 vols. New York: Harper Colophon Books, 1969 [1962].

Hick, John. *A Christian Theology of Religions: The Rainbow of Faiths.* Louisville, Ky: Westminster/John Knox Press, 1995.

―――. *God Has Many Names: Britain's New Religious Pluralism.* London: Macmillan, 1980.

―――. *An Interpretation of Religion: Human Responses to the Transcendent.* New Haven and London: Yale University Press, 1989.

Hodgson, Marshall G. S. *The Venture of Islam.* 3 vols. Chicago and London: University of Chicago Press, 1974.

Hopkins, Jasper. *Nicholas of Cusa's De Pace Fidei and Cribatio Alkorani: Translation and Analysis.* Minneapolis: Arthur J. Banning, 1990.

―――. *Nicholas of Cusa on God as Not-Other: A Translation and Appraisal of De Li Non Aliud.* Minneapolis: University of Minnesota Press, 1979.

―――. *Nicholas of Cusa On Learned Ignorance: A Translation and Appraisal of De Docta Ignorantia.* 2nd ed. Minneapolis: Arthur J. Banning, 1985.

Horsley, Richard A. *Jesus and the Spiral of Violence: Popular Jewish Resistance in Roman Palestine.* Minneapolis: Fortress, 1993 [1987].

Horsley, Richard A., and Neil Asher Silberman. *The Message and the Kingdom: How Jesus and Paul Ignited a Revolution and Transformed the Ancient World.* New York: Grosset/Putnam, 1997.

Isaac, Jules. *The Teaching of Contempt: Christian Roots of Anti-Semitism.* Ed. Claire Huchet-Bishop. New York: Holt, Rinehart & Winston, 1964.

Ives, Christopher, ed. *Divine Emptiness and Historical Fullness: A Buddhist-Jewish-Christian Conversation with Masao Abe.* Valley Forge, Pa.: Trinity Press International, 1995.

Jaspers, Karl. *The Great Philosophers.* Vol. 2, *The Original Thinkers.* Ed. Hannah Arendt. New York: Harcourt, Brace & World, 1966.

————. *The Origin and Goal of History.* Trans. Michael Bullock. New Haven: Yale University Press, 1953.

John Paul II. "The Challenge and the Possibility of Peace." *Origins* 16/21 (Nov. 6, 1986): 370.

————. *The Gospel of Life [Evangelium Vitae].* New York: Random House Times Books, 1995.

————. *Tertio Millennio Adveniente. Origins* 24/24 (Nov. 24, 1994): 401, 403-16.

Johnson, Marshall D. "Reflections on a Wisdom Approach to Matthew's Christology." *Catholic Biblical Quarterly* 36 (1974): 44-64.

Johnston, William. *Christian Zen.* New York: Harper Colophon Books, 1971.

————. *The Still Point: Reflections on Zen and Christian Mysticism.* New York: Fordham University Press, 1970.

Jonas, Hans. *The Gnostic Religion: The Message of the Alien God and the Beginnings of Christianity.* 2nd ed., rev. Boston: Beacon, 1963.

Jones, Ken. *Beyond Optimism: A Buddhist Political Ecology.* Oxford: Jon Carpenter, 1993.

Kasimow, Harold, and Byron L. Sherwin, eds. *No Religion Is an Island: Abraham Joshua Heschel and Interreligious Dialogue.* Maryknoll, N.Y.: Orbis, 1991.

Kasulis, T. P. *Zen Action, Zen Person.* Honolulu: University of Hawaii Press, 1981.

Katz, Stephen T. *Post-Holocaust Dialogues: Critical Studies in Modern Jewish Thought.* New York: New York University Press, 1983.

Kayatz, Christa. *Studien zu Proverbien 1-9.* Wissenschaftliche Monographien zum alten und neuen Testament 22. Neukirchen-Vluyn: Neukirchener Verlag, 1966.

Kitagawa, Joseph Mitsuo. *The Quest for Human Unity: A Religious History.* Minneapolis: Fortress, 1990.

Knitter, Paul. *One Earth Many Religions: Multifaith Dialogue and Global Responsibility.* Maryknoll, N.Y.: Orbis, 1995.

Koester, Helmut. *Introduction to the New Testament.* 2 vols. Philadelphia: Fortress, 1982.

Kohn, Livia. *The Taoist Experience: An Anthology.* Albany: State University of New York Press, 1993.

The Koran. Trans. H. J. Dawood. 4th rev. ed. Harmondsworth, England: Penguin, 1974.

Küng, Hans, and Julia Ching. *Christianity and Chinese Religions.* New York: Doubleday, 1989.

Küng, Hans, and Karl-Josef Kuschel, eds. *A Global Ethic: The Declaration of the Parliament of the World's Religions.* New York: Continuum, 1993.

Lang, Bernhard. *Wisdom and the Book of Proverbs: An Israelite Goddess Redefined.* New York: Pilgrim Press, 1986.

Leclercq, Jean. *Bernard of Clairvaux and the Cistercian Spirit.* Cistercian Studies 16. Kalamazoo, Mich.: Cistercian Publications, 1976.

Lefebure, Leo D. *The Buddha and the Christ: Explorations in Buddhist-Christian Dialogue.* Maryknoll, N.Y.: Orbis, 1993.

————. *Life Transformed: Meditations on the Christian Scriptures in Light of Buddhist Perspectives.* Chicago: ACTA Publications, 1989.

Levenson, Jon D. "Is There a Counterpart in the Hebrew Bible to New Testament Antisemitism?" *Jounal of Ecumenical Studies* 22 (1985): 242-60.

———. *Sinai and Zion: An Entry into the Jewish Bible.* San Francisco: Harper & Row, 1985.

Lewis, Bernard, ed. and trans. *Islam from the Prophet Muhammad to the Capture of Constantinople.* New York and Oxford: Oxford University Press, 1987.

Lindblom, J. *Prophecy in Ancient Israel.* Philadelphia: Fortress, 1962.

Macy, Joanna. "In Indra's Net: Sarvodaya and Our Mutual Efforts for Peace." In *The Path of Compassion: Writings on Socially Engaged Buddhism,* ed. Fred Eppsteiner Rev. 2nd ed. Berkeley, Calif.: Parallax, 1988.

———. *World as Lover, World as Self.* Berkeley, Calif.: Parallax, 1991.

Manselli, Raul. *St. Francis of Assisi.* Chicago, Ill.: Franciscan Herald Press, 1988.

McGinn, Bernard, ed. and trans. *Apocalyptic Spirituality.* New York: Paulist, 1979.

Meer, F. Van der. *Augustine the Bishop: Religion and Society at the Dawn of the Middle Ages.* New York: Harper Torchbooks, 1961.

Mejía, Jorge. "World Religions: Together to Pray." *Origins* 16/21 (Nov. 6, 1986): 369.

Merton, Thomas. *The Way of Chuang Tzu.* New York: New Directions, 1965.

———. *The Wisdom of the Desert: Sayings from the Desert Fathers of the Fourth Century.* New York: New Directions, 1960.

Mitchell, Donald W., ed. *Masao Abe: A Zen Life of Dialogue.* Boston: Charles E. Tuttle, 1998.

Mitchell, Donald W., and James A. Wiseman, eds. *The Gethsemani Encounter: A Dialogue on the Spiritual Life by Buddhist and Christian Monastics.* New York: Continuum, 1997.

Moffett, Samuel Hugh. *A History of Christianity in Asia.* Vol. 1, *Beginnings to 1500.* San Francisco: HarperSanFrancisco, 1992.

Moran, Gabriel. *Uniqueness: Problem or Paradox in Jewish and Christian Traditions.* Maryknoll, N.Y.: Orbis, 1992.

Murphy, Roland E. "The Interpretation of Old Testament Wisdom Literature." *Interpretation* 23 (1969): 289-301.

———. *The Tree of Life: An Exploration of Biblical Wisdom Literature.* Anchor Bible Reference Library. New York: Doubleday, 1990.

———. "Wisdom and Creation." *Journal of Biblical Literature* 104 (1985): 3-11.

Musurillo, Herbert, ed. and trans. *The Acts of the Christian Martyrs.* Oxford: Clarendon Press, 1972.

National Conference of Catholic Bishops. *The Challenge of Peace: God's Promise and Our Response: A Pastoral Letter on War and Peace.* Washington, D.C.: United States Catholic Conference, 1983.

Nessan, Craig L. "Sex, Aggression, and Pain: Sociobiological Implications for Theological Anthropology." *Zygon* 33 (1998): 443-54.

Nhat Hanh, Thich, et al. *For a Future to Be Possible: Commentaries on the Five Wonderful Precepts.* Berkeley, Calif.: Parallax, 1993.

Nhat Hanh, Thich. *Breathe! You Are Alive: Sutra on Full Awareness of Breathing.* Berkeley, Calif.: Parallax, 1990.

———. *Vietnam: Lotus in a Sea of Fire.* New York: Hill & Wang, 1967.

————. *Zen Keys*. Garden City, N.Y.: Anchor Books, 1974.

Nicholas of Cusa. *The Vision of God*. New York: Frederick Ungar Publishing Co., 1978 [1928].

Niditch, Susan. *War in the Hebrew Bible: A Study in the Ethics of Violence*. New York and Oxford: Oxford University Press, 1993.

O'Collins, Gerald. *Retrieving Fundamental Theology*. New York: Paulist, 1993.

O'Flaherty, Wendy Doniger, ed. and trans., with Daniel Gold, David Haberman and David Shulman. *Textual Sources for the Study of Hinduism*. Chicago: University of Chicago Press, 1988.

Oppenheim, A. Leo. *Ancient Mesopotamia: Portrait of a Dead Civilization*. Rev. ed. completed by Erica Reiner. Chicago: University of Chicago Press, 1977.

Origen. *Contra Celsum*. Trans. Henry Chadwick. Cambridge: Cambridge University Press, 1980 [1953].

————. *An Exhortation to Martyrdom, Prayer, First Principles Book IV, Prologue to the Commentary on the Song of Songs Homily XXVII on Numbers*. Trans. Rowan A. Greer. New York: Paulist, 1979.

Otto, Rudolf. *The Idea of the Holy: An Inquiry into the Non-rational Factor in the Idea of the Divine and Its Relation to the Rational*. 2nd ed. Oxford: Oxford University Press, 1975 [1950].

Overholt, Thomas. *Channels of Prophecy: The Social Dynamics of Prophetic Activity*. Minneapolis: Fortress, 1989.

Parrinder, Geoffrey. *Avatar and Incarnation*. New York: Oxford University Press, 1982.

————. *Mysticism in the World's Religions*. London: Sheldon, 1976.

Perdue, Leo G. *The Collapse of History: Reconstructing Old Testament Theology*. Minneapolis: Fortress, 1994.

————. *Wisdom and Creation: The Theology of Wisdom Literature*. Nashville: Abingdon, 1994.

Perdue, Leo G., Bernard Brandon Scott, and William Johnston Wiseman, eds. *In Search of Wisdom: Essays in Memory of John G. Gammie*. Louisville: Westminster/John Knox Press, 1993.

Peters, Edward, ed. *The First Crusade: The Chronicle of Fulcher of Chartres and Other Source Materials*. Philadelphia: University of Pennsylvania Press, 1971.

The Philokalia: The Complete Text Compiled by St. Nikodimos of the Holy Mountain and St. Makarios of Corinth. Trans. G. E. H. Palmer et al. 3 vols. London: Faber & Faber, 1979.

Pieris, Aloysius. *Love Meets Wisdom: A Christian Experience of Buddhism*. Maryknoll, N.Y.: Orbis, 1988.

Pierre, Abbé, and Bernard Kouchner. *Dieu et les Hommes: Dialogue et propos recueillis par Michel-Antoine Burnier*. Paris: Robert Laffont, 1993.

Pixley, George V. *On Exodus: A Liberation Perspective*. Trans. Robert R. Barr. Maryknoll, N.Y.: Orbis, 1987.

Pontifical Council for Interreligious Dialogue and the Congregation for the Evangelization of Peoples, *Dialogue and Proclamation*. *Origins* 21/8 (July 4. 1991): 121, 123-35.

Preuss, H. D. "Erwägungen zum theologischen Ort alttestamentlicher Weisheitsliteratur." *Evangelische Theologie* 30 (August 1970): 393-417.

———. "Das Gottesbild der älteren Weisheit Israels." In *Studies in the Religion of Ancient Israel,* 117-45. Leiden: E. J. Brill, 1972.

Price, Theron D. *Revelation and Faith: Theological Reflections on the Knowing and Doing of Truth.* Macon, Ga.: Mercer University Press, 1987.

Pritchard, James D., ed. *Ancient Near Eastern Texts Relating to the Old Testament.* 3rd ed. with supplement. Princeton, N.J.: Princeton University Press, 1969.

Pushparajan, A., ed. *Pilgrims of Dialogue.* Munnar, India: Sangam Dialogue Centre, 1991.

Race, Alan. *Christians and Religious Pluralism: Patterns in the Christian Theology of Religions.* Maryknoll, N.Y.: Orbis, 1982.

Rad, Gerhard von. *Holy War in Ancient Israel.* Grand Rapids: Eerdmans, 1991.

———. *Old Testament Theology.* 2 vols. New York: Harper & Row, 1962, 1965.

———. *Wisdom in Israel.* Nashville: Abingdon, 1972.

Radhakrishnan, Sarvepalli. *The Hindu View of Life.* London: Unwin Paperbacks, 1980 [1927].

———. *Indian Religions.* New Delhi and Bombay: Orient Paperbacks, 1979.

Radhakrishnan, Sarvepalli, and Charles A. Moore, eds. *A Sourcebook in Indian Philosophy.* Princeton, N.J.: Princeton University Press, 1957.

Rahman, Fazlur. *Islam.* 2nd ed. Chicago and London: University of Chicago Press, 1979.

———. *Major Themes of the Qur'an.* Minneapolis and Chicago: Bibliotheca Islamica, 1980.

Rahner, Karl. "Christianity and the Non-Christian Religions." In *Theological Investigations,* 5:115-34. Baltimore: Helicon, 1966.

———. *Foundations of Christian Faith: An Introduction to the Idea of Christianity.* New York: Crossroad, 1982.

———. "The Incomprehensibility of God in Thomas Aquinas." *Journal of Religion* 58 Supplement (1978): S107-25.

———. "The One Christ and the Universality of Salvation." In *Theological Investigations,* 16:199-224. New York: Crossroad, 1983.

———. *The Practice of Faith: A Handbook of Contemporary Spirituality.* Ed. Karl Lehman and Albert Raffelt. New York: Crossroad, 1986.

———. "Reflections on the Experience of Grace." In *Theological Investigations.* London: Darton, Longman & Todd; New York: Seabury Press, 1974.

Rahula, Walpola. *What the Buddha Taught.* New York: Grove Press, 1959.

Rambachan, Anantanand. *Accomplishing the Accomplished: The Vedas as a Source of Valid Knowledge in Shankara.* Society for Asian and Comparative Philosophy 10. Honolulu: University of Hawaii Press, 1991.

———. *The Limits of Scripture: Vivekananda's Reinterpretation of the Vedas.* Honolulu: University of Hawaii Press, 1994.

Ratzinger, Joseph Cardinal. "Commentary on Profession of Faith's Concluding Paragraphs." *Origins* 28/8 (July 16, 1998): 116-19.

Redford, Donald B. *Egypt, Canaan, and Israel in Ancient Times.* Princeton, N.J.: Princeton University Press, 1992.

Rescher, Nicholas. *Pluralism: Against the Demand for Consensus.* Oxford: Clarendon, 1993.

———. *The Strife of Systems.* Pittsburgh: Pittsburgh University Press, 1985.

Ricoeur, Paul. *Symbolism of Evil.* Boston: Beacon, 1967.

The Rig Veda: An Anthology. Ed. and trans. Wendy Doniger O'Flaherty. Harmondsworth, England: Penguin, 1981.

Ringgren, Helmer. *Word and Wisdom: Studies in the Hypostatization of Divine Qualities and Functions in the Ancient Near East.* Lund: Ohlsson, 1947.

Robinson, James M., ed. *The Nag Hammadi Library in English.* Rev. ed. San Francisco: Harper & Row, 1988.

Robinson, Neal. *Christ in Islam and Christianity.* Albany, N.Y.: State University of New York Press, 1991.

Rowley, H. H. *Prophecy and Religion in Ancient China and Israel.* New York: Harper and Brothers, 1956.

Rubenstein, Richard L. *After Auschwitz: Radical Theology and Contemporary Judaism.* Indianapolis: Bobbs-Merrill Educational Publishing, 1966.

————. "Emptiness, Holy Nothingness, and the Holocaust." In *Masao Abe: A Zen Life of Dialogue,* ed. Donald W. Mitchell, 184-95. Boston: Charles E. Tuttle, 1998.

Rudolph, Kurt. *Gnosis: The Nature and History of Gnosticism.* Trans. and ed. Robert McLachlan Wilson. San Francisco: Harper & Row, 1983.

Ruether, Rosemary Radford. *Faith and Fratricide: The Theological Roots of Anti-Semitism.* New York: Seabury, 1979.

Runciman, Steven. *A History of the Crusades.* Vol. 3, *The Kingdom of Acre and the Later Crusades.* Cambridge: Cambridge University Press, 1954.

Ruokanen, Miika. *The Catholic Doctrine of Non-Christian Religions According to the Second Vatican Council.* Leiden: E.J. Brill, 1992.

Saggs, H. W. F. *The Encounter with the Divine in Mesopotamia and Israel.* London: University of London/Athlone, 1976.

Sahn, Seung. "True God, True Buddha." *Primary Point* 9/2 (Sept. 1992): 3-4.

The Sayings of the Desert Fathers: The Alphabetical Collection. Trans. Benedicta Ward. Kalamazoo, Mich.: Cistercian Publications, 1975; rev. ed. 1984.

Schillebeeckx, Edward. *Christ: The Experience of Jesus as Lord.* New York: Crossroad, 1981.

————. *Church: The Human Story of God.* New York: Crossroad, 1990.

Schmid, H. H. *Wesen und Geschichte der Weisheit.* Beihefte zur Zeitschrift für die alttestamentliche Wissenschaft 101. Berlin: Alfred Töpelmann Verlag, 1966.

Schoeps, Hans Joachim. *The Jewish-Christian Argument: A History of Theologies in Conflict.* New York: Holt, Rinehart and Winston, 1963.

Schwartz, Benjamin I. *The World of Thought in Ancient China.* Cambridge, Mass., and London, England: Belknap Press of Harvard University Press, 1985.

"Seminaire de recherche sur l'oeuvre de René Girard tenu au RIER (Regroupement Interuniversitaire pour l'Etude de la Religion)." *Studies in Religion/Sciences Religieuses* 10, no. 1 (1981): 67-107.

Sharma, Arvind, ed. *Our Religions.* San Francisco: HarperSanFrancisco, 1993.

Shih, J. "The Tao: Its Essence, Its Dynamism, and Its Fitness as a Vehicle of Christian Revelation." In *L'Eglise et les Religions,* 117-33. Studia Missionalia 15. Rome: Gregorian University Press, 1966.

Shinran. *Tannisho: A Shin Buddhist Classic.* Trans. Taitetsu Unno. Honolulu: Buddhist Study Center Press, 1984.

Siker, Jeffrey S. *Disinheriting the Jews: Abraham in Early Christian Controversy.* Louisville, Ky.: Westminster/John Knox Press, 1991.

Smith, Mark S. *The Early History of God: Yahweh and the Other Deities in Ancient Israel.* San Francisco: Harper & Row, 1990.

Smith, Morton. "The Common Theology of the Ancient Near East." *Journal of Biblical Literature* 71 (1952): 135-47.

Smith, Wilfred Cantwell. *Towards a World Theology: Faith and the Comparative History of Religions.* Philadelphia: Westminster, 1981.

Stark, Rodney. *The Rise of Christianity: A Sociologist Reconsiders History.* Princeton, N.J.: Princeton University Press, 1996.

Stendahl, Krister. *Paul among Jews and Gentiles and Other Essays.* Philadelphia: Fortress, 1976.

Streng, Frederick J. *Emptiness: A Study in Religious Meaning.* Nashville: Abingdon, 1967.

Suggs, M. Jack. *Wisdom, Christology, and Law in Matthew's Gospel.* Cambridge, Mass.: Harvard University Press, 1970.

Suzuki, D. T. *Outlines of Mahayana Buddhism.* New York: Schocken Books, 1963 [1907].

Swartley, Willard M. *The Love of Enemy and Nonretaliation in the New Testament.* Louisville, Ky.: Westminster/John Knox Press, 1992.

Swift, Louis J. *The Early Fathers on War and Military Service.* Wilmington, Del.: Michael Glazier, 1983.

Tanner, Norman P., ed. *Decrees of the Ecumenical Councils.* 2 vols. London: Sheed & Ward; Washington, D.C.: Georgetown University Press, 1990.

Tao Te Ching. Trans. Ch'u Ta-Kao. London: Unwin Paperbacks, 1989.

Taylor, Rodney L. "Confucianism: Scripture and Sage." In *The Holy Book in Comparative Perspective,* ed. Frederick M. Denny and Rodney L. Taylor. Columbia: University of South Carolina Press, 1993.

Tellenbach, Gerd. *Church, State and Christian Society at the Time of the Investiture Contest.* Atlantic Highlands, N.J.: Humanities Press, 1979[1940].

Theissen, Gerd. *Biblical Faith: An Evolutionary Approach.* Philadelphia: Fortress, 1985.

Tilley, Terrence W. "'Christianity and the World Religions,' A Recent Vatican Document." *Theological Studies* 60, no. 2 (1999): 318-37.

Tracy, David. *Dialogue with the Other: The Inter-Religious Dialogue.* Louvain Theological and Pastoral Monographs. Louvain: Peeters; Grand Rapids: Eerdmans, 1990.

Tu Wei-Ming. *Centrality and Commonality: An Essay on Confucian Religiousness.* Rev. ed. Albany: State University of New York Press, 1989.

Ullman, Walter. *A Short History of the Papacy in the Middle Ages.* London and New York: Methuen, 1972.

Upanishads. Trans. Patrick Olivelle. Oxford and New York: Oxford University Press, 1996.

Valeri, Valerio. *Kingship and Sacrifice: Ritual and Society in Ancient Hawaii.* Chicago and London: University of Chicago Press, 1985.

Van Seters, John. *In Search of History: Historiography in the Ancient World and the Origins of Biblical History.* New Haven: Yale University Press, 1983.

Vivekananda. "Hinduism." In *The Dawn of Religious Pluralism: Voices from the World's Parliament of Religions, 1893,* ed. Richard Hughes Seager. LaSalle, Ill.: Open Court, 1993.

Vorländer, Hermann. "Der Monotheismus Israels als Antwort auf die Krise des Exils." In *Der einzige Gott: Die Geburt des biblischen Monotheismus,* ed. B. Lang. Munich: Kösel, 1981.

———. *Mein Gott: Die Vorstellungen vom persönliche Gott.* Kevelaer: Butzon and Bercker, 1975.

Waldenfels, Hans. *Absolute Nothingness: Foundations for a Buddhist-Christian Dialogue.* Trans. J. W. Heisig. New York: Paulist, 1980.

Watson, Burton, ed. and trans. *The Complete Works of Chuang Tzu.* New York and London: Columbia University Press, 1968.

Watt, W. Montgomery. *Muhammad: Prophet and Statesman.* London and Oxford: Oxford University Press, 1974.

Wellhausen, Julius. *Prolegomena to the History of Ancient Israel.* Cleveland: Cleveland World, 1957 [1885].

Wertz, William F., Jr., trans. and ed. *Toward a New Council of Florence: "On the Peace of Faith" and Other Works by Nicholas of Cusa.* Washington, D.C.: Schiller Institute, 1993.

Wilken, Robert L. *John Chrysostom and the Jews: Rhetoric and Reality in the Late 4th Century.* Berkeley: University of California Press, 1983.

———. "Religious Pluralism and Early Christian Thought." *Pro Ecclesia* 1 (1992): 89-103.

Williams, James G. *Those Who Ponder Proverbs: Aphoristic Thinking and Biblical Literature.* Sheffield, England: Almond, 1981.

Wilson, Robert R. *Prophecy and Society in Ancient Israel.* Philadelphia: Fortress, 1980.

Wink, Walter. *The Powers.* Vol. 1, *Naming the Powers: The Language of Power in the New Testament;* Vol. 2, *Unmasking the Powers: The Invisible Forces that Determine Human Existence;* Vol. 3, *Engaging the Powers: Discernment and Resistance in a World of Domination.* Philadelphia and Minneapolis: Fortress, 1984, 1986, 1992.

Wright, G. Ernest. *God Who Acts: Biblical Theology as Recital.* London: SCM, 1952.

———. *The Old Testament against Its Environment.* London, SCM, 1950.

Wu, John C. H. *Chinese Humanism and Christian Spirituality.* Ed. Paul K. T. Sih. Jamaica, N.Y.: St. John's University Press, 1965.

Zaehner, R. C. *The Bhagavad Gita with a Commentary Based on the Original Sources.* London: Oxford University Press, 1969.

———. *The City within the Heart.* New York: Crossroad, 1981.

———. *Concordant Discord: The Interdependence of Faiths.* Oxford: Clarendon Press, 1970.

———. *Mysticism Sacred and Profane.* London: Oxford University Press, 1978 [1957].

General Index

Abe, Masao, 185-200
agapē (selfless love), 81, 161
Aitken, Robert, 179
Albrektson, Bertil, 28
Ambrose of Milan, 119-20
anti-Judaism: in New Testament, 70-73. *See also* anti-Semitism
anti-Semitism: Christian religions and, 3-4; of early church fathers, 3-4
Arinze, Francis Cardinal: ecumenical messages of, 8
Arjuna, 148-51
Augustine: anti-Semitism of, 4; and biblical interpretation, 120; and Hellenism, 94-95; and original sin, 120-22; and repression of religious opponents, 122
awakening, Buddhist, 158; and Christian revelation, 185-200
Axial Age, 131; meaning of, 39, 224
axial religions, 164-65; dialogue among, 131

Barr, James: on wisdom tradition, 44
Barth, Karl: anti-Semitism and, 4; and biblical revelation, 26; debate of, with Emil Brunner, 44; and natural theology, 44
Batto, Bernard F.: on myth, 33-34, 36
Bernardin, Joseph Cardinal: and anti-Judaism, 73
Bernard of Clairvaux, 127-28
Bhagavad Gita, 147-51; religious pluralism and, 10
Bible: holy war in, 57-58; images of God in, 55; interpretation of,

113-14; prophetic books of, 37-38; and religion of ancient Israel, 26-29; revelation and, 26, 55-82; violence and, 29, 55-82, 113-15
Biblical Theology Movement, 27-28, 32
bodhisattva (future Buddha), 155, 224
brahman (ultimate reality), 143; meaning of, 146, 224
Briggs, John, 175, 179, 185
Bright, John, 32
Brown, Raymond E.: and anti-Judaism of the New Testament, 71, 73
Brueggemann, Walter: on revelation and violence, 59-61; on wisdom tradition, 27-28
Brunner, Emil: debate of, with Karl Barth, 44
Buber, Martin: on ideology of holy war, 61; on Jesus, 168
Buddha. *See* Shakyamuni Buddha
Buddhism, 130-42, 153-64, 185-200; Ch'an (Zen), 140; divine revelation and, 6, 11, 131; Four Noble Truths of, 154; Pure Land, 11; and René Girard, 162-64; Theravada, 163
Buddhist-Christian Colloquium: ecumenical statement of, 6-7
Burkert, Walter: ideas about sacrifice and the holy of, 13

categorical revelation, 186, 224. *See also* Rahner, Karl
Catholic Church: anti-Semitism and, 3; transformation of attitudes of, 3